Islam & Christianity

IN Prophecy

To order additional copies of
Islam and Christianity,
by Tim Roosenberg, call **1-800-765-6955**.

Visit us at
www.reviewandherald.com
for information on other Review and Herald® products.

Islam & Christianity in Prophecy

Tim Roosenberg
With Tim Lale

REVIEW AND HERALD® PUBLISHING ASSOCIATION
Since 1861 | www.reviewandherald.com

Copyedited by James Cavil
Designed by Review and Herald Design Center
Cover art and interior © by Steve Creitz
Cover design by Bryan Gray
Typeset: Bembo 9/10

Unless otherwise noted, Bible texts in this book are from the New King James Version. Copyright © 1979, 1980, 1982 by Thomas Nelson, Inc. Used by permission. All rights reserved.

Bible texts credited to KJV are from the King James Version of the Bible.

Scripture quotations credited to NIV are from the *Holy Bible, New International Version.* Copyright © 1973, 1978, 1984, 2011 by Biblica, Inc. Used by permission. All rights reserved worldwide.

PRINTED IN U.S.A.
15   14   13   12   11   5   4   3   2   1

Library of Congress Cataloging-in-Publication Data
Roosenberg, Tim.
   Islam and Christianity : the coming holy war / Tim Roosenberg with Tim Lale.
      p. cm.
   ISBN 978-0-8280-2592-8
   1. Bible. O.T. Daniel XI-XII--Prophecies. 2. Bible. O.T. Daniel XI-XII—Criticism, interpretation, etc. 3. Christianity and other religions—Islam. 4. Islam—Relations—Christianity. 5. Seventh-day Adventists--Doctrines. I. Lale, Tim, 1964- II. Title.
   BS1556.R66 2011
   236'.9—dc23
                                          2011030669

ISBN 978-0-8280-2592-8

Contents

Introduction

Some Things to
Know About This Book

Where I'm Coming From

I am a big-picture forest person, not a tree person. I study the trends and avoid getting bogged down in the details. After being immersed in history and Bible prophecy for more than 30 years, I've come to have a feel for it. In 2002 I had an ah-ha moment, an epiphany of sorts, about the central meaning of Daniel 11. Following that ah-ha moment I spent several years testing my findings, and I have now, I believe, confirmed them after checking sources and consulting with scholars and researchers.

I got into this study during the 1970s as a freshman in college. Since I didn't enjoy writing, I decided that if I had to do a composition paper, I would write about something that I like—Bible prophecy.

As I studied the various methods of prophetic interpretation, I discovered that the way of the Reformers (Luther, Calvin, the Wesleys, and others) for understanding Bible prophecy, known as historicism, is much more accurate and true to the Bible text than the methods used by most prophecy teachers of North America today. Historicism is a method of interpretation based on the idea that biblical predictions, instead of something reserved solely for the future, have not only been fulfilled throughout history but continue to be fulfilled today. Because of my study, this book is built on history and Scripture, illuminated by the Reformers' understanding of prophetic interpretation.

The resulting picture is clear. Our world is about to go through great change. Are you ready for the war that will engulf this world? Or for what will come after it? *Islam and Christianity* will show you what to expect. That knowledge will give you the chance to survive both spiritually and physically.

The prophecies that God placed in the Bible have proved reliable since the beginning of human history. Bible prophecy helps people to know with certainty what events are coming, and causes them to believe when they see the predicted events actually happening. In all cases when God has revealed the future to human beings, the prophecies have played out as foretold.

This book does not attempt to explain every prophecy in the Bible. Rather, it presents a commonsense big picture of where the human race has come from and where it is going next. Nor does it seek to be politically correct. My goal is to be biblically correct—faithful to the Bible text. It is not my goal to offend you, but if I do, I hope you will take the time to find out for yourself whether what I say is true to the Bible. If you do conclude that the book's message and conclusions do agree with the Bible, I hope you will be open to making changes in your life that will bring you into harmony with God and His words. That is the purpose of Bible prophecy: to help each of us be prepared for the future. The prophecy cannot help us if we don't act on it.

How Much Do You Know Already?

While the more you know about the Bible the easier it will be to connect some of the ideas I present to your general understanding of God's Word, don't be concerned if you have little Bible knowledge. This book explains the prophecies of Daniel step by step.

Whom Is This Book For?

The great news about the Daniel prophecies concerning the end of the world is that the truth fits all people. Assuming that you and I are still alive when the end of the world comes, we can live through the most catastrophic times without fear or uncertainty and come out safely (at least spiritually) on the other side.

You do not have to be surprised by world events as they happen. Nor do you need to be overwhelmed by anxiety and bewilderment. Great trouble will fill the time ahead, but God tells us clearly what is coming and what to do in the face of it.

The Best Place to Start

If you have not read the book of Daniel all the way through, now is a good time to do it. Even if you've read it before, you will appreciate the review. Though you may not understand everything you read, keep on going through it. Then, when you read *Islam and Christianity,* the book of Daniel will become clearer to you.

Basic Terms to Know

I will use some terms frequently in this book. Here are the most common ones and their meaning:

- *the Bible:* the Old and New Testaments of the sacred Scriptures, the written Word of God
- *Bible prophecy:* predictions about the future, given by God to individuals, who wrote them down in Scripture
- *geopolitical:* political aspects of nations, especially having to do with international relations, as influenced by geography
- *spiritual:* the parallel religious aspects of nations or political powers
- *the king of the north:* geopolitical powers in prophecy that come against Israel from the north
- *the king of the south:* geopolitical powers in prophecy that attack Israel from the south
- *the Papacy:* the ecclesiastical system of governance in the Roman Catholic Church, one headed by the pope
- *Islam:* the religion of Muslims, a monotheistic faith regarded as revealed through Muhammad as the prophet of Allah
- *the Reformation:* the sixteenth-century religious movement that rejected or modified some Roman Catholic doctrines and practices, and resulted in the creation of Protestant churches
- *the Reformers:* the leaders of the Protestant Reformation

The Key Bible Text of the Book

If you have just read the book of Daniel again, you may be wondering why succeeding chapters appear to repeat some parts of the prophecies. Daniel 2, 7, and 8 seem to be talking about the same powers and events but with details added or omitted. What you need to know is that the chapters are layers, each one adding more detail than the previous one. Daniel 11 provides the road map you need to understand the prophecies. It is a chronological guide to all of the prophecies described in previous chapters of Daniel—and even for those in the book of Revelation.

All Doom and Gloom?

End-time scenarios turn off many people. Why even talk about the end of the world as we know it? Why spread fear and anger and sadness, they say, when we could be looking for the good in the world and making a positive difference? Think about this: the study of Bible prophecy is a *both/and* activity. A faithful and accurate take on Bible prophecy shows us what is really happening in our world, prompts us to take positive action now, and brings to light the promises of much better things to come.

It raises the question Why look to the future for better things to come? Why not just work for the good of people in the world today? Bible prophecy has a both/and application here as well. Good and evil are at war in the world. The only way to avoid that reality is to pretend it isn't there. Working for the good of people in the world today is extremely important—a must-do—but it must be done in the context of a world in the grip of spiritual and physical conflict. It is a giant mistake for anyone to live in denial of the spiritual and political aspects of our world.

Rather, it is extremely important for us to understand what God has revealed. Bible prophecy lifts the veil from what will happen in the near future. Today's complicated realities, both good and bad, find an explanation in the revelations of the prophet Daniel and other Bible writers.

Let's Find the Truth

In *Islam and Christianity in Prophecy* we are on a quest for truth. Not my truth or your truth. Not the truth of one church or one religion, nor of one political ideology or political party. Not liberal truth or conservative truth. We are looking for Bible truth, the truth that God gave to all people.

Why is that important? God's Word in the Bible transcends all human manipulation. And your life depends on it! Follow God and His Word, and you will live. Ignore it, twist it, misrepresent it, neglect it, and you will not survive the coming trouble. So let's find the truth in Bible prophecy.

CHAPTER 1

The Coming Holy War

People no longer trust their leaders and governments, a sad reality we see illustrated by an ad for a recent movie thriller, *2012*. It declared:

"How would the governments of our planet prepare 6 billion people for the end of the world?"

"They wouldn't."

However, God has told us what to expect in the future, and unlike world leaders, He has a perfect track record of honesty.

The mayhem portrayed in movie thrillers is sometimes eerily similar to the visions described by the Bible prophets in several places. The Bible has the advantage of being reliable in its predictions, however. As we look into the prophecies in the books of Daniel and Revelation we will uncover the plain truth about what is in store for our world.

Introducing Daniel

The statesman Daniel was one of the most important Bible prophets. Prime minister of two world powers, he began his civic career in his youth, about 605 B.C., when taken into exile in Babylon from the tiny country of Judah. His captors trained him to serve in the court of Nebuchadnezzar, the new emperor of Babylon. Through his long career Daniel endeared himself to the kings he served because he had a relationship with his God that gave him access to reliable knowledge and wisdom, and his integrity was unshakable.

God entrusted him with prophecies about the future. His first one, recorded in Daniel 2, explains Nebuchadnezzar's dream about a giant statue. The later prophecies, revealed in Daniel 7 and 8, build on that first prophecy like layers on a cake, adding more detail and extending the time line. The frosting on the cake is Daniel 11. That chapter defines and explains in chronological order the prophecies of world history from Daniel's time to the end of the world.

Islam and Christianity

I believe that the prophecies of Daniel predict three holy "wars" between Islam and Western Christianity. In the sense used here, "war" means a lengthy conflict between two broad powers in the world. The first war was the Arab expansion of Islam and seven major Christian Crusades from A.D. 1095 to 1291. The second was the growth of the Islamic Ottoman Empire during the period of the Reformation and following, roughly A.D. 1449 to 1840.[1] These two major Christian/Islamic "wars" have already happened. But the third holy war could begin at any time.

In the third and final holy war, Islam will attack Western Christianity. Western Christianity, including the United States and Europe, will counterattack. How can we know that the third war will happen? And what will it look like? We will explore the biblical evidence in this book.

But I am not the only one who has come to this conclusion. Others have also noticed similar trends from history and current events. Boris Johnson, in his 2008 British Broadcasting Corporation documentary *After Rome: Holy War and Conquest,* sees a north–south split of the Roman Empire and continuing conflict between Islam and Christianity.[2] Samuel P. Huntington in his major *Foreign Affairs* article in 1993 indicated that the coming conflicts are likely to be between civilizations, such as the Christian West and Islam.[3] Many news commentators have alluded to a possible holy war.

A Prophecy of the Third Holy War

Daniel 11 gives the prophecy predicting the third holy war. To understand what the chapter says, keep in mind that the king of the north represents Western Christianity and the king of the south represents Islam. The "Glorious Land" (Dan. 11:41) and "the glorious holy mountain" (verse 45) are names for Jerusalem and/or the state or region of Israel. In places where the words "he" or "him" are not clearly connected to one of the kings, I have indicated the correct king in brackets.

"At the time of the end the king of the South shall attack him [the king of the north]; and the king of the North shall come against him [the king of the south] like a whirlwind, with chariots, horsemen, and with many ships; and he [the king of the north] shall enter the countries, overwhelm them, and pass through.

"He [the king of the north] shall also enter the Glorious Land, and many countries shall be overthrown; but these shall escape from his hand: Edom, Moab, and the prominent people of Ammon.

"He [the king of the north] shall stretch out his hand against the countries, and the land of Egypt shall not escape. He shall have power over the treasures of gold and silver, and over all the precious things of Egypt; also the Libyans and Ethiopians shall follow at his heels.

"But news from the east and the north shall trouble him [the king of the north]; therefore he shall go out with great fury to destroy and annihilate many. And he [the king of the north] shall plant the tents of his palace between the seas and the glorious holy mountain; yet he [the king of the north] shall come to his end, and no one will help him" (Dan. 11:40-45).[4]

The third war will result in the destruction of Islam, a change that will likely be much more dramatic and pivotal than the Crusades of the Middle Ages or World Wars I and II. As depicted in Daniel 11, the third holy war will dramatically alter the world and our freedoms as we have known them. And then, in the aftermath of the third war, God will rescue a small part of Christianity as well as a small part of Islam, with the majority of the people in both groups being destroyed.

Please note: the prophecy and its interpretation is neither anti-Muslim nor anti-Christian. Rather, it is a straightforward prediction of what will happen in the future.

Daniel 11: A Chronological Prophecy

The entire prophecy that includes predictions of the three major conflicts between Christianity and Islam appear in Daniel 11:2-12:3. It starts in the time of Daniel (seventh century B.C.), moves in a straightforward way through human history, and concludes with the end of the world and God's people living with Him forever after the return of Jesus Christ and the resurrection.

Because this chapter of Daniel is chronological, it gives us a time line of major events in history. Many of the predicted events have already occurred, so in this book we will check them against the historical record. The final events of Daniel 11 remain as yet unfulfilled.

Although most Bible scholars have considered Daniel 11 a difficult passage, many of them are reaching conclusions similar to those presented here. It has been my experience that once people learn certain keys of interpretation, the Daniel 11 prophecy will become clear to most.

People in the world today worry about the possibility of nuclear war. Let me set your mind at ease: I am certain that nuclear war will not destroy the human race. How do I know that? When Jesus returns to earth, the prophet tells us in Revelation 1:7 that human beings will be alive to see His coming. No all-out nuclear war will annihilate humanity.

That does not rule out limited nuclear war, however. The United States has already used such weapons against Japan in 1945, and it could happen again with other countries.

Many are concerned about terrorism. They wonder, Where could it hit next? The Bible does not say where it will happen next, but it does, I believe, tell us that the Islamic south will be pushing against or attacking the Christian north. So we can expect continued terrorism until the Christian powers destroy radical Islam.

The Signs to Watch For

The Bible talks about signs that will indicate the progression of these events. Some, the Bible says, will increase in intensity and frequency as the time of Jesus Christ's coming gets close, and therefore no one needs to be surprised by the events as they happen. Scripture compares the increasing intensity to the contractions of a woman giving birth:

"Concerning the times and the seasons, . . . you yourselves know perfectly that the day of the Lord so comes as a thief in the night. For when they say, 'Peace and safety!' then sudden destruction comes upon them, as labor pains upon a pregnant woman. And they shall not escape. But you . . . are not in darkness, so that this Day should overtake you as a thief" (1 Thess. 5:1-4).

No one needs to be surprised by either the turbulent events that lead up to the return of Jesus Christ or the Second Coming itself. But we must be watching for the signs.

When Jesus lived on earth during the early first century A.D., He explained some of the signs:

"As He sat on the Mount of Olives, the disciples came to Him privately, saying, 'Tell us, when will these things be? And what will be the sign of Your coming, and of the end of the age?'

"And Jesus answered and said to them: 'Take heed that no one deceives you. For many will come in My name, saying, "I am the Christ," and will deceive many. And you will hear of wars and rumors of wars. See that you are not troubled; for all these things must come to pass, but the end is not yet'" (Matt. 24:3-6).

History has witnessed countless wars through the centuries as well as frequent rumors of impending or potential ones. It is important for us to establish a general picture of the present world situation. Recent history shows that the tension between the Islamic world and other powers has been growing for many decades. The flash points are familiar to anyone who keeps track of world news. As an example, notice a typical report about Iran and Israel from November 2008.

"Senior Tehran officials are recommending a preemptive strike against Israel to prevent an Israeli attack on Iran's nuclear reactors, a senior Islamic Republic official told foreign diplomats two weeks ago in London.

"The official, Dr. Seyed G. Safavi, said recent threats by Israeli authorities strengthened this position, but that as of yet, a preemptive strike has not been integrated into Iranian policy."[5]

Iran suggested that it might launch a preemptive attack on Israel, because Israel had declared that it might attack Iran before Iran could get a nuclear weapon to strike Israel. Each side seeks to preempt a preemptive attack! That's the kind of world we live in today—one full of wars and rumors of wars.

The rumors are there, but we want to figure out whether we live in a time of increasing "labor pains." Are the pressures mounting in frequency and strength? Labor pains start out soft and slow and get more and more intense until the birth. We are seeing indications that history's "labor pains" are growing more severe.

A Word of Caution

People have been looking at and evaluating the signs and rumors of wars for a long time. One of the dangers of focusing on such events in the news is that it's easy to jump to the conclusion that the ones apparent right now represent the very intense labor pains just before the birth. But are they really?

The book *Heralds of the Morning,* written by Asa Oscar Tait and published in several editions at the end of the nineteenth century, shows what happens when a student of prophecy believes that events in his or her day represent those final labor pains. *Heralds of the Morning* includes a long chapter titled "And the Nations Were Angry." It describes in great detail the capabilities of the United States military during the 1890s. The author writes: "The prophetic declaration is that the war spirit will prevail over the whole world; and what may be seen among the nations today? Does the outlook indicate a universal peace? Are not the greatest armies being hastily gathered, and the most marvelous implements of war being forged, that could ever have been conceived in the wildest realm of imaginative fancy?"[6] Further on, he adds: "The weapons with which Napoleon and the great generals of all former times fought were mere toys when compared with the weapons that are now being prepared."[7] And marveling at the many guns of his time, he observed: "In 1861 Dr. R. J. Gatling invented the gun that bears his name, and the ingenious mechanism of this weapon enables it to fire from 600 to 1,200 shots per minute."[8]

But today the United States has gone far beyond the destructive capability of the late nineteenth century, including such devices as smart bombs. A pilot in an airplane several miles above the earth's surface can by remote control drop a bomb down a vent stack into a bunker. The military has missiles that can hit anywhere in the world to within a couple feet of the target and devastate vast areas. We are no longer talking about just rapid-firing guns.

What is my point here? Be careful in looking at such things and using them to announce, "Jesus will be here in a very short time, because this sign is being fulfilled." Many people have made that mistake. Christ Himself said: "Nation will rise against nation, and kingdom against kingdom. And there will be famines, pestilences, and earthquakes in various places. All these are the beginning of sorrows" (Matt. 24:7, 8). He did not say that such events indicate His immediate return, but rather that they were just the beginning of the signs. The wars are preliminary birth pains. We need to be looking at what is going on around us and be getting ready, but there are some things in Scripture that are more solid indicators than the "wars and rumors of wars."

Famines, diseases, and earthquakes in various places are sadly commonplace in the world. Can we find anything that helps to measure whether the intensity of such catastrophes is increasing? Consider, for example, this news release:

"New research compiled by Australian scientist Dr. Tom Chalko shows that global seismic activity on Earth is now five times more energetic than it was just 20 years ago. The research proves that destructive ability of earthquakes on Earth increases alarmingly fast and that this trend is set to continue. . . . The analysis of more than 386,000 earthquakes between 1973 and 2007 recorded on the U.S. Geological Survey database proved that the global annual energy of earthquakes on Earth began increasing very fast since 1990."[9]

The point of looking at such signs is not that we are all the way there but rather that we are getting closer, and that the labor pains are intensifying. Sooner or later the final event is going to happen—Jesus will return.

Continuing in Matthew 24, we discover more of the signs:

"Then they will deliver you up to tribulation and kill you, and you will be hated by all nations for My name's sake. And then many will be offended, will betray one another, and will hate one another. Then many false prophets will rise up and deceive many. And because lawlessness will abound, the love of many will grow cold. But he who endures to the end shall be saved. And this gospel of the kingdom will be preached in all the world as a witness to all the nations, and then the end will come" (verses 9-14).

What is the major sign of the return of Jesus? The gospel truth about Jesus being communicated to all the world. That's the big one! Watch for that one.

A Message for You

The words of Jesus declare that those who endure to the end will be saved. It means that we might go through some hard times. The labor pains might get a little tough to take. But if we hang in there, we will receive something really good at the end: a new life. When the gospel has gone to the whole world, then we get to spend eternity with Jesus. That is something really, really good. The good news about Jesus Christ is now spreading across the world in a multitude of ways right now—through the Internet, through radio, through individual people with great courage on the ground in areas where it is not easy to share the gospel.

Who Are the Real Christians?

God in 2 Timothy 3:1-4 reveals more about what the situation will be like at the end of the world. "But know this, that in the last day"—the last day, meaning toward the end—"perilous times will come: For men will be lovers of themselves, lovers of money, boasters, proud, blasphemers, disobedient to parents, unthankful, unholy, unloving, unforgiving, slanderers, without self-control, brutal, despisers of good, traitors, headstrong, haughty, lovers of pleasure rather than lovers of God."

While it sounds like the world of today, it's not referring to the society or culture in which we live. If we keep reading, we find that verse 5 speaks of people "having a form of godliness but denying its power. And from such people turn away!"

Unfortunately, Paul is talking about the Christian church! Proud, blasphemers, lovers of pleasure, growing cold in their love . . . those verses describe people who have a form of godliness and claim to be Christians but are really not.

How can that be possible? Consider the findings of George Barna, the Christian researcher. He found that 62 percent of Protestants are "born again" and 22 percent of Catholics are "born again." By "born again" he simply means that "a person has a relationship with Christ that causes them to believe that they have been forgiven of their sins and expect to live with Him forever." That's a pretty simple definition. But Barna's survey found that only 62 percent of Protestants and 22 percent of Catholics consider themselves born again.

Then, in a recent study,[10] Barna asked how many of these people have a biblical worldview. He settled on a minimum of six beliefs that make up a biblical worldview. They included:
• Absolute moral truth exists.
• The Bible is totally accurate in all of the principles it teaches.
• Satan is a real being or force, not merely symbolic.
• People cannot earn their way into heaven by trying to be good or doing good works.
• Jesus Christ lived a sinless life on earth.
• God is the all-knowing, all-powerful Creator of the world who still rules the universe today.

How many born-again Christians actually affirmed all six concepts? Only 9 percent! So, among people who profess to be Christian, only a small percentage are born again and have a biblical worldview. It's probably safe to say that some of them claim it but don't really live it, so the real figure is probably worse. Barna sums it up this way: "Although most Americans consider themselves to be Christian and say they know the content of the Bible, less than one out of ten Americans demonstrate such knowledge through their actions."

This reminds me of what Mahatma Gandhi said: "I like your Christ. I do not like your Christians. Your Christians are so unlike your Christ."

Now, you may be one who has given up on the Christian church, because you met some of those that weren't really Christian, and you said, "Forget it!" But I want to encourage you: don't give up. Keep digging into God's Word. Keep looking for a real, true Christian who follows God's

Word, has a biblical worldview, and trusts in Jesus Christ so that you can see what a real Christian looks like.

The apostle Paul said something important to Christians in 1 Corinthians 10:31: "Therefore, whether you eat or drink, or whatever you do, do all to the glory of God." If you are a Christian, make sure that you are doing that, because if you are not, you are going to lead somebody else to reject Christianity.

The Time for Understanding Is Now

The end of the Daniel 11 prophecy, which actually appears in Daniel 12, says: "But you, Daniel, shut up the words, and seal the book until the time of the end; many shall run to and fro, and knowledge shall increase" (verse 4). God said the prophecy wouldn't be understood for a long while, or, as verse 4 states, "until the time of the end." Therefore, you can expect the book of Daniel to be fully comprehended right about the time period indicated in Daniel 11:40.

As I was working on this volume, someone shared study materials with me on the book of Daniel. Interestingly, they did not include chapter 11 at all. Why? Because many have considered it a really difficult chapter to interpret. But at the end of the prophecy of Daniel 11 (which, as I said, runs into chapter 12), the angel presenting the vision declares that it will be comprehended (Dan. 12:4). That just really excites me, because people are beginning to grasp Daniel 11, and that puts us right about the time of verse 40 in Daniel 11.

Daniel 11 takes us through the same empires as those found in the statue prophecy of Daniel 2. As we will see, it starts in Daniel's day and works step by step through the Persian Empire, the Greek Empire, the time of Christ, the Roman Empire, and right up to a final struggle between the kings of the north and south. And then it shows Jesus rescuing His people, describes a resurrection, and then declares that God's people will live with Him forever. It is the only prophecy in the Bible with that much detail, beginning way back in history, approximately 535 B.C., and continuing all the way to the return of Christ.

In some ways Daniel 11 also acts like a filing system. We can take all of the other prophecies of Daniel and those from other books of the Bible, and find where each of them fits in the Daniel 11 chronology. Although it's really not that difficult to understand, God just did not open people's minds on it until recently.

How the Filing System Works

Daniel 11:2 says: "Now I will tell you the truth: Behold, three more kings will arise in Persia." Daniel was its prime minister at the time, and so this verse indicates that the prophecy begins in his era. "Three more kings will arise in Persia, and the fourth shall be far richer than them all; by his strength, through his riches, he shall stir up all against the realm of Greece." Unfortunately, that led to the downfall of the fourth king. When Xerxes (called Ahasuerus in the Bible) did that, the Greeks defeated him in battle. We have here a switch from the Persian to the Greek Empire, and Alexander takes control. Daniel 11 will not stay with one political power but will track the succeeding ones as it advances through time. This transition sets up a pattern for similar ones elsewhere in the chapter. Whenever the current world power challenges the next rising power and does not win, the focus will shift to the new power even though the old one may continue for some time. In the case of Persia a number of additional kings reigned after Greece entered the scene.

Verses 3 and 4: "Then a mighty king shall arise, who shall rule with great dominion, and do according to his will. And when he has arisen, his kingdom shall be broken up and divided toward the four winds of heaven, but not among his posterity nor according to his dominion with which he ruled; for his kingdom shall be uprooted, even for others besides these." Not only do we have a shift from Persia to Greece, but verse 4 says that the new kingdom will fragment into four segments. When Alexander the Great died at age 32, four of his generals split up his empire into four Greek or Hellenistic kingdoms. God's prophecies are right on the mark with the details.

Now I want to demonstrate how the Daniel 11 "filing system" works. We will look at some other chapters in Daniel to show how to expand our understanding of chapter 11.

In Daniel 2 King Nebuchadnezzar had a dream one night, and during it he saw something really amazing. Then he woke up and forgot the dream. Puzzled, he summoned his counselors and said, "Tell me the dream, and I will give you great riches. Don't tell me the dream, and you're dead."

"You want us to tell you what you dreamed last night?" they asked. "Oh, king, nobody does that."

"But you are going to," their ruler retorted. Why? The counselors claimed to have a connection with the gods. Thus they could interpret dreams, because the gods would explain to them what the dreams meant.

And so, if the gods sent the dreams and the interpretation, surely the counselors should be able to tell Nebuchadnezzar what the dream had been. Basically the king was saying, "If you can't do this, then you are a bunch of frauds, and you're done."

Since the wise men still hedged, the king sent soldiers to round them up and execute them all.

The troops came to Daniel's house (he had not been invited to the meeting) and knocked on his door. When he inquired what was going on, they told him.

"Take me to the king," he announced when they had finished.

Requesting some additional time from Nebuchadnezzar, he assured him that his God could reveal to Daniel what the dream had been.

The prophet returned home, and with his friends Meshach, Shadrach, and Abednego had a serious prayer meeting. In essence they were saying, "God, either give us the dream or we are dead!"

The Lord showed Daniel the dream, and so the young man went back to the court and announced, "King, here is the dream you had. You were thinking about the future, and you dreamed about a statue with a head of gold, chest of silver, belly and thighs of brass, legs of iron, and feet of iron and clay. As you looked at that, a rock that was cut out without hands came crashing down on the statue and destroyed it. The statue just blew away as dust in the wind, and then the Rock took over the whole world.

"Here's the interpretation," Daniel announced to the king. "You are the head of gold—Babylon. After you will rise another kingdom, one inferior to you." (This was actually Medo-Persia.) "And then a third power will take over." By the time we get to Daniel 11 the book of Daniel actually identifies most of the powers by name. But in Daniel 2 the prophet named only Babylon and then symbolically described the rest.

Continuing, Daniel said, "King, after the third one will come a very strong kingdom, with legs of iron." This was Rome. History tells us that when it began to decline, it wasn't conquered as a whole. Instead, it fell apart, and remnants of the Roman Empire remained afterward. As time passed it went from being the Roman Empire to the various countries of Europe, North Africa, and the Middle East. We are still living in that time of divided Europe and other areas of the former Roman Empire, a condition that will continue until the second coming of Jesus Christ.

The prophecy predicts four major empires, and after them, a collection of weaker countries, and nobody would be able to reunite them. If you look at the most important family trees of Europe, for example, "they [would] mingle with the seed of men," as Daniel 2:43 puts it. The leading families of the nations intermarried, trying to keep peace between the different parts of the region. And then they would have a family feud and go to war anyway! It didn't work, just as Daniel said it wouldn't.

Several emperors and conquerors tried to unite Europe and hold it together, but nobody could. Some of the fragments of other former parts of the Roman Empire, such as Egypt and Syria under Gamal Abdel Nasser during the twentieth century, also tried to unite but eventually failed. Daniel said that no one would be able to do this after the Roman Empire, and nobody has. That puts us down in the "toenails" of time. We are right down at the end somewhere, during which those "labor pains" are becoming more intense.

In Daniel 7 the prophet goes over the same material, only this time the prophecy depicts the powers as animals. Those four beasts are God's cartoons. We use animals in cartoons all the time. Americans depict Democrats as donkeys and Republicans as elephants. You can glance at a political cartoon and know right away what it is talking about.

Daniel starts out with Babylon as a lion with eagle's wings. If you had entered the Ishtar Gate and processional way in Babylon, you would have seen blue-tiled walls with animals on them.[11] They are beautiful, and on the walls are lions with wings. The winged lion was a symbol of Babylon in Daniel's day. Everybody knew whom the prophet was talking about when he mentioned the lion with eagle's wings.

Following that in the vision was a bear, which represented Medo-Persia. It was humped up on one side. What did that mean? That one side would be more powerful. And it was the case in that the Persians were the stronger element of the Medo-Persian coalition. The first king was a Mede, but after that, the Persians took control.

Then emerged Greece, depicted by a leopard that rapidly conquered the world that the people of the Bible knew. The leopard had four heads. After the death of Alexander the Great, his kingdom split into four major segments. Again, the detail is correct.

Later in Daniel 7 a nondescript and fearsome beast with 10 horns comes up, which represents Rome.

These are important points to keep in mind as we go through Daniel 11.

I am not going to give you every last detail of the history in Daniel 11. Anyone not especially interested in history would get bored and fall asleep. For the complete list of historical events and the corresponding verses in Daniel 11, see Appendix A, pp. 203-212.

Kings of the North and South

While there seems in Daniel's prophecies a direct correlation between an animal or beast symbol and a particular power, that is apparently not always the case in Daniel 11. It employs the terms "king of the North" and "king of the South" for different powers at different times, depending on which nations controlled the areas to the north and south of Palestine and could make incursions into it from those directions. For instance, Daniel 11:4-19 talks about Alexander's kingdom and how it split four ways, but then it focuses on two of them.

The two that it concentrates on are called the king of the north (the black arrow) and the king of the south (the gray arrow). One of the powers invaded from the north of Jerusalem, and the other attacked from the south.

This is not the first designation of the king of the north in prophecy. The first empire so named was Babylon, according to the prophet Jeremiah. Now, the Babylonian Empire lay mostly to the east of Jerusalem, so why would anyone refer to Babylon in the east as the king of the north? Because when the Babylonian army approached Israel, it had to march northwest around the desert regions and then down to Jerusalem from the north. No army commander would be foolish enough to cut through the desert.

At this point we can say from what happened in history that in Daniel 11 the king of the north is a power that would invade Jerusalem from the north. And we can conclude that the king of the south would be a power coming from the south of Israel.

In Daniel 11:4 and following we begin to see the imagery of the king of the north and the king of the south applied to the time of the Greeks. The armies of Alexander the Great marched around by land from the west and attacked Jerusalem from the north. After his empire split up, the two powers north and south of Israel comprised the dynasties of two of Alexander's generals, Ptolemy and Seleucus. Ptolemy was made governor of Egypt, but later declared it the Ptolemaic kingdom. Calling himself pharaoh, he took the title of Ptolemy I. Seleucus, given the governorship of what had been Babylonia, proved even more ambitious. In less than 10 years he conquered a vast territory from the middle of present-day Turkey east to the Indus River, the western frontier of India, creating the Seleucid empire.

In relation to the position of Jerusalem, the Seleucid empire was to the north and the Ptolemaic kingdom to the south. If the two powers got into a fight, who found themselves caught in the middle? Jerusalem. As it happened, Ptolemy I took over the area around Jerusalem in violation of an agreement that had given the territory to Seleucus. That prompted a series of six conflicts called the Syrian Wars.

Seleucus' grandson Antiochus II tried to take back the territories of Israel, Judah, and Syria in the second Syrian War, and Ptolemy II, the son of Ptolemy I, fought to keep them. In an attempt to make peace, Ptolemy II sent his daughter Berenice to marry Antiochus II. So Antiochus II divorced his wife, Laodice, and sent her into exile. With his new wife, Queen Berenice, Antiochus II had a son.

Ptolemy II died and was succeeded by his eldest son, Ptolemy III. Up in the Seleucid Empire, Antiochus II thought, *Berenice's father is gone,* and so he dumped her and again took up with his first wife, Laodice. Soon after that, Antiochus II died (likely poisoned by his angry first wife). She then declared her son Seleucus II the new emperor and succeeded in having Berenice and her son poisoned.

Consider how accurately Daniel 11:5, 6 depicts the events:

"Then the king of the South shall become strong, as well as one of his princes; and he shall gain power over him and have dominion. His dominion shall be a great dominion. And at the end of some years they shall join forces, for the daughter of the king of the South shall go to the king of the North to make an agreement; but she shall not retain the power of her authority, and neither he nor his authority shall stand; but she shall be given up, with those who brought her, and with him who begot her, and with him who strengthened her in those times."

Isn't that exactly what happened to Berenice and her son? The authority of Antiochus II did not last, and Berenice did not retain her power, and she was given up, along with those who brought her to the Seleucid court.

Ptolemy III, Berenice's brother, was extremely upset about what had happened. Wouldn't you be if someone had just poisoned your sister? The marriage was supposed to be a peace treaty. So Ptolemy III marched back up through Judea, fought a battle, and won. Then the conflict swung back and forth for some time. (I'm not going to describe all of those encounters here.) Daniel 11:7-9 gives the picture:

"But from a branch of her [Berenice's] roots one shall arise in his place, who shall come with an army, enter the fortress of the king of the North, and deal with them and prevail. And he shall also carry their gods captive to Egypt, with their princes and their precious articles of silver and gold; and he shall continue more years than the king of the North. Then the king of the North shall come to the kingdom of the king of the South, but shall return to his own land."

Daniel 11:7 declares: "From a branch of her roots one shall arise in his place." This points back to the root, Ptolemy I, and the succeeding kings are each a different branch from Ptolemy I. The passage clearly shows the symbolism of "a branch of her roots."

Then in verses 17-19 Antiochus III tries to do the same thing as Ptolemy II. He thinks that with a marriage he can establish peace.

"He shall also set his face to enter with the strength of his whole kingdom, and upright ones with him; thus shall he do. And he shall give him the daughter of women to destroy it; but she shall not stand with him, or be for him. After this he shall turn his face to the coastlands, and shall take many. But a ruler shall bring the reproach against them to an end; and with the reproach removed, he shall turn back on him. Then he shall turn his face toward the fortress of his own land; but he shall stumble and fall, and not be found."

Let's see if, once again, the prophecy matches history. Antiochus III, the Seleucid king in the north, said, "OK, I'm going to send my daughter down to Egypt to marry a Ptolemy, to make a peace treaty." He sent his daughter, by the name of Cleopatra I, down to the south, where she married the king of the south but had no intention of being true to her father or husband. Assuming control of the Ptolemy government, she then played the Seleucids and the Romans (the new power emerging in Europe) against each other. With Cleopatra in the south, Antiochus III turned against the western powers and was defeated by the Roman commander Lucius Cornelius Scipio Asiaticus in 190 B.C. Antiochus III died while trying to plunder a pagan temple near Susa (187 B.C.) just a year after signing peace accords with Rome (188 B.C.). Thus, as Scripture says, he stumbled and was found no more. The role of the king of the north now switches to Rome. As Roy Gane has pointed out,[12] when a ruler from the current kingdom (Greece, in this case) attacks the rising kingdom and does not do well, the prophetic focus will switch to the new emerging kingdom (now Rome).

The Rise of Rome

In verses 20-22 we have the Roman phase. After Antiochus III's time the Romans gained power in Europe and the Middle East. And here we find mention of the prince of the covenant.

Some people ask me, "How can you be sure there is a change from the Greeks to the Romans?" Jeremiah 1:15 tells me to expect one kingdom to replace another: " 'For behold, I am calling all the families of the kingdoms of the north,' says the Lord; 'they shall come and each one set his throne at the entrance of the gates of Jerusalem, against all its walls all around, and against all the cities of Judah.' " When Nebuchadnezzar captured the city, he had his throne placed at the gate of Jerusalem for a little while to show that he was the new ruler. But notice that the verse says "kingdoms." Several kingdoms would seize Jerusalem and, as each conquered it, set up their throne. Daniel's prophecies of chapters 2 and 7 say that a series of powers would emerge: Babylon, Medo-Persia, Greece, Rome, and a divided former Roman Empire. One after another they are the kingdoms that represent the king of the north from Daniel's era all the way through to the time of the end.

The book of Jeremiah repeatedly refers to the Babylonian invasion of Jerusalem as coming from the north. Also Jeremiah 50:9 declares that Babylon's conqueror will arrive from the north. This would make Medo-Persia the second king of the north. Then Daniel 11 calls the Seleucids, a part of the Greek Empire, as the king of the north, and introduces another part of the empire, the Ptolemaic kingdom, as a new power from the south. Finally, Rome, the fourth major power from Daniel 2 and 7, also advances from the north as it takes Jerusalem. Our conclusion, then, is that the powers of Daniel 2 and 7 all attack Jerusalem from the north, and each is correctly identified as the king of the north.

Jesus, the Center of Prophecy

We need to go back now and take a look at Daniel 11:20-22, to revisit the time of Rome and the prince of the covenant. Again we are examining the match between the prophecy and what actually happened in history.

"There shall arise in his place [the Greek king of the north] one who imposes taxes on the glorious kingdom; but within a few days he shall be destroyed, but not in anger or in battle. And in his place shall arise a vile person, to whom they will not give the honor of royalty; but he shall come in peaceably, and seize the kingdom by intrigue. With the force of a flood they shall be swept away from before him and be broken, and also the prince of the covenant."

At the beginning of this passage we find someone in power imposing taxes on the "glorious kingdom," which is Israel. We find confirmation of such taxation in Luke 2: "And it came to pass in those days that a decree went out from Caesar Augustus [the Roman emperor] that all the world should be registered [taxed]." Here you have a link from the New Testament to Daniel 11. The birth of Jesus happened when that person taxed the "glorious kingdom." Jesus was broken (killed) during the time of the Roman Empire. He is the prince of the covenant spoken of in Daniel 11:22.

Now we go to another part of Daniel that expands on what the prince of the covenant does when He arrives. Daniel 9 contains a prophecy about the prince of the covenant, who will die to take away the sins of humanity. Who does that? Jesus Christ! Here is what Daniel 9:24-27 announces:

"Seventy weeks are determined for your people and for your holy city, to finish the transgression, to make an end of sins, to make reconciliation for iniquity, to bring in everlasting righteousness, to seal up vision and prophecy, and to anoint the Most Holy.

"Know therefore and understand, that from the going forth of the command to restore and build Jerusalem until Messiah the Prince, there shall be seven weeks and sixty-two weeks; the street shall be built again, and the wall, even in troublesome times.

"And after the sixty-two weeks Messiah shall be cut off, but not for Himself; and the people of the prince who is to come shall destroy the city and the sanctuary. The end of it shall be with a flood, and till the end of the war desolations are determined. Then he shall confirm a covenant with many for one week; but in the middle of the week he shall bring an end to sacrifice and offering. And on the wing of abominations shall be one who makes desolate, even until the consummation, which is determined, is poured out on the desolate."

The prophecy needs some explanation. First of all, in Ezekiel 4:6 and in Numbers 14:34 we find a principle for interpreting time prophecies, which states that a prophetic day equals a year. Keep this in mind whenever you run into a time prophecy. It works very well in Daniel 9.

"Seventy weeks are determined for your people." How many days in 70 weeks? 7 x 70 = 490 days. Applying the principle of a day for a year, we have 490 years. And so, "from the going forth of the command to restore and build Jerusalem until Messiah the Prince" (the prince of the covenant), you have 62 weeks, or 483 years.

Notice that the verse says there are 7 and 62, and the Messiah comes after the 62. The 7 weeks represented the first jubilee cycle of 49 years of rebuilding the Temple and city, and the 62 weeks symbolized the long time period from the rebuilding of the Temple and city until the coming of the Messiah. You add those together, and it brings you 483 years to Messiah the Prince.

Did that actually happen? The book of Ezra announces the decree that authorized the rebuilding of the Temple. Archaeology has pinned that date to 457 B.C. Doing the math (457 B.C. plus 490 years) brings us to A.D. 34. Or, if we use the 483 years, that brings us to A.D. 27. (Don't forget that in going from B.C. to A.D., you have to add one year, because there was no zero year.) So according to the prophecy, Jesus the Messiah, the prince of the covenant, should enter the picture in A.D. 27, and the time of probation for the Israelite nation should be over in A.D. 34.

What happened in A.D. 27? Jesus began His ministry. Here is what Luke recorded: "Now in the fifteenth year of the reign of Tiberius Caesar," "when all the people were baptized, it came to pass that Jesus also was baptized; and while He prayed, the heaven was opened" (Luke 3:1, 21). When Jesus is baptized, He comes up out of the water, the Holy Spirit descends on Him, anointing Him for ministry, and He begins the ministry of the Messiah. Luke pinpoints the anointing of Messiah the Prince at the fifteenth year of Tiberius Caesar, which was A.D. 27.

What else does this tell us? If we count the Passover cycles in the Gospel of John, we find three and a half Passover cycles during Jesus' ministry, which meant that He died in or about A.D. 31. Daniel 9:27 declares, "Then he shall confirm a covenant with many for one week; but in the middle of the week he shall bring an end to sacrifice and offering." If you are a Christian, have you offered a sacrifice recently? killed a lamb to atone for your sins? Why not? Because Jesus is the Lamb of God. He died on the cross for our sins. Jesus brought an end to sacrifice—that is why you are not offering them.

Mark 15:38 records the end of sacrifice this way: "The veil of the temple was torn in two from top to bottom." When Jesus said, "It is finished" on the cross, an unseen hand from heaven grabbed that huge Temple veil and ripped it apart. From God's perspective, sacrifices no longer mattered, because Jesus, the Lamb of God, had just died to take away your sins and mine and every sin that has ever been committed on earth, for all who will let Him remove their sins from them. Jesus put an end to sacrifices. Yes, the Jewish priests still offered them for a few more years before the destruction of the Temple, but from heaven's perspective, they ceased when Jesus said, "It is finished."

When Jesus left earth and went back to heaven, He told His disciples to work first in Jerusalem, next in Judea, then in Samaria, and finally the uttermost parts of the world. Why did He tell them to focus on Judea first? Because, according to the prophecy, three and a half years still remained for the nation to decide if it would fully accept Jesus and His gift.

At the end of those three and a half years, the religious leaders of Judea stoned Stephen to death (read about it in Acts 7). Saul, who had actively participated in the execution, headed out to persecute Christians. Jesus called to him from heaven, knocked him down with a bright light, and asked why he was persecuting Him. When Saul saw the wrong he was doing, Jesus said to him, "Depart, for I will send you from here to the Gentiles." The time period was up—the 70 weeks were over. The gospel now also went to the non-Jews, not just the Jews.

Without question Jews can still be saved in God's kingdom. But the special focus on them as a nation was gone—it was now on anyone who would accept Jesus Christ. The prophecy of Daniel 9 was completely fulfilled in the ministry of Jesus Christ, and that is the prophecy alluded to in verses 20-22 of Daniel 11. Daniel 9 talked about Jerusalem being destroyed like "a flood." Those are the same words used in Daniel 11:20-22 for the destruction of Jerusalem. Scripture clearly links the death of Jesus and the destruction of Jerusalem under Rome. It ties in directly with the fact that both Jesus and the Roman power were active then. We have firm evidence that it is Rome as the king of the north here and Jesus as the prince of the covenant.

Who is really the center point of prophecy? After His resurrection, Jesus said to the two He met on the road to Emmaus: "Don't you know that all those prophecies from the Old Testament point to Me?" (See Luke 24:13-27.) Jesus is the one who ties it all together. Some people wonder if Christians should even study Daniel 11, because it is in the Old Testament. But Jesus said that all those prophecies pointed to Him.

Don't shortchange your study by throwing out or neglecting any part of the Bible. It's true that we don't need to offer sacrifices anymore, but all of the Bible points to Jesus Christ. You can be sure of this: if you know all about Bible prophecy and don't know Jesus, you will have missed both its meaning and its fulfillment.

---

[1] The historical basis of this chapter comes from a variety of sources, but any reputable book of world history will bear it out.

[2] Boris Johnson, *After Rome: Holy War and Conquest,* directed by Grace Chapman and Francis Hanley, two-part series aired Nov. 29 and Dec. 6, 2008 (London: BBC, 2008).

[3] See Samuel P. Huntington, "The Clash of Civilizations?" *Foreign Affairs* 72, no. 3 (Summer 1993): 22-49.

[4] The Daniel 11 prophecy with detailed explanation appears in Appendix A on pp. 203-212, with Bible texts on the left and interpretation on the right.

[5] www.haaretz.com/news/top-iran-officials-recommend-preemptive-strike-against-israel-1.255799.

[6] Asa Oscar Tait, *Heralds of the Morning* (Oakland, Calif.: Pacific Press., 1899), pp. 183, 184.

[7] *Ibid.,* pp. 186, 187.

[8] *Ibid.,* p. 187.

[9] www.cbsnews.com/stories/2008/06/18/tech/main4191556.shtml.

[10] www.barna.org/barna-update/article/21-transformation/252-barna-survey-examines-changes-in-worldview-among-christians-over-the-past-13-years.

[11] You can walk through those gates today, but you can't go to Babylon to do it. You have to visit the Pergamon Museum in Berlin, Germany. The Germans took the gate down piece by piece, transported it to their country, and rebuilt it.

[12] "The Un-Manifestation of Antiochus IV Epiphanes in Daniel 11:1-22."

CHAPTER 2

The King of the North: Roman to Holy Roman Empire

In chapter 1 we had a quick overview of Daniel 11 through 12:4 from the time of the prophet Daniel to the end of sin and suffering. We found that the kings of the north and south go through phases of conflict. The first phase was the struggle between the Greek Ptolemies and the Greek Seleucids, and then came Rome from the north. As we got up to verses 20-22 we saw that the prince of the covenant is Jesus Christ. Daniel 9 expanded on that, giving us a time frame for when His ministry would begin, the dates for His baptism and His death, and how He would bring an end to sacrifice. Jesus is the ultimate sacrifice for sin, and that makes Him the focal point of Bible prophecy.

When Jesus lived on earth, the pagan phase of the Roman Empire was the king of the north. We also saw that power depicted in the legs of iron in the statue of Daniel 2. Because the legs of iron turn into feet of iron and clay, there is some continuation of the iron into the feet. In a match to this prophecy, Daniel 7 explains how the attention turns from the pagan Roman Empire as it changes from a beast with iron teeth and claws to a focus on the beast's 10 horns that develop after it. The 10 horns of the beast rise in Europe after the breakup of the western Roman Empire, and a little horn comes up after that.

Daniel 2, 7, and 8 are parallel prophecies with Daniel 11. It means that the king of the north after the breakup of the Roman Empire will be the same as the feet of iron and clay in Daniel 2 and the same as the little horn of Daniel 7 and 8. Most Bible commentators believe that the little horn of Daniel 7 and 8, the "man of sin" in 2 Thessalonians 2, and the beast of Revelation 13 are one and the same power that emerges from within the western Roman Empire, an entity often called the antichrist. The commentators do not all agree on exactly what or who this power is, but most Bible commentary and prophecy books of today agree that the three Bible references refer to the same agency. The power described in those Bible references is the same as the king of the north that appears after the Roman Empire in Daniel 11.

Among the descriptions in 2 Thessalonians, Daniel, and Revelation are 16 characteristics that reveal the identity of the little horn/king of the north/man of sin/antichrist power. Let's examine the characteristics and then see which historical power they match up with. In this chapter and in the rest of the book I will refer to the antichrist, the little horn, and the king of the north interchangeably as the same power.

First Characteristic

According to 2 Thessalonians 2:1-3, the antichrist power rises before the return of Jesus, when He gathers His believers. "Now, brethren, concerning the coming of our Lord Jesus Christ and our gathering together to Him, we ask you, not to be soon shaken in mind or troubled, either by spirit or by word or by letter, as if from us, as though the day of Christ had come. Let no one deceive you by any means; for that Day will not come unless the falling away comes first, and the man of sin is revealed, the son of perdition."

The antichrist will manifest itself before Jesus returns. The man of sin must appear, and then Jesus will come. Remember the sequence, because that is important in determining the identity of this power.

Second Characteristic

Later in 2 Thessalonians 2 Paul tells us that the antichrist power had already begun to manifest itself in the first century. The apostle writes: "For the mystery of lawlessness is already at work; only He who now re-strains will do so until He is taken out of the way. And then the lawless one will be revealed, whom the Lord will consume with the breath of His mouth and destroy with the brightness of His coming" (verses 7, 8). Since this power had already emerged in the time of the early church, Paul could write about it.

Third Characteristic

The antichrist surfaces among the 10 horns, which means it rises from somewhere in the European part of the former Roman Empire. Daniel 7:8 says: "I was considering the [10] horns, and there was another horn, a lit-tle one, coming up among them."

The 10 horns are kingdoms that developed out of the breakup of the Roman Empire. The following 10 were the major tribes: Ostrogoths,

Visigoths, Vandals, Alemanni, Burgundians, Franks, Lombards, Anglo-Saxons, Suevi, and Heruli. As the old empire fell apart, these tribes took over. The little horn—the antichrist—rose from among them.

Fourth Characteristic

The little horn, or the antichrist, would manifest itself after the establishment of the 10 horns. Daniel 7:24: "The ten horns are ten kings who shall arise from this kingdom. And another shall rise after them; he shall be different from the first ones." The date generally accepted by historians for the end of the Roman Empire is A.D. 476. The little-horn power develops within the geographical area of the Roman Empire but after the time the 10 horns bring an end to the old empire itself.

Fifth Characteristic

It is a little horn, or a little kingdom. Scripture mentions several times that sizewise it is a little horn. "There was another horn, a little one, coming up among them" (verse 8). While it will be a smaller or younger power, it will still have a vast amount of influence.

Sixth Characteristic

The little-horn power would uproot three of the 10 horn powers formed out of the Roman Empire. "There was another horn, a little one, coming up among them, before whom three of the first horns were plucked out by the roots" (verse 8). Verse 24 adds: "And shall subdue three kings." Three powers would be deposed to make room for the little-horn power—exactly what happened in the century after Rome shattered. The emperor Justinian subjugated the Heruli, the Vandals, and the Ostrogoths, because of their Arian theology (they did not believe that Jesus was fully God), and their kingdoms faded away.

Seventh Characteristic

The little-horn power has a human being as its head. Verse 8 states: "There, in this horn, were eyes like the eyes of a man, and a mouth speaking pompous words." Revelation 13:8 follows suit: "All who dwell on the earth will worship him, whose names have not been written in the Book of Life of the Lamb slain from the foundation of the world." And finally, 2 Thessalonians 2:3 talks about the man of sin: "That Day will not come unless the falling away comes first, and the man of sin is revealed." Almost all Bible scholars view the antichrist power as being led by a man.

Eighth Characteristic

It would be unlike all the other kingdoms preceding it. "The ten horns are ten kings who shall arise from this kingdom. And another shall rise after them; he shall be different from the first ones" (Dan. 7:24). We will see what that means as we go along.

Ninth Characteristic

The antichrist would speak "great words," or blasphemy. What is blasphemy? Jesus helps us understand it. While He was on earth, He said, "Before Abraham was, I Am" (John 8:58). God is the "I Am" of Scripture. But then, according to John 10:31, "the Jews took up stones again to stone Him," because they thought He was claiming to be God. Blasphemy happens when a person claims to be God and really is not. (The catch for Jesus' accusers was that He really is God.)

Jesus faced another accusation of blasphemy in Mark 2:5-7. "When Jesus saw their faith, He said to the paralytic, 'Son, your sins are forgiven you.' But some of the scribes were sitting there and reasoning in their hearts, 'Why does this Man speak blasphemies like this? Who can forgive sins but God alone?'" Blasphemy happens when a sinful human being claims a prerogative limited only to God. Here, only God can forgive sin.

Notice the description of the "great words" or blasphemy in the three Bible references we are comparing. Daniel 7:8 refers to "a mouth speaking pompous words," verse 20 mentions "a mouth which spoke pompous words," and verse 25 declares that "he shall speak pompous words against the Most High." In 2 Thessalonians 2:4 we find someone "who opposes and exalts himself above all that is called God or that is worshiped, so that he sits as God in the temple of God, showing himself that he is God." And Revelation 13:5 describes a being who "was given a mouth speaking great things and blasphemies." The man of sin claims the prerogatives or attributes of God. The little horn speaks pompous words against God. And Revelation combines the two types of speech—the pompous words and the blasphemy. From these descriptions you can start to see how Bible commentators end up seeing this power as the same entity, because it repeatedly displays the same characteristics.

Tenth Characteristic

The little-horn power would persecute the saints, or God's people. Daniel 7:25 says: "[He] shall persecute the saints of the Most High."

Revelation 13:7: "It was granted to him to make war with the saints and to overcome them." One of its hallmarks is that the antichrist would attack God's people.

Eleventh Characteristic

The little horn would take upon itself to change what God had established. Daniel 7:25: "[He] shall intend to change times and law." While the other two Bible books do not mention this aspect, it is key to the definition of the little-horn power.

Twelfth Characteristic

The antichrist power has a 1260-day or -year rule. Daniel 7:25 states: "Then the saints shall be given into his hand for a time and times and half a time." How do we get 1260 days out of that? We take "time" as one year, and "times" (the Hebrew word means "twice," or "two") gives us two more, for a total of three. "Half a time" is the half year to finish it. That adds up to three and a half years.

You may be thinking, *Pastor Tim, you're starting to push it there. How do you know that is definite?*

To corroborate this figure, in Revelation 12:14 we find the time period again. "The woman was given two wings of a great eagle, that she might fly into the wilderness to her place, where she is nourished for a time and times and half a time, from the presence of the serpent." There you have "times" again, but does it really signify three and a half years? Revelation gives the figure in a different way in still another verse. Revelation 12:6: "The woman fled into the wilderness, where she has a place prepared by God, that they should feed her there one thousand two hundred and sixty days." The same woman goes to the same place for the specified period of time. Calculating in reverse using the biblical day/year principle (see Eze. 4:6), 1260 days equals three and a half years.

But the book of Revelation hits it a third way, just to make sure we have got it. "He [the antichrist] was given a mouth speaking great things and blasphemies, and he was given authority to continue for forty-two months" (Rev. 13:5). How many years is forty-two months? Three and a half years. And 42 months times 30 equals 1260, which means the years had only 360 days, indicating that they were symbolic, not literal.

All of these references have the same three-and-a-half-year time prophecy, which equals 1260 years. The antichrist receives authority for the 1260 years, and then its power ceases.

35

Thirteenth Characteristic

The little horn, or antichrist entity, would receive a deadly wound, and later it would come back to life, but now with great worldwide power. Revelation 13:3 explains: "I saw one of his heads as if it had been mortally wounded, and his deadly wound was healed. And all the world marveled and followed the beast." One of the marks of the beast power portrayed here is that it will recover from a deadly wound and have a global following.

Fourteenth Characteristic

The least important of the characteristics, in my opinion, but the most widely popularized, is the number 666. "Let him who has understanding calculate the number of the beast, for it is the number of a man: His number is 666" (Rev. 13:18).

I have heard all kinds of ideas about 666, such as "It's a credit card." No, it's not a credit card. "It's a bar code." Again, no, it's not a bar code. It is none of those things. The issue is something else, far more important and fundamental. But we will explore that later in the chapter.

Fifteenth Characteristic

Another mark of identification is that the antichrist would receive "the dragon's throne." "The dragon gave him his power, his throne, and great authority" (Rev. 13:2). The dragon in Revelation symbolizes Satan, but it also represents a power that he worked through.

"The dragon stood before the woman who was ready to give birth, to devour her Child as soon as it was born" (Rev. 12:4). The Child born to the woman ends up ruling the world with a "rod of iron," as King of kings, and He is taken up to heaven to be with God. Who fits that description? Jesus Christ.

After Jesus' birth Herod tried to kill Him. As a vassal king, Herod was part of the Roman government, and he sent soldiers into Bethlehem to kill the infant boys in an attempt to kill Jesus. Since Herod ruled under the authority of Rome, it is the nondescript, dragonlike power that Satan was working through. We can expect that the Roman power will eventually give the little horn some kind of seat or throne.

Sixteenth Characteristic

The sixteenth trait comes along a little too late for us to use in confirming the identity of the antichrist, because it is still in the future. However, it is an important one to keep in mind. Daniel describes what he saw in vision: "I watched then because of the sound of the pompous words which the horn was speaking; I watched till the beast was slain, and its body destroyed and given to the burning flame" (Dan. 7:11). When the little-horn power finally ceases to be, he will perish in fire. When might that happen? "And then the lawless one will be revealed, whom the Lord will consume with the breath of His mouth and destroy with the brightness of His coming" (2 Thess. 2:8). The flame is the coming of Jesus, and it will annihilate the antichrist at that time.

The prophet John, in Revelation 19:19 and 20, talks further about the fate of the little horn when Jesus returns.

"And I saw the beast, the kings of the earth, and their armies, gathered together to make war against Him who sat on the horse and against His army. Then the beast was captured, and with him the false prophet who worked signs in his presence, by which he deceived those who received the mark of the beast and those who worshiped his image. These two were cast alive into the lake of fire burning with brimstone."

Later we will discuss the false prophet and the mark of the beast. For now, we can see that the beast power—the antichrist—will be destroyed by fire at Jesus' second coming. With this final characteristic we can see that the books of Daniel, 2 Thessalonians, and Revelation all describe the same agency.

The Power That Is the Antichrist or King of the North

Who, then, is this little-horn/antichrist/beast power? Luther, Calvin, Wycliffe, and the Wesleys taught that it was the Roman Catholic papal system (its ecclesiastical structure), and I agree with them.

That does not mean the little horn is the Roman Catholic membership. (When God calls those within every fallen church "My people" in Revelation 18:4, that would apply to those within the Catholic Church as well.) We can expect lots of Roman Catholic people to be in heaven, because for centuries it has had faithful Christians within it. And that will continue to be the case until just before the end of the world.

It is the papal system—the governmental structure and teachings of the Roman Catholic Church—that have some very serious problems with Scripture. The church places the authority of tradition ahead of that of Scripture, and anytime you do that, dangerous things can happen.

We will now go back through the 16 characteristics, and as we do, we will see whether or not they match the papal system.

First, did the Papacy arise before the return of Jesus Christ? We need to ask ourselves one question: Has Jesus come back to earth yet?

Second, the Christian church in the first century was already seeing the beginning of a system of ideas that valued tradition above Scripture. Paul was fighting it, and he said it would be held back. Who restrained it during the apostle's day? The pagan Roman Empire had ironfisted control, and because it was persecuting Christians, it inadvertently blocked many of those errors. As soon as Christianity became acceptable in the empire and it was no longer facing persecution, the errors rushed in, and aspects of paganism crept into the church. Christianity became mixed with other traditions. So the problem of "the mystery of lawlessness," as Paul called it, had already begun in the first century.

Concerning the third characteristic, we must ask, Did the Roman Catholic Church, or the papal system, emerge within the Roman Empire? Yes, the city of Rome, which became the seat and center of papal influence, was the empire's focal center.

Number four: Did the little-horn power arise after the breakup of the Roman Empire? Yes, it gained its power soon after the demise of the western Roman Empire. So that's a match.

How about number five? Is the little horn a small kingdom? While today Vatican City has a land mass of about 110 acres (tiny compared to previous papal territory), it has power way beyond its size. Small kingdom, large power. That matches all of the descriptions in Daniel, 2 Thessalonians, and Revelation. Furthermore, in Daniel 11:23, 24 we find that the next power that represents the king of the north lacks an army and acquires the kingdom through intrigue. While the passage does not specifically name any entity, we do know that the Papacy originally possessed no military forces but had the city of Rome left to it when Emperor Constantine moved away. The legs of iron had given way to the feet of iron and clay.

According to characteristic number six, the antichrist power uproots three horns. As mentioned earlier, the emperor of the eastern empire subjugated the Heruli, the Vandals, and the Ostrogoths for a very simple reason. Although they had accepted Christianity, they followed the teachings of Arius. Emperor Justinian believed that Arian theology was heretical and unorthodox, and he issued edicts that forbade anyone in his empire to espouse Arius' views. His armies conquered the three tribes to enforce his decrees. Their destruction made the Papacy the leader of Christianity and gave it full reign in Europe.

Number seven: Does the power have a human being at its head? Clearly, the individual called the pope. Considered the supreme leader of the church, his word is law within it.

Number eight asks whether it is different from the other prophetic kingdoms. Think back to Babylon, Medo-Persia, Greece, and Rome. They were all primarily political entities, but the post-Roman Roman Empire coalitions (especially the papal territories) were primarily religious in nature, bound together by the type of Christianity that the emperor and the pope enforced, and only secondarily political. It is diverse or different from the previous kingdoms because it is primarily a religious power. Through the course of Daniel 11:23-45 the king of the north takes on religious characteristics. Again we have a match with the references in Daniel, 2 Thessalonians, and Revelation.

Number nine talks about speaking great words or blasphemy. Daniel 11:36, 37 links this power to the king of the north, who is speaking great words and blasphemy. We have already seen in Mark 2 and John 10 that blasphemy is either someone putting themselves in the place of God when they are not or claiming to be able to forgive sin, solely a divine prerogative. Let's see what the Roman Catholic Church leadership says about its authority and abilities in these areas. The following are quotations from Roman Catholic materials. They are not from people who have an ax to grind against that church.

"The Pope is of so great dignity and so exalted, that he is not mere man, but as it were, God, and the vicar of God. . . . The Pope is called the most holy because he is rightfully presumed to be such. He is, likewise, the divine monarch, and supreme emperor, and king of kings. Hence the Pope is crowned with a triple crown as king of heaven and of earth and of hell."[1]

Look at the names for the pope listed here: divine monarch, supreme emperor, and king of kings! But Jesus Christ is the real King of kings in Scripture, so in essence the quotation attributes to the pope characteristics limited to Jesus Christ alone. When anyone claims that a human being has divine prerogatives and they are not God, then it meets the biblical definition of blasphemy.

Another statement from the same article in *Prompta Bibliotheca* says: "The Pope is as it were God on earth, Sole sovereign of all the faithful of Christ, chief king of kings, having a plentitude of unbroken power, entrusted by the omnipotent God to govern the earthly and heavenly kingdoms."[2] Here he is chief king of kings. That would put him above Jesus, if Jesus is the King of kings. And then it says, "God on earth." You have noticed, I am sure, that popes come and go. They die, and therefore are not God—but that is the claim.

The book *On the Authority of the Councils* declares, "All names which in the Scriptures are applied to Christ, by virtue of the which it is established that He is over the church, all the same names are applied to the Pope."[3] You get the overall drift with these words: "Thou art the shepherd, thou art the physician, thou art the director, thou art the husbandman, finally thou art another God on earth."[4]

In a 1984 article in the Los Angeles *Times* entitled "No Forgiveness 'Directly From God,' Pope Says," Don Schanche wrote: "Rebutting a belief widely shared by Protestants and a growing number of Roman Catholics, Pope John Paul II on Tuesday dismissed the 'widespread idea that one can obtain forgiveness directly from God' and exhorted Catholics to confess more often to their priest."[5] What, then, is the Catholic Church's teaching on forgiveness? That you must obtain it from a priest.

Another source for the church's claims about the power of the priests is Michael Müller: "Seek where you will, throughout heaven and earth, and you will find but one created being who can forgive the sinner, who can free him from the chains of sin and hell: and that extraordinary being is the priest, the Catholic priest. . . . Yes, the priest not only declares that the sinner is forgiven, but he really forgives him. The priest raises his hand, he pronounces the words of absolution, and in an instant, quick as a flash of light, the chains of hell are burst asunder, and the sinner becomes a child of God. So great is the power of the priest, that the judgments of heaven itself are subject to his decision."[6]

If this were true, it would place great power into the hands of a human being. But Mark 2:7 indicates that if a person claims they can forgive sin, it is blasphemy, because only God can do that.

Furthermore, Catholic doctrine not only teaches that the priest forgives sins but that God has to do what the priest tells Him to do. Think of it this way: if you are friends with the priest and the priest forgives you, then God has to do the same, even if you did not mean it. If, on the other hand, you are enemies with the priest and ask to be forgiven, and he says, "No, I will not forgive you," then, according to the doctrine, God cannot forgive you either. That teaching has brought untold trouble through the centuries.

Thankfully, as the Scripture says, any one of us can go to Jesus, confess our sins, and know that we are forgiven and thus have eternal life. I am thrilled that God's Word is simple and straightforward on that point, and that we do not have to seek forgiveness through a human being.

The tenth characteristic: persecuting the saints. We have already seen how the books of Daniel and Revelation talk about persecution against the people of God. In Daniel 11:30-33 the king of the north "shall be grieved, and return in rage against the holy covenant, and do damage. . . . The people . . . know their God shall be strong, . . . [but] they shall fall by sword and flame." Remember the three tribes (horns) uprooted? They were destroyed because they did not hold the same Christian beliefs as the dominant religious authorities did. Through the centuries millions faced suffering and death because they disagreed with church positions. If you believed that you should have the Bible in your own language and be able to read it, for example, you could die by the sword or be burned at the stake.

In a 1994 letter Pope John Paul II acknowledged the history of persecution by the church. He wrote that a "painful chapter of history to which the sons and daughters of the Church must return with a spirit of repentance is that of the acquiescence given, especially in certain centuries, to *intolerance and even the use of violence* in the service of truth."[7] In March 2000 John Paul urged forgiveness for centuries of wrongs that the Roman Catholic Church had perpetrated on others. In a daylong ceremony called the "Day of Forgiveness," he and seven senior church leaders read prayers that asked forgiveness for the Crusades, the Inquisitions, forced conversions, and acts committed against women, indigenous peoples, and Jews, among other things. "We humbly ask for forgiveness for the part that each of us with his or her behaviors has played in such evils, thus contributing to disrupting the face of the church," John Paul said.[8] Clarifying the purpose of the prayers, the pope said the next day: "The Church does not cease to implore God's forgiveness for the sins of her members."[9]

Do such persecuting practices continue today? I have experienced it myself. In South America I recently presented some Bible lectures, and that upset the local Catholic priest. He sent some police officers with automatic rifles to our hotel in the middle of the night. That is not a fun way to wake up in your hotel room. Such things still happen.

Considering characteristic number 11, Daniel 7:25 tells us that "[they] shall intend to change times and law." Daniel 11:28, 30, and 32 state that the king of the north would be against God's covenant. In other words, it would think to change or do away with it. Has that happened? Here is what Ferraris' eighteenth-century *Prompta Bibliotheca* says: "The Pope is of so great authority and power that he is able to modify, declare, or interpret even divine laws. The Pope can modify divine law, since his power is not of man but of God, and he acts as vicegerent of God upon earth with most ample power of binding and loosing his sheep."[10] Based on that claim, the pope can alter God's Word whenever he wants to. That is why the Catholic Church announces that its authority and traditions can supersede God's written Word.

I believe in *sola scriptura* ("the Bible only") as the primary guide for life. I listen to other people, but I always test what they present by the Bible. Make it a habit to check everything. Ask yourself, "What does the Bible really say?" Always be sure that what people teach about Scripture actually reflects the message of the Bible.

Has the Roman Catholic Church changed times and laws? To answer, first let us consider a simple example. Peter Geiermann's *Convert's Catechism of Catholic Doctrine* discusses the Ten Commandments: "The First Commandment is: I am the Lord thy God; thou shalt not have strange gods before Me."[11] If you were reading along in Exodus 20, you would find that, yes, that is the first commandment.

Then the catechism continues: "The Second Commandment is: Thou shalt not take the name of the Lord thy God in vain."[12] Whoops! If you are reading along in your Bible, you will see that what should be the second commandment appears in Exodus 20:4. It states that we should not bow down to images. The catechism's list of the Ten Commandments ignores the verse, not stressing it as a separate commandment. Why would the church do that? If you have been in a Roman Catholic cathedral, you will have seen the statues lining the walls. People bow and pray before them. Perhaps the church's teaching glosses over the injunction because of this. It is still there in the explanation of the first one, but it is not treated as a separate commandment.

So in the catechism the first commandment is "I am the Lord thy God; thou shalt not have strange gods before Me." The second one is "Thou shalt not take the name of the Lord thy God in vain." From that point on, the commandment list in this catechism is one off from the traditional Protestant list until you get to the tenth one. They had to split the one about coveting into two commandments to make 10 separate commandments.

But now let us look at what is clearly the most extreme example. Here's what the same catechism says:

"Q. *What is the Third Commandment?*

A. The Third Commandment is: Remember that thou keep holy the Sabbath day.

42

Q. *Which is the Sabbath day?*

A. Saturday is the Sabbath day.

Q. *Why do we observe Sunday instead of Saturday?*

A. We observe Sunday instead of Saturday because the Catholic Church transferred the solemnity from Saturday to Sunday. . . .

Q. *By what authority did the Church substitute Sunday for Saturday?*

A. The Church substituted Sunday for Saturday by the plenitude of that divine power which Jesus Christ bestowed upon her."[13]

The church claims authority over Scripture so that it has the ability to change divine law. But I do not believe that any human institution has such power.

Daniel said that the little-horn power would alter times and laws. The examples I have cited fit the prophecy.

Characteristic number 12: the 1260 day/year prophecy. In A.D. 533 Justinian declared the pope to be the head of all the churches in the empire. The Code of Justinian, book 1, title 1, proclaims the bishop of Rome as "head of all the holy churches" and "head of all the holy priests of God."[14] The year of key prophetic importance, however, is 538. In that year Justinian defeated the Ostrogoths, who had held Italy and brought Rome under his protection. "Vigilius . . . ascended the papal chair under the military protection of [General] Belisarius (538-554)."[15] It removed the last of the three Arian tribes that had stood in the way of papal authority. Now the little horn had gained religious and political power across the empire, and the pope was the generally acknowledged and undisputed leader of the Christian church.

From A.D. 538, 1260 years takes us to 1798. That year the Napoleonic general Louis-Alexandre Berthier and his French Republican troops entered Italy and invaded the Vatican. Berthier proclaimed a Roman republic. Napoleon abolished the Papal States (those areas directly under the control of the pope). (The Papal States were temporarily reconstituted several times, until they were finally incorporated into a unified Italy in 1870.) When Pope Pius VI refused to surrender, Berthier arrested him and carried him off to France, where the pope died in captivity. The world thought that the Papacy as a political power had met its end.

Number 13: As successor to the Roman Empire, the Papacy had both political and religious power until 1798 and then received a "deadly wound." But the Bible also says the wound would be healed, and the antichrist would then hold power until the end of time. That king of the north will continue until the coming of Jesus Christ, and unless we can find another entity that replaces the king of the south, Islam will maintain its influence until almost the end as well.

Revelation 13:3 describes the healing of the deadly wound. "I saw one of his heads as if it had been mortally wounded, and his deadly wound was healed. And all the world marveled and followed the beast." Newspapers around the world reported a remarkable development in 1929. The San Francisco *Chronicle* of February 12, 1929, put it this way: "The Roman question tonight was a thing of the past and the Vatican was at peace with Italy. The formal accomplishment of this today was the exchange of signatures in the historic Palace of St. John Lateran by two noteworthy plenipotentiaries, Cardinal Gasparri for Pope Pius XI and Premier Mussolini for King Victor Emmanuel III. In affixing their autographs to this memorable document, healing the wound which has festered since 1870, extreme cordiality was displayed on both sides."[16]

Revelation says that the wound would be healed. The San Francisco *Chronicle* actually uses the words "healing the wound." From 1798 until 1929 the Papacy had been in trouble. It had not been in control of Vatican City itself since 1870. Not until 1929 did the church regain jurisdiction of even its small territory. The treaty with the Italian government in 1929 was of utmost importance to the church, because now it again had political authority of its own.

From that time on, the power of the Papacy began to rebuild. In the twentieth century John Paul II was a major mover in restoring its authority. His death brought together almost every national leader in the world for his funeral, along with the president of the United States and several past presidents.[17]

Number 14: What about the number 666? Many Protestants have seen in the title "Vicarius Filii Dei" a name attributed to the pope that might match the number. I have read a whole book written on just that title.[18] It records the times that the Catholic Church's own documents employ the words Vicarius Filii Dei. Today the Roman Catholic Church denies that Vicarius Filii Dei is a title employed by the pope, but that it appeared only as a title of the pope in a document called the Donation of Constantine and accepted by the church from about the ninth century A.D. until 1440, when scholars demonstrated that it was a forgery.

Vicarius Filii Dei means vicar or representative of the Son of God. The letters in the name can be seen as Roman numerals:

VICARIVS: V = 5, I = 1, C = 100, A = 0, R = 0, I = 1, V = 5, S = 0. (Latin has no U; a V took its place.)

FILII: F = 0, I = 1, L = 50, I = 1, I = 1.

DEI: D = 500, E = zero, I = 1.

The numbers of the name equal 666. The sum works as follows:

VICARIVS FILII DEI = 5 + 1 + 100 + 1 + 5 + 1 + 50 + 1 + 1 + 500 + 1 = 666.

Through the years people have tried to figure out if the numeric value of the letters of some prominent leader's name represents 666. But it does not matter what the numbers of any name add up to if the other characteristics do not match. If all the other characteristics correspond to a particular person, only then would it be worth checking the numbers of their name.

Number 15: The little-horn power receives the dragon's throne. In the first and second centuries A.D. Rome became recognized as an important center of Christianity, especially because of its association with the apostolic tradition of Peter and Paul. Gradually the Roman church manifested authority over other churches. Pope Leo the Great declared in A.D. 445: "The care of the universal Church should converge towards Peter's one seat, and nothing anywhere should be separated from its Head."[19] After Emperor Constantine built a new capital for the Roman Empire and named it Constantinople, he spent little time in Rome. In his absence the head of the Roman church became the leader of Christianity and increasingly had civic power in Rome as well. As one scholar noted: "The Roman church pushed its way into the place of the Western empire, of which it is 'the actual continuation.' Thus the empire did not perish; it only changed its form. The pope became Caesar's successor."[20] In the power vacuum resulting from the collapse of the Roman Empire the former capital city of Rome continued to exercise great authority, but the one in the seat of power was the pope. The Bible says the beast would receive the seat of the dragon, and that, too, was fulfilled.

Number 16: Christ's return destroys the antichrist power. This is the one characteristic we must wait for since it is still in the future, but we still have a match with the first 15. The little horn of Daniel 7, the man of sin of 2 Thessalonians, and the beast of Revelation are all symbols representing the Papacy. Also, the king of the north in Daniel 11 matches that power.

The Church's Reaction

What did the Papacy do in response to being cast as the antichrist by the Protestant Reformers? If you were the pope, would you be happy when Luther, Calvin, and others pointed out what the Bible says about the little horn that echoed characteristics of the Papacy?

For one response, Luis De Alcasar, a priest during the Counter-Reformation, came up with a concept now called preterism. He said that the books of Daniel and Revelation focus on the past. The prophecies are not about the Papacy when they describe the little horn. Instead, Daniel foretells the activity of Antiochus Epiphanes IV, a Seleucid king ruling before the time of Jesus. And for the book of Revelation, it is not talking about the Papacy when it portrays the beast, but rather points to the Roman emperor Nero.

A second response came from Francisco Ribera, a Jesuit priest, who created the concept termed futurism. He taught that Daniel and Revelation have no current application to the Papacy. The prophecies will all be fulfilled in the future, when an individual will appear as the antichrist just before the second coming of Jesus. Therefore, he said, the Papacy is not the little horn or the beast power or the man of sin.

The Vatican 100-lira coin pictured here was minted in the late 1950s and early 1960s. Look at it closely. Do you know what "*Vaticano*" means? It comes from a Latin root meaning "prophecy." I have to wonder about the art department that created this coin. When they placed the woman with a cup in one hand and a cross in the other, I imagine they were thinking about Ephesians 5:23-27, which talks about the bride of Christ "not having spot or wrinkle." Or perhaps they were looking at Revelation 12:1-6 and verse 17, which describes a pure woman, dressed in white, representing God's people. I am sure that is probably what they had in mind.

However, unfortunately, another woman also appears in the book of Revelation. Revelation 17:3-6 states: "Then the angel carried me away in the Spirit into a wilderness. There I saw a woman sitting on a scarlet beast that was covered with blasphemous names and had seven heads and ten horns. The woman was dressed in purple and scarlet, and was glittering with gold, precious stones and pearls. She held a golden cup in her hand, filled with abominable things and the filth of her adulteries. The name written on her forehead was a mystery:

BABYLON THE GREAT
THE MOTHER OF PROSTITUTES
AND OF THE ABOMINATIONS OF THE EARTH.

I saw that the woman was drunk with the blood of God's holy people, the blood of those who bore testimony to Jesus" (NIV).

Of great interest here is that the pure woman of Revelation 12 hid in the wilderness. The woman in Revelation 17 is found in the wilderness, but she is no longer a pure woman, dressed in white. She now wears scarlet. The woman is an adulterer. God's bride—His people—was supposed to remain true to Him, but they mixed paganism and Christianity together. The church comes out of this time period as a scarlet woman—a harlot. God's people have fallen away from Him.

The woman on the coin has a cup in her hand. Which one of the women in Revelation is a better match to the image on the coin? It's not the woman with nothing in her hands, but rather the one holding a cup full of abominations. Not only that, but the woman with the cup was dressed in scarlet. Ironically, what are the papal colors? Usually scarlet over white. In the prophecy the woman started out with clothing of white that became scarlet.

King of the North

In Daniel 11:23-45 we have the time period of the reign of the Roman Catholic Church as the king of the north. Verse 23 says: "And after the league is made with him he shall act deceitfully, for he shall come up and become strong with a small number of people." As we noted previously, the Vatican took control of Western Europe without an army of its own. The Roman emperor Constantine simply moved away from Rome to Constantinople and left the Papacy in the power vacuum created by his departure. Here is the beginning of the Vatican in control.

The end of verse 24 announces: "but only for a time." We also learned earlier that according to Daniel and Revelation the Papacy would have a 1260 day/year rule—it was only for a time.

During the 1260 years the Papacy as the king of the north engaged in battles with the king of the south. "He shall stir up his power and his courage against the king of the South with a great army. And the king of the South shall be stirred up to battle with a very great and mighty army; but he shall not stand, for they shall devise plans against him. Yes, those who eat of the portion of his delicacies shall destroy him; his army shall be swept away, and many shall fall down slain. Both these kings' hearts shall be bent on evil, and they shall speak lies at the same table; but it shall not prosper, for the end will still be at the appointed time" (verses 25-27).

These encounters—nine major crusades and many minor ones—went on for several centuries. Large armies took part, and the casualties were high.

When the papal armies were successful, they would return with relics, and they would get people worshipping them instead of worshipping according to God's Word. "While returning to his land with great riches, his heart shall be moved against the holy covenant; so he shall do damage and return to his own land" (verse 28). All the booty the armies brought back and all the knowledge and ideas they learned about the East from their incursions into the Holy Land greatly enriched Europe.

Verses 30, 31 indicate a naval battle: "For ships from Cyprus shall come against him; therefore he shall be grieved, and return in rage against the holy covenant, and do damage. So he shall return and show regard for those who forsake the holy covenant. And forces shall be mustered by him, and they shall defile the sanctuary fortress; then they shall take away the daily sacrifices, and place there the abomination of desolation."

Pope Pius V best represents the actions depicted here. During his time as pope the Ottoman Turks had control of the island of Cyprus and the eastern end of the Mediterranean Sea. Pius brought together the Holy League of 1571, a European navy that defeated the Ottomans and put a temporary stop to the naval hegemony of Islam. Because of his political victories in gathering Europe together to push Islam back, Pius V gained power, and he used that influence to ramp up the Inquisition and to enforce the liturgical Mass throughout Europe.

Verse 32 and following, I believe, describe the pre-Reformation and Reformation periods, still within the 1260 day/years. "Those who do wickedly against the covenant he shall corrupt with flattery; but the people who know their God shall be strong, and carry out great exploits. And those of the people who understand shall instruct many; yet for many days they shall fall by sword and flame, by captivity and plundering."

During the Reformation came the reawakening of personal Bible study. People began to trust in Scripture again, rather than religious traditions. Many in the Roman Catholic Church opposed those who desired to put the Bible into common languages. The verse says, "Those of the people who understand shall instruct many," but as a result, the king of the north would destroy by the sword and the flame. The papal powers would come in with the sword and destroy whole cities that had gone against Roman Catholicism and its teachings. They would take the leaders and burn them at the stake, something we find clearly described in Daniel. "Now when they fall, they shall be aided with a little help; but many shall join with them by intrigue. And some of those of understanding shall fall, to refine them, purge them, and make them white, until the time of the end; because it is still for the appointed time" (verses 34, 35). God appointed the Reformation to take place sometime during the 1260 years of the papal power's dominance. The Lord also promises in these verses that at the time of the end He will resurrect those who were faithful to Him.

Verse 36: "Then the king shall do according to his own will: he shall exalt and magnify himself above every god, shall speak blasphemies against the God of gods, and shall prosper till the wrath has been accomplished; for what has been determined shall be done." The power that speaks blasphemy will dominate until the "wrath has been accomplished." Later in the chapter on the plagues we will see that the seven last plagues are God's wrath. The book of Revelation depicts how the beast power is destroyed at the end of the plagues.

By now you understand that all of these prophecies come together and point to one and only one power: the papal system. The prophecies do not point to the Roman Catholic people, many of whom are true Christians. Because of this, we share God's truth to everyone with kindness and love.

---

[1] Translated from the Latin in F. Lucius Ferraris, "Papa, Articulus II," *Prompta Bibliotheca: Canonica, Juridica, Moralis, Theologica, Ascetica, Polemica, Rubristica, Historica* (Paris: J. P. Migne, 1858), vol. 5, pp. 25. Retrieved from www.aloha.net/~mikesch/prompta.htm.

[2] *Ibid.*

[3] *On the Authority of the Councils*, book 2, chap. 17.

[4] Philippe Labbe and Gabriel Cossart, "History of the Councils," Vol. XIV, col. 109.

[5] Abstract available at http://pqasb.pqarchiver.com/latimes/access/675039382 .html?dids=675039382:675039382&FMT=ABS&FMTS=ABS:AI&type=historic&date= Dec+12%2C+1984&author=DON+A+SCHANCHE&pub=Los+Angeles+Times+(1886- Current+File)&edition=&startpage=B11&desc=No+Forgiveness+%27Directly+From+ God%2C%27+Pope+Says.

[6] Michael Müller, *God, the Teacher of Mankind* (New York: Benziger Brothers, 1882), vol. 6, p. 332.

[7] "Apostolic Letter *Tertio Millennio Adveniente* of His Holiness Pope John Paul II, to the Bishops, Clergy, and Lay Faithful on Preparation for the Jubilee of the Year 2000." Available online at www.vatican.va/holy_father/john_paul_ii/apost_letters/documents/hf_jpii_apl_10111994_tertio-millennio-adveniente_en.html.

[8] Quoted in the CNN "Sunday Morning News" transcript for March 12, 2000. http://transcripts.cnn.com/TRANSCRIPTS/0003/12/sm.06.html.

[9] Pope John Paul, Angelus, March 12, 2000. Quoted in *Growth in Agreement III,* ed. Jeffrey Gros, Thomas F. Best, and Lorelei F. Fuchs (Geneva: WCC Publications, 2007), p. 255.

[10] Translated from the Latin in Lucius Ferraris.

[11] Peter Geiermann, *The Convert's Catechism of Catholic Doctrine* (St. Louis: Herder Book Co., 1946), p. 48.

[12] *Ibid.*, p. 49.

[13] *Ibid.*, p. 50.

[14] *The Seventh-day Adventist Bible Commentary* (Washington, D.C.: Review and Herald, 1976), vol. 4, p. 827; S. P. Scott, *The Civil Law* (Cincinnati: Central Trust Co., 1932), Vol. XII.

[15] Philip Schaff, *History of the Christian Church* (New York: Scribner, 1867), vol. 3, p. 327.

[16] San Francisco *Chronicle*, Feb. 12, 1929, p. 1. Retrieved from http://biblelight.net/lateran1.gif.

[17] Daniel 11:40-45 covers the time period we are talking about here, after the healing of the deadly wound, when the Papacy is resurgent, until the Papacy's destruction. We will study that in detail in a later chapter.

[18] Jerry A. Stevens, *Vicarius Filii Dei* (Berrien Springs, Mich.: Adventists Affirm, 2009).

[19] Leo, bishop of the city of Rome, letter to Anastasius, bishop of Thessalonica. www.newadvent.org/fathers/3604014.htm.

[20] LeRoy E. Froom, *The Prophetic Faith of Our Fathers* (Washington, D.C.: Review and Herald, 1950), vol. 1, p. 498.

CHAPTER 3

The Actors and Powers of the Time of the End

At the time of the end the king of the South shall attack him; and the king of the North shall come against him like a whirlwind, with chariots, horsemen, and with many ships; and he shall enter the countries, overwhelm them, and pass through. He shall also enter the Glorious Land, and many countries shall be overthrown; but these shall escape from his hand: Edom, Moab, and the prominent people of Ammon. He shall stretch out his hand against the countries, and the land of Egypt shall not escape. He shall have power over the treasures of gold and silver, and over all the precious things of Egypt; also the Libyans and Ethiopians shall follow at his heels" (Dan. 11:40-43).

The Players

This book takes the position that from the breakup of the Roman Empire to the end of time, most, if not all, of the symbols/players are both political and religious powers. We can see the dual role through the geopolitical and religious aspects of the prophecy, through other passages of Scripture, and in the record of history. Let us define some of the prophecy's elements.

1. The king of the north: geopolitically, the king of the north is the Holy Roman Empire and other entities that emerged in the former Roman Empire and that attack Israel from the north during the Crusades. Religiously, it also opposed any group that rejected the concept of allowing church traditions to overrule Scripture.

2. The king of the south: geopolitically, the king of the south is the Islamic powers that conquered the southern part of the former Roman Empire and invaded Israel from the south. Religiously, it also opposed Christianity and the divinity of Jesus.

3. The Glorious Land and the glorious holy mountain: geopolitically,

this would be Israel and Jerusalem. Religiously, the New Testament indicates that true Christians are included in Israel, as they are the sons of Abraham and citizens of God's true people.

4. Many countries: the Islamic nations defeated by the king of the north and mostly not mentioned by name in the prophecy, though it does specifically name Egypt, Libya, Ethiopia (most likely the ancient region now included in southern modern Egypt and Sudan), and the western part of Jordan.

5. Edom, Moab, and Ammon: geopolitically, these regions now make up part of western Jordan. Historically they are related to Abraham and were once a part of the Davidic kingdom. This book takes the position that, spiritually speaking, they represent the people within Islam who are true believers in God, trust in Jesus as Savior, and do not follow the king of the north at the end.

6. Egypt: geopolitically, this is the nation of Egypt, and it will be overthrown in the third and final conflict between Christianity and Islam. Religiously, Egypt and the many countries may represent those who take up radical Islam and would prefer death to following any form of Christianity. I suggest this indicates that during the third and final conflict Egypt will be in opposition to the "Christian" nations.

7. Libya and Ethiopia: geopolitically, they represent the nations of Libya and Ethiopia (though see note under number 4 above). If we consider their ancient boundaries instead of the modern ones, the two countries would take up most of north Africa. They represent people who are not willing to die for Islam but would rather follow the king of the north than be overthrown or destroyed.

It is important to keep in mind that throughout our examination of the Daniel 11 prophecy the players in the prophecy, whether countries or powers or individuals, have both a geopolitical and religious definition that comes into play and affects the outcome. Both roles must be acknowledged and interpreted in order for us to understand what God has revealed.

CHAPTER 4

The United States in Bible Prophecy

A wide range of beliefs exists about the United States and its potential role in biblical prophecy. Some people see America in the end-time prophecies, and others don't.

Take, for instance, the author Joel Rosenberg. In his novel *Dead Heat* he gets rid of the United States so that it is not a player at the end of time. His way that the United States gets wiped out goes something like this.

The Republican National Convention is in session in Los Angeles. It has been a rocky, tumultuous period in history. The president has already served two terms, and he has a vice president whom he wants to see elected. The president walks out on the stage at the convention to give a speech and hand over the mantle, so to speak, to the vice president, whom he is hoping will win the election. Suddenly there is a warning. Then, before anyone can get the president into a safe room, a nuclear missile hits the convention center and destroys the elected government. Simultaneously, missiles launched from container ships off the East Coast strike Washington, D.C., causing chaos on both sides of the United States and wiping the country out as a political and military player for the end-times. (I'm not giving away the book, because this is just the beginning of the story.)[1]

Why did Rosenberg employ that particular plot device to present his ideas about the end-times? He does not find any role for the United States in Bible prophecy, so in his novel he has to get rid of the nation somehow, and that's how he does it.

But since I do see the United States in Bible prophecy, it leads me to some very different conclusions about end-time events. I believe that what I have found is in harmony with the Bible and the teaching of the Reformers. I'm going to show you how one of them, John Wesley, was pointing in the same direction that I am looking.

I love the United States. Having traveled outside of the country many times, I always appreciate getting back home. When the airplane touches down, I know a couple things for sure: I have religious freedom again, by and large, and I have police officers that are normally more honest than corrupt—something that is not always true in other parts of the world. And then I also have plumbing that works and water I can drink.

Now, I cannot give you extremely detailed specifics about the United States in prophecy, because the Bible simply doesn't provide them. Instead, Scripture just gives a general outline. The more specific and detailed students try to get in explaining prophecy, the more likely they are going to be wrong. So I am going to stick to what the Bible says and try not to go much beyond that.

Second Peter 1:19 declares: "We also have the prophetic word made more sure, which you do well to heed as a light that shines in a dark place, until the day dawns and the morning star rises in your hearts." What could there be better than when Jesus brings a whole new day to our world at His second coming, when He puts away sin and suffering once and for all? But in the meantime God's prophetic Word is a good light to follow and keep an eye on.

So far we have seen that Daniel 11 covers the time of the prophet Daniel all the way to the end of sin and suffering, and we have noticed that the kings of the north and the south go through phases. The clashes between north and south started with Greece and then switched to Rome when Jesus was on earth as the prince of the covenant.

We saw that the identity of the king of the north in Daniel 11:23 and following is the same as the little horn, the man of sin, and the beast power of the book of Revelation. Those four terms or images (the king of the north, the little horn, the man of sin or "lawless one," and the beast of Revelation) are different symbols representing the same power: the Papacy. All share common characteristics, and the description of each of the symbols added a little more information not given in the others. The papal power arises after the pagan Roman Empire, and it will perish at the coming of Jesus Christ. It holds power during the time period in between. Furthermore, we noticed that the pagan Roman Empire becomes those entities represented by the legs of iron changing to the iron and clay in the feet, powers that last until the coming of Jesus Christ.

Think about this, though. Does the fact that the beast of Revelation is the Papacy mean that Roman Catholics are bad somehow? No! Countless true Christians belong to the Roman Catholic Church. The Bible has a problem with the Papacy and its teachings, not the Catholic people. Revelation 18:4 says: "Come out of her, my people." God sees faithful Catholics as His people "within," until just before the very end, when He calls them out.

In Daniel 11:25-31 we saw that the Papacy is the king of the north during the Crusades against Islam, and Islam in prophetic terms has become the king of the south. Verses 32-39 dealt with the Reformation. The Reformers were strong for God and stood up for Him. Some were put in prison, killed by the sword, and burned at the stake.

Daniel 11:40-45, the section that we are now looking at, describes the Papacy after the healing of the deadly wound it received in 1798. That process, as we saw earlier, began in 1929 with the Lateran Treaty between the state of Italy and the Vatican, signed by Benito Mussolini. As a result, the passage outlines the time of the resurgence to power of the Papacy from the healing of the deadly wound until its destruction at the return of Christ. Now we are going to slow down and spend several chapters just on these five verses.

Allies of the Papacy

Daniel 11:40, 41 says: "At the time of the end the king of the South shall attack him; and the king of the North shall come against him like a whirlwind, with chariots, horsemen, and with many ships; and he shall enter the countries, overwhelm them, and pass through. He shall also enter the Glorious Land, and many countries shall be overthrown." If the king of the north is the Papacy at the time of the end, who does the Bible say will be its allies? That's an important question. In the final conflict, who stands with the Papacy and who doesn't? Where does the pope get all those armies, since it does not have one of its own? If you visit the Vatican, do you find that it has its own police force? No, it has only the Swiss Guard. The police force from the surrounding city of Rome patrols St. Peter's Square.

The verse continues by saying that some would "escape from his hand," apparently referring to areas of the southern kingdom that the king of the south controls. These parts escape: "Edom, Moab, and the prominent people of Ammon." We will explore what that might mean in chapter 7.

Continuing on: "He [the king of the north] shall stretch out his hand against the countries, and the land of Egypt shall not escape. He shall have power over the treasures of gold and silver, and over all the precious things of Egypt; also the Libyans and Ethiopians shall follow at his heels. But news from the east and the north shall trouble him; therefore he shall go out with great fury to destroy and annihilate many" (verses 42-44).

Where does the Papacy get its armies? That's where we find the role of the United States. Revelation 13:1-10 describes the rise of the Papacy through the symbolism of the beast power. Then, in verses 11-17, the prophecy depicts the beast's helper, the one who is the strong arm (or police force) of the world, if you will. Let's see what Revelation 13:11-17 says about the helper of the beast power: "Then I saw another beast coming up out of the earth, and he had two horns like a lamb and spoke like a dragon. And he exercises all the authority of the first beast [the Papacy] in his presence, and causes the earth and those who dwell in it to worship the first beast [the Papacy], whose deadly wound was healed. He performs great signs" (verses 11-13).

Daniel 11:40 and following describe the time period after the wound to the first beast. The Papacy appears to go down in Daniel 11, and it drops out of sight. Then it resurfaces at the time of the end. Likewise, the book of Revelation reveals that the beast receives a deadly wound and then comes back when the wound is healed. So Revelation 13, speaking of the second beast, is talking about the time of the end:

"He [the second beast] performs great signs, so that he even makes fire come down from heaven on the earth in the sight of men. And he deceives those who dwell on the earth by those signs which he was granted to do in the sight of the beast, telling those who dwell on the earth to make an image to the beast who was wounded by the sword and lived. He was granted power to give breath to the image of the beast, that the image of the beast should both speak and cause as many as would not worship the image of the beast to be killed. He causes all, both small and great, rich and poor, free and slave, to receive a mark on their right hand or on their foreheads, and that no one may buy or sell except one who has the mark or the name of the beast, or the number of his name" (verses 14-17).

Who or what is the second beast power? Notice that it seeks to police the world. It forces humanity to follow the leading of the first beast.

Rise of the Second Beast Power

Keep a couple characteristics in mind. The second beast rises out of the earth, while the first one emerged from the sea. They have different origins. Revelation 17:15 says: "And he said to me, 'The waters which you

saw, where the harlot sits, are peoples, multitudes, nations, and tongues.'"
The harlot is sitting on the first beast, which came out of water. The water
represents lots of people and different nationalities. The beast that she's riding on—the first beast power—has traits of a lion, a leopard, and a bear,
and it has the horns from a nondescript beast. Those are the creatures of
Daniel 7 and 8 that appeared out of the sea. That's telling you the beast
power had its origin in the Mediterranean Basin, the cradle of civiliza-
tion—the sea of humanity.

The second beast power does not come up from that source. It
emerges from "the earth," which apparently symbolizes a place with relatively few people. It's not the heavily populated Old World.

A second characteristic is that the beast with lamblike horns in
Revelation 13 does not have crowns on its horns. That suggests that it does
not have kings as the Old World kingdoms did. Also, it is "like a lamb,"
possibly lamblike or Christlike—peace-loving. But it ends up speaking like
a dragon. It has the "might makes right" attitude that pagan Rome, papal
Rome, and Satan had: they have the power, so they are right. In other
words: "You had better do it our way, or else!"

The second beast surfaces after the healing of the fatal wound of the
first beast. The period of papal supremacy went from A.D. 538 to 1798.
Keep those dates in mind, because the second beast is going to be a player
after that second date.

In 1754 John Wesley had no question in his mind that the Papacy was
the first beast of Revelation 13. And when he was thinking about the second beast of Revelation 13, he said this: "He [the second beast] is not yet
come, though he can not be far off; for he is to appear at the end of the
forty-two months of the first beast."[2] So in 1754 Wesley believed that the
second beast was about to surface on the scene. I have a lot of respect for
his confidence to look at just Bible prophecy (without having history behind him) to conclude what was coming!

Is this second beast the United States? I believe it is. It makes its appearance after the first beast receives the "deadly wound." That was in
1798. The United States began to gain power about the same time.

You might protest, "The United States Declaration of Independence
was in 1776." The prophecy doesn't say the second beast was born on an
exact date—just that it comes into existence about the same time. The
United States was no world power at the beginning. For a parallel, look at
the Papacy. It was in existence before 538, but it did not have its full power
before then. The Bible does not necessarily go by the beginning date of an

entity's existence. It focuses on when the beast acquires its power. About 1798 the United States arrives on the scene and grows in power after that time. And it emerges from the "earth," someplace where there were relatively few people.

The United States took its place as a world player at the time of World War II, soon after 1929, when the Papacy recovered its sovereignty of Vatican City. Thus America had begun as a nation about the time the papal power received its wound, and it gained global influence right about the time the wound was healed. So we have some good matches on this prophecy.

Revelation 13:11 says the second beast power has its origin in the "earth." The United States definitely did not come up out of the Old World. If we look at other options besides the United States in the New World, we have Canada, South America, and Australia. Which one of them is playing police officer of the world today—the apparent role of the second beast of Revelation 13? Today the United States is the primary power seeking to maintain peace and order in international affairs. And it has no crown and no king. Americans have been very clear about not wanting a monarch.

Has the United States been lamblike or peace-loving? It depends on how you look at it. The nation has been pretty rough on other countries in some of the wars in the past 100 years. But there is something unique about the United States, something different than any other power before it. When the United States wins a war, it rebuilds the enemy's lost infrastructure and gives back the country! Japan and Germany offer prime examples. Which countries are some of the primary economic competitors of the United States? Japan and Germany—countries that it rebuilt. The United States is a very different kind of nation. It is peace-loving in a particular way. If you leave the United States alone, it by and large does not bother you. But according to the prophecy, it becomes the world's police officer and ends up "speaking like a dragon."

Lamblike could also mean Christlike. We could possibly say that the United States is a Christlike or Christ-connected nation. To much of the non-Christian world, the United States represents Christianity. That also is a match to the second beast.

Here is the catch, though—when the Islamic world looks at the United States, it focuses on Hollywood and the rest of American culture and concludes, "That's what Christianity is." No wonder Islam has a warped view of Christianity.

Fall of Religious Freedom

Revelation 13 says that the second beast would "speak like a dragon." Speak means expressing in legislation, which eventually involves enforcement. Right now the U.S. still has good laws that provide religious freedom. But the laws have been eroding. You know how things have gone: we have a few acts of terrorism, and we then hurriedly give up certain rights. Call it the Patriot Act or whatever, society can become dangerous as we lose our rights. Religious rights and national safety find themselves in constant tension.

Could religious repression emerge in the United States? I hear people saying they want to make or remake America as a Christian nation. It sounds like a good idea to some, but I hope it does not happen. Robert Grant, director of Christian Voice, said: "If Christians unite, we can do anything. We could pass any law or any amendment. And that's exactly what we intend to do."[3] Here's the question: Whose version of Christianity would it enforce by law if the United States is a Christian nation? Back in medieval times the Papacy decided what form of Christianity was acceptable and then persecuted all who held dissenting views. I would rather have the U.S. as a nation of complete religious liberty, in which each one of us can share as we believe and are not restricted by any church's or politician's definition of what it means to be a Christian. I do not trust politicians or church leaders to decide who or what a true Christian is. That would be real trouble!

W. A. Criswell, a Baptist pastor, said on the *CBS Evening News,* "I believe this notion of the separation of church and state was the figment of some infidel's imagination." Baptists used to be in favor of the separation of church and state. Back at the founding of the United States the denomination was among the primary players that brought about separation of church and state. But Criswell said it was a figment of some infidel's imagination. He seems to be implying that the early Baptist founders were infidels. But I agree with the early Baptists. Separation is a good idea.

Unfortunately, most of the people seated on the United States Supreme Court in the twenty-first century would agree with what Justice William Rehnquist said, that "the 'wall of separation between church and state' is a metaphor based on bad history, a metaphor which has proved useless as a guide to judging. It should be frankly and explicitly abandoned."[4] That is a dangerous thought for the United States Supreme Court to have. But the prophecy said that a time will come when the United States would "speak like a dragon" and force people to worship in a certain way, which is something the nation has not yet done. I encourage you to resist that trend. We are now in a volatile period of religious liberty in our country.

Wesley hinted at the coming of the second beast in the 1750s, but the first time that I am aware of anyone naming the United States as the second beast was in the early 1850s. J. N. Andrews, a Bible scholar, wrote that the United States is the second lamblike beast in Revelation 13.[5] Think of the courage it took to make that statement in his day. Before the Civil War, when the United States was at risk of falling apart and splitting down the middle, he said (and I paraphrase), "The United States is going to be the worldwide player to enforce the wishes of the Papacy." Just as many do today, some thought that America was not going to survive at that time. But Andrews proclaimed, based on Bible prophecy, that the United States was the second beast power from Revelation 13:11-17.

Signs and Wonders

Most of the world views the United States as Christian, and the nation is the powerhouse, not so much of Catholicism, but of Protestantism. You might wonder if the United States and the Papacy would ever work together. But they already have. The two powers may have contributed to a major change of history by working together in Europe. Here is a quote from *Time* magazine: "'This was one of the great secret alliances of all time.' . . . Reagan and the pope agreed to undertake a clandestine campaign to hasten the dissolution of the Communist empire. . . . Step by reluctant step, the Soviets and the Communist government of Poland bowed to the moral, economic, and political pressure imposed by the pope and the president" (Feb. 24, 1992).

Pope John Paul II and President Ronald Reagan had gotten together and laid their plans. They had both quietly supported the labor unions in Poland against the Communist government. Through them, and those in other parts of Eastern Europe, they were able to bring down Communism by working together. Nobody knew about it when it was happening. Not until after the fall of Communism did *Time* magazine break the story. Could the United States and the Papacy work together to change the world? They already have. And I believe they will again.

Some people say, "What about Revelation 13 saying the second beast calls fire down from heaven? Is that referring to the United States using nuclear weapons?" I have heard people suggest that, but I don't agree. Revelation 13:13, 14 says: "He [the United States] performs great signs, so that he even makes fire come down from heaven on the earth in the sight of men. And he deceives those who dwell on the earth by those signs which he was granted to do in the sight of the beast." Do nuclear weapons deceive people or kill them? They kill them. So I do not believe the fire refers to nuclear weaponry. I think there is a better answer. The verse continues: "Telling those who dwell on the earth to make an image to the beast who was wounded by the sword and lived." What is a better answer than nuclear weapons? This lamblike beast—this Christianlike beast—actually calls fire down from the heavens to deceive people.

Fire Comes Down

Is it possible that fire would flash down from heaven? Think back in the Scriptures to other times that someone summoned fire from heaven. In all of those instances it was to show who was the true God, the one who should be worshipped. First Kings 18 reports an encounter on Mount Carmel between the God of heaven and the pagan god Baal. One guy, Elijah, was on God's side. On Baal's side was the king of Israel, much of the Israelite nation, and 450 Baal prophets. Three and a half years of famine had desolated the land, because Elijah had said, "There won't be any rain until I say so." The nation was in serious trouble from the lack of dew or rain. Think about how the United States would look with no rain for three and a half years. It would devastate the country.

After three and a half years Elijah showed up and said, "OK, now that we've got your attention, let's meet on Mount Carmel for a showdown." Once the nation had gathered there, he said to the prophets of Baal, "Here's the deal. You build an altar and put a sacrifice on it. I'll build an altar and put a sacrifice on mine. Then we'll see which deity can rain fire down from heaven and burn up the sacrifice. The real God can send fire from heaven. That's the test."

The priests of Baal didn't have much of a choice. Everybody was there, and they didn't want to lose face, so they agreed. They built an altar and placed a sacrifice on it, and the 450 prophets started running around, yelling and cutting themselves to get Baal's attention. Elijah had a sense of humor. As he stood nearby, he said, "Hey, shout a little louder. Your god must be asleep." They did, but to no avail. A little bit later he suggested, "He must not be asleep—he must be on vacation! Shout louder!" Finally their half of the day was gone, and Elijah announced, "Now it's my turn. Be quiet."

Erecting his altar, he set his sacrifice on it and told his help to get four barrels of water. After he poured the water over the sacrifice, he added, "That's not enough. Do it again." Then he dug a trench around the altar and filled the trench with water. Finally, he said, "OK, Lord. Show them who is God." *Flash!* Fire from heaven! It burned up the sacrifice, consumed the rocks, and vaporized the water. And the nation of Israel responded, "The God of Elijah is the real God." There was a showdown, and the God of heaven won.

According to Revelation 13 another confrontation will take place at the end, but God has already warned that this time around He's not answering with fire—at least not till later. The counterfeit power will do that. Do not be deceived by the counterfeit.

In Acts 2 we also find a story about fire from heaven, and it is even more appropriate to Revelation 13. On the day of Pentecost tongues of fire settled on the heads of the disciples. As a result of being baptized by the Holy Spirit and being filled with the Holy Spirit, they went out and worked "signs and wonders" to take the gospel to the world. Compare this to the lamblike beast, or second beast of Revelation 13. It performs signs and wonders to deceive people into false worship instead of the true worship of Jesus Christ. People follow the one who claims to be in the place of Jesus Christ. What have we seen that the Papacy has claimed? To be in the place of Jesus on earth. So be careful. At the end, those who profess to work through the Holy Spirit will perform "signs and wonders," counterfeit miracles, and/or even bringing fire down from the sky, which will lead people to follow the beast.

Second Thessalonians 2:9-12, using the phrase "the lawless one" for the beast power, the king of the north power, gives this warning: "The coming of the lawless one is according to the working of Satan, with all power, signs, and lying wonders, and with all unrighteous deception among those who perish" (verses 9, 10). Those who listen to the lawless one are going to die "because they did not receive the love of the truth." Jesus said that His Word is truth. You either believe God's Word and base everything on that, and not on tradition, or you will be deceived and perish. The passage in Thessalonians concludes: "And for this reason God will send them strong delusion, that they should believe the lie, that they all may be condemned who did not believe the truth but had pleasure in unrighteousness" (verses 11, 12).

God says in His Word that He is going to let Satan look as though he is doing real miracles with real powers. But if you are reading the Word, you also know the truth. When the false powers throw a curveball and try to take you away from what God declares, you can say, "No, I know what God's Word teaches, and I am going to stick with it!"

Following Tradition Is Fatal

Why does God allow such a counterfeit? It separates those who are true believers from those who are not. Right before Jesus returns there will emerge a clear dividing line between those who are truly following God's Word and those who accept tradition—be it Islamic, Christian, Buddhist, or anything else. If you do not let God and His Word guide you, it's going to sort you out. That's why God said He would allow "strong delusion"—false wonders and signs and miracles.

You don't find the lamblike horned beast mentioned after Revelation 13, because the name of the power changes. The lamblike beast power is still there, but it is now under a different name. The new name is the false prophet, and it is also the United States. If Revelation 13 describes the United States, then the "false prophet" is the same power. Here's how we know that. Revelation 19:20 is a quote right out of Revelation 13: "Then the beast was captured, and with him the false prophet who worked signs in his presence, by which he deceived those who received the mark of the beast and those who worshiped his image." In Revelation 19 the second beast works signs and wonders, deceives people, and forces them to worship the beast. Same actions, same beast. Continuing in Revelation 19:20: "These two were cast alive into the lake of fire burning with brimstone." The Papacy is destroyed at the coming of Jesus Christ, and the second beast, his right-hand helper, perishes at the same time.

The name change has a reason behind it. The United States is pushing a false prophetic message—one already being presented by many Christians in the United States.

A little while back I saw a headline: "The Demise of the United States as a World Power." I laughed. While I don't know all the details of prophecy, I do know the general principles, and according to the broad outline, the United States remains in power until Jesus Christ comes and destroys it with fire at the very end. The U.S. will not disappear before then. That is not to say that it will not go through some rocky times. It probably will. But the U.S. will survive as the major world power right up until the end. I might add that a superpower in decline can be more dangerous than one at its zenith. The former tends to get more volatile.

Revelation 16 talks about the "false prophet" at the end of time: "I saw three unclean spirits like frogs coming out of the mouth of the dragon, out of the mouth of the beast, and out of the mouth of the false prophet. For they are spirits of demons, performing signs, which go out to the kings of the earth and of the whole world, to gather them to the battle of that great day of God Almighty" (verses 13, 14). The verse describes the period of the plagues right before the destruction of the beast power and the false prophet. Again prophecy portrays the beast power and the false prophet as performing signs and "lying wonders" at the very end of time.

A False Trinity

We are looking at three powers—the dragon, the beast, and the false prophet. What is the name for a trio of powers? A trinity. We call the trio of God the Father, God the Son, and God the Holy Spirit the Trinity. You might be aware that some people question whether there really is a holy Trinity of the Father, the Son, and the Holy Spirit. But I believe that the Bible teaches exactly that. When He was on earth, Jesus got baptized, and at the same time the Holy Spirit descended as a dove. As Jesus emerged from the water, the Father said, "This is My beloved Son" (Matt. 3:17). Here all three members of the Trinity are active in the same verse.

Here is another reason I believe in the true Trinity: Satan has a counterfeit one. If you have never noticed it before, look at how interesting this counterfeit trinity is.

TRUE TRINITY	FALSE TRINITY
Father	Dragon
Gives Power and Authority	
Son	Beast
1260 Day/Year—Fatal Wound—Revives With Power	
Holy Spirit	False Prophet
Fire From Heaven—Signs, Wonders, and Miracles—Enables Work of the "Son"	

Down the left-hand column of the table you see the true Trinity, while down the right-hand column you find the false trinity. According to Scriptures, in the true Trinity God the Father gives power and authority to the Son (John 5:19-30; Matt. 28:18). In the false trinity the dragon extends power and authority to the beast (Rev. 13:4). Remember, the beast power—the Papacy—claims to be Jesus Christ on earth. The Papacy gets its power from the dragon, Satan. So if you follow the beast, you place yourself under the control of the dragon. And if you worship the beast, you are really worshipping the dragon. The dragon was, in a symbolic way, Rome, but according to Revelation, it was ultimately Satan. So Satan is the powerhouse—he gives authority to the others in the false trinity. But God the Father, the true powerhouse, bestows the authority in the true Trinity.

Parallel Prophecies

Jesus Christ the Son had a three-and-a-half-year ministry, as described in Daniel 9 and the Gospels. Three and a half years equals 1260 days, or 42 months. According to Bible prophecy and history, the beast power had a 1260-day/year reign and then received a fatal wound. Jesus had a three-and-a-half-year ministry and died on the cross. He also had a fatal wound. What happens to Jesus right after His crucifixion? In a short time He is resurrected. All of the world should be worshipping Him, but it does not. The beast, on the other hand, at the end of the 1260 days/years, received a fatal wound when the French general Berthier marched in and seized the pope. The general took him to France, where the pope died in captivity. But with the Lateran Treaty in 1929 papal power received a resurrection and a new life.

These are not accidental parallels. This kind of imagery is not coincidence. But most Bible scholars and prophecy students have missed it. Why? Because most of them follow one of the two prophetic methods that emerged during the Counter-Reformation. They gave up the historicist method of interpretation as employed by the Reformers. If you stick with the Reformers' method, though, you will be like John Wesley and see things coming before they happen!

We have seen the parallel of the Father and the Son, the dragon and the beast. Next comes the Holy Spirit. In Acts 2 the Holy Spirit arrives with fire from heaven, working signs and wonders, enabling the work of the Son, Jesus Christ. The Holy Spirit lifts up Jesus Christ and spreads the gospel to the world. In the false trinity the false prophet emerges on the scene and works false signs, wonders, and miracles to cause people to worship the beast. When they worship the beast, they are really worshipping Satan. That's a counterfeit!

The Christian Counterfeit

I challenge you to dig into God's Word. Make sure that what you are doing and what you believe is based on the Bible and not on some kind of counterfeit. The counterfeit is strong, and it seeks, by and large, to deceive Christians.

Some people say, "You have got to be kidding me! How can the beast power, the antichrist power, arise from within the Christian church?" That's exactly from where 2 Thessalonians said it would emerge—in the temple of God (2 Thess. 2:4). The temple in the New Testament is the church (Eph. 2:20-22). In Revelation the beast power takes over the role of the pure woman, the pure church. Revelation 12 declares that the pure woman hides in the wilderness. Then in Revelation 17 John looks and sees the church coming out of the wilderness now as a harlot. Christianity changes.

Remember that according to George Barna, the majority of Christians today apparently do not hold biblical worldviews. That tells you that the majority are vulnerable to follow the false prophet. A few signs and wonders, and they are had! Many of them are already following the beast anyway, and the deception will just finish them off. It will continue until the very end of the time of the plagues.

People often ask me, "How could the United States become dragonlike?" Dragonlike speech and actions could come from either the political left or the political right. I already described how the Christian Coalition might do it. But think back to September 12, 2001. Everybody was saying, "God bless America." The churches were full. The government was out to destroy whoever hit the towers, and conservatives came up pretty strong. Now, if the conservative right were to take control, I would say, just knowing history, that only politically religious-right people would do well under its influence. It could become a time of religious persecution.

On the other hand, if politically liberal people are in charge, they might tend to give Islam a pass. But if they are attacked, the liberals may retaliate even more because their peace overtures had been spurned.

I conclude that the change of the United States into a persecuting power could come from either the religious right, the political right, or the political left. But I'm not so much worried about figuring out who would be in office at that time or which group might cause the change. Instead, I'm watching and wondering, "When does that attack from the king of the south against the king of the north happen?"

The role of the United States as the second beast makes more sense to me than anything else I can find—a lot more than the nation being blown away by nuclear weapons and not being a power at the end of time. The Papacy must have a military arm, and the prophecy answers that question.

---

[1] Joel Rosenberg, *Dead Heat* (Tyndale, 2008).

[2] John Wesley, *Explanatory Notes Upon the New Testament* (London: Epworth Press, 1929), p. 1010.

[3] In Roland R. Hegstad, "Down the Road to a Christian Republic," *Liberty,* May/June 1980, p. 4.

[4] *Wallace v. Jaffree,* 472 U.S. 38 (1985), at 107 (Rehnquist, J., dissenting opinion).

[5] J. N. Andrews, "Thoughts on Revelation XIII and XIV," in *Second Advent Review and Sabbath Herald,* May 19, 1851, pp. 81-86.

CHAPTER 5

The Role of Europe and China

Besides the United States, the Papacy has other allies. In Daniel 11:40 the king of the south attacks, and the king of the north responds with a huge military operation that decimates the south. What are the rest of the Papacy's allies? Revelation 17:7-14 tells us.

"But the angel said to me, 'Why did you marvel? I will tell you the mystery of the woman and of the beast that carries her, which has the seven heads and the ten horns. The beast that you saw was, and is not, and will ascend out of the bottomless pit and go to perdition. And those who dwell on the earth will marvel, whose names are not written in the Book of Life from the foundation of the world, when they see the beast that was, and is not, and yet is.

"'Here is the mind which has wisdom: The seven heads are seven mountains on which the woman sits. There are also seven kings. Five have fallen, one is, and the other has not yet come. And when he comes, he must continue a short time. And the beast that was, and is not, is himself also the eighth, and is of the seven, and is going to perdition. And the ten horns which you saw are ten kings who have received no kingdom as yet, but they receive authority for one hour as kings with the beast. These are of one mind, and they will give their power and authority to the beast. These will make war with the Lamb, and the Lamb will overcome them, for He is Lord of lords and King of kings; and those who are with Him are called, chosen, and faithful.'"

The beast power that claims to be king of kings will one day meet the real King of kings. When that happens, the counterfeit power does not prosper. Both Jesus the Son of God and the Papacy, the beast power, claim to be King of kings and Lord of lords. But only one can be. Thus one is true, and the other is false.

Revelation 17 talks about the beast power having seven heads. That

68

power consists of the four characters from Daniel 7 and 8. Count the heads from Daniel 7: the lion with wings (1), the bear (1), the leopard (4), and the nondescript beast (1). Added together, they equal seven! No big mystery here. Also, Revelation 13:1–10 describes the beast as part leopard, lion, and bear, and with 10 horns like the last of the four Daniel 7 beasts. The last head is going to die and come back again.

Who is the last head? It began as pagan Rome and turned into papal Rome. It receives a deadly wound and then comes back again. The "one who was" is the Papacy during the 1260 years. Then the Papacy "was not" from 1798 to the 1920s. And then it "is" when it regains power at the end of time. This power is the king of the north in Daniel 11:40 and following.

Revelation 17 also mentions that "those seven heads were seven hills," on which the woman sits with her throne. The city widely known as the "city of seven hills" is Rome.

The passage also said that 10 kings would give their power and authority over to the beast for a short time at the end. Which part of the world had 10 horns that were 10 kingdoms? Divided Europe. At the end of time, although Europe is never truly united under one ruler, a period comes when the 10 powers are working together in such a way that they can give their power and authority to the beast. I believe that I am watching that develop as the European Union continues to evolve. Those 10 kings of Europe from the past will have power again.

What do we have if we put the kings of Christian Europe (the 10 horns of Revelation 17) together with the United States (Revelation 13's beast with lamblike horns)? It is plain and simple. You have a prophetic description of NATO—the U.S. and Western Christian Europe—that will hand its power and its military might over to the Papacy and be directed by the Papacy in the third and final conflict between Islam and the Christian world. In case you are thinking we just went looking for a possible description of NATO, remember that Bible prophecy shows that at the time of the end there would be a strong Papacy, a strong United States, and European powers that would be willing to give power over to the Papacy. Doesn't that sound familiar?

This third and final conflict during the time of the end could happen anytime. Scripture offers no time prophecy about when it will happen. But if we have our eyes open, we can sense what's approaching. I hope you can see it, to better know how to handle life in the toughest period in human history.

But, you may wonder, hasn't Europe backed off from Afghanistan and Iraq? As I write this book, yes, they are doing so. Do you realize, though, that some years ago, just before Jacques Chirac left the leadership of France, he warned radical Islam. He said in so many words, "You use a nuclear weapon on us, and we will obliterate you." France has quite a few nuclear weapons. Daniel 11:40 tells us the king of the south keeps pushing until he makes the king of the north angry. We may be seeing an example of that in France. The French government has banned the Islamic burkas. Elsewhere, the German government has said to Islamic immigrants, "OK, if you're going to live here, you're going to learn to speak German—you will not just speak your own languages." In the Netherlands Geert Wilders has been leader of the third-most-powerful political party, the Party for Freedom. Anti-Islamic in nature, it has been gaining seats in the Netherlands parliament. That is the kind of change brewing in Europe. NATO may yet be used as a tool when the king of the north goes after Islam.

The little horn, or beast, had 1260 years of power, lost its power, but came back. Clearly we are in the "toenails of time" right before Jesus returns. We cannot know when the final conflict will happen, cannot tell if it will be this year or next year or 50 years from now. But I do know this: we are headed the direction that the prophecy foretells. All that was predicted and that is now history was fulfilled exactly as foretold. So you can trust the prophecy of what is yet to come. I certainly do.

What would unite Europe, the United States, and the Papacy? The biggest enemy that those three powers have is radical Islam. Daniel says that something in particular is the "match" that ignites the tumultuous time of the end. It could take the form of terrorism or financial collapse—any of those kinds of things. But Daniel 11:40 tells us what unites those powers. "At the time of the end, the king of the south shall attack him."

Let's take the imagery out of it for a moment. The king of the south for the previous 20 verses of Daniel 11 was Islam. Then verse 40 declares: "At the time of the end the king of the South [Islam] shall attack him [the Papacy and its Christian alliance]; and the king of the North [the Papacy and its alliance] shall come against him [Islam] like a whirlwind, with chariots, horsemen, and with many ships; and he [the papal alliance] shall enter the countries, overwhelm them, and pass through." The passage goes on to describe the destruction that follows. According to Daniel 11, it is aggressive behavior by Islam that unites the papal alliance.

What would bring Europe, the United States, and the Papacy into one massive coalition? Islam pushing hard against them: nuclear weapons somewhere, an attack on Israel, or massive terrorism in Europe. All kinds of things could do it. I don't know where it is going to come from. But according to the prophecy that's what will happen.

Are the powers of the papal alliance united yet? Only partially. I don't believe that what happened on September 11, 2001, fulfilled Daniel 11:40. But I do believe that it was a warning or small sample of what yet awaits us. Interestingly, when the United States retaliated and entered Iraq, it was the Papacy that tried to hold the United States back from that war. Daniel 11 describes what happens when the war between the Christian West (in the book of Daniel, the north) and Islam changes from political to holy war, and that's when the time of the end is unleashed. We should note that for radical Islam it already is a holy war. Just think what it will be like when both sides view it that way!

"When will that happen?" you may ask me. I don't know. It could be tomorrow or 20 or 30 years from now. Perhaps it could be longer than that. But it could happen anytime. Everything could change in a few moments.

China

Another question people sometimes ask me is "What about China?" The only place that I can perhaps see a role for China is in Revelation 18. When the Papacy and the United States and the 10 kings perish, a certain group stands in the distance, watching and crying because they've lost their markets. Who is becoming the new economic powerhouse in the world? China. At the moment that country is still in a rapid growth mode.

Revelation 18:3 says: "For all the nations have drunk of the wine of the wrath of her fornication, the kings of the earth have committed fornication with her, and the merchants of the earth have become rich through the abundance of her luxury." Earlier we described NATO as the military might of the king of the north. Who are the customers of China? NATO countries. The Eastern merchants have gotten rich off the Western world.

Verse 11: "And the merchants of the earth will weep and mourn over her, for no one buys their merchandise anymore." When things go bad for the Christian empire, things don't go well for the merchants. They weep because no one is in a position to buy anymore.

Which side would China take if there were a showdown between Islam and Christianity? Well, who is their major market? I expect that they will side with them. The Chinese have a lot invested in the United States. If they turn against America, the United States could write off its debt to the Chinese. Europe could do the same. "And all the world follows the beast," Revelation 13:3 states, because that is seemingly in their best interest.

What about Russia? Russia has a Christian history, and in the twenty-first century it also faces an Islamic threat.

We can see how the powers of the world are jostling together. According to prophecy the Papacy is the primary beast, the United States is the second-most-important player, and then the rest of the world will support them. What was the major challenge to Christian powers in the past? Islam. And who contends against Christian powers today? Militant Islam.

CHAPTER 6

The Role of Israel in Prophecy

A List of Tribes

One of the keys for understanding Daniel 11 is to know whether a power is attacking Israel from the north or the south. Israel is always the country in the middle. We will look at some of the implications from the Old and New Testament for understanding Israel in Bible prophecy.

What does it mean when Daniel 11:41 and 45 talk about "the Glorious Land"? Verse 41: "He shall also enter the Glorious Land, and many countries shall be overthrown." "He" is the king of the north advancing into Israel. Verse 45: "And he shall plant the tents of his palace between the seas and the glorious holy mountain." Geographically, we do find a mountain between the Dead Sea and the Mediterranean Sea, the mountain where Jerusalem sits. So when the verse says "between the seas and the glorious holy mountain," I believe it is talking about Israel and/or Jerusalem.

Previously we have gone to other parts of the Bible, especially Revelation, to understand elements of the prophecies of Daniel, and we find that Revelation explains Israel as well. Revelation 7:1 states: "After these things I saw four angels standing at the four corners of the earth, holding the four winds of the earth, that the wind should not blow on the earth, on the sea, or on any tree."

Have you ever wondered why we don't have more terrorist attacks than we do? Or why the world doesn't spin out of control? If I were a terrorist, I could think of all kinds of nifty ideas that would cause massive death and destruction. But many of their plans get stopped, and some of them simply fall apart. Why? God declares that He is holding back the "winds" of trouble until a certain time when He says, "That's it!" and He lets them blow. I don't know how long it will take before He releases those winds. We have no time prophecy that tells us. But it will happen when God and His people are ready.

Revelation 7:2, 3: "Then I saw another angel ascending from the east, having the seal of the living God. And he cried with a loud voice to the four angels to whom it was granted to harm the earth and the sea, saying, 'Do not harm the earth, the sea, or the trees till we have sealed the servants of our God on their foreheads.'" Keep in mind that seal, or the distinguishing mark, on their foreheads. It will come up again later.

Next, in Revelation 7, we find a list of the 12 tribes of Israel:

"And I heard the number of those who were sealed. One hundred and forty-four thousand of all the tribes of the children of Israel were sealed:

of the tribe of Judah twelve thousand were sealed;
of the tribe of Reuben twelve thousand were sealed;
of the tribe of Gad twelve thousand were sealed;
of the tribe of Asher twelve thousand were sealed;
of the tribe of Naphtali twelve thousand were sealed;
of the tribe of Manasseh twelve thousand were sealed;
of the tribe of Simeon twelve thousand were sealed;
of the tribe of Levi twelve thousand were sealed;
of the tribe of Issachar twelve thousand were sealed;
of the tribe of Zebulun twelve thousand were sealed;
of the tribe of Joseph twelve thousand were sealed;
of the tribe of Benjamin twelve thousand were sealed" (verses 4-8).

To understand this list, we need to get some context in Revelation 14, in which we find the 144,000 mentioned again. "Then I looked, and behold, a Lamb standing on Mount Zion, and with Him one hundred and forty-four thousand, having His Father's name written on their foreheads. And I heard a voice from heaven, like the voice of many waters, and like the voice of loud thunder. And I heard the sound of harpists playing their harps. And they sang as it were a new song before the throne, before the four living creatures, and the elders; and no one could learn that song except the hundred and forty-four thousand who were redeemed from the earth. These are the ones who were not defiled with women, for they are virgins. These are the ones who follow the Lamb wherever He goes. These were redeemed from among men, being firstfruits to God and to the Lamb. And in their mouth was found no deceit, for they are without fault before the throne of God" (Rev. 14:1-5).

Here are the servants of God, 144,000 people, categorized as the 12 tribes of Israel. The list raises many questions. What is its purpose? Why does each tribe have exactly 12,000? Are they a literal group of people, or are they symbolic of something? And what does this tell us about Israel at the time of the end?

To begin answering these questions, we need to resolve some apparent problems with the list of tribes. Look at the table below to see how the Bible cites the tribes elsewhere.

The first column comes from Genesis 49, at the beginning of the nation of Israel. The second one is from Ezekiel 48, and the last one appears in Revelation 7, both end-time scenarios. One would assume that Ezekiel and Revelation would agree and match the first list, but they cite the tribes differently. In Genesis 49 we have the 12 sons of Jacob (or Israel, as God later calls him). As we go down Ezekiel's list, we get to where Levi should be, but he

Gen. 49	Eze. 48	Rev. 7
Reuben	Reuben	Reuben
Simeon	Simeon	Simeon
Levi	Manasseh	Levi
Judah	Judah	Judah
Zebulun	Zebulun	Zebulun
Issachar	Issachar	Issachar
Dan	Dan	Manasseh
Gad	Gad	Gad
Asher	Asher	Asher
Naphtali	Naphtali	Naphtali
Joseph	Ephraim	Joseph
Benjamin	Benjamin	Benjamin

adds Manasseh instead—one of the sons of Joseph. When he gets to Joseph, he puts in Ephraim, the other son. By leaving out Levi and Joseph, he can add the two half tribes of Manasseh and Ephraim and still get 12 tribes. Then in Revelation we have Levi back in the list. Dan drops out, and Manasseh takes his place. Ephraim is not there, and Joseph is back. What's going on?

Before we can answer that, we must look at some other problems. If 144,000 is a literal number of people, how is it that an even 12,000 of a big tribe and an even 12,000 of a small one end up saved? Does God choose who is going to be saved, and it doesn't matter what they think or what they believe? How is it that exactly 12,000 get redeemed from each of the tribes?

And then a third problem: they are all virgins. If it is a literal number of specific individuals, they are people who never married, never had sexual relations with anybody.

To take the number and the tribes as literal means missing what

Revelation 1 says: "The Revelation of Jesus Christ, which God gave Him to show His servants—things which must shortly take place. And He sent and *signified it* by His angel to His servant John, who bore witness to the word of God, and to the testimony of Jesus Christ, to all things that he saw" (Rev. 1:1, 2). Revelation has a lot of symbols in it. Think of the beast with seven heads, made up of different kinds of animals and 10 horns. I do not believe that we will actually see that literal beast walk out of the water somewhere. It is all the symbols of Daniel 7 merged into one. Since we know that we have symbols in Revelation, when we start running into problems with a literal interpretation of a passage, we could rightly conclude, "This might be one of those symbols."

I have a hunch that the 144,000 are symbolic of something, if nothing else because of the many problems that we run into with a literal interpretation. The people are all virgins, each tribe has an even 12,000, and the names of the tribes here don't match other lists in the Bible. To figure it out, I go to the rest of the New Testament to find out what it teaches on the topic.

The Israel of Faith

In Galatians 3:7-9 Paul writes: "Therefore know that only those who are of faith are sons of Abraham. And the Scripture, foreseeing that God would justify the nations by faith, preached the gospel to Abraham beforehand, saying, 'In you all the nations shall be blessed.' So then those who are of faith are blessed with believing Abraham."

All who are of faith are sons of Abraham, including Gentiles by faith! Abraham is the true father of the faithful—the true father of Israel, so to speak.

Paul then adds, "You are all sons of God through faith in Christ Jesus. For as many of you as were baptized into Christ have put on Christ. There is neither Jew nor Greek, there is neither slave nor free, there is neither male nor female; for you are all one in Christ Jesus. And if you are Christ's, then you are Abraham's seed, and heirs according to the promise" (verses 26-29).

Paul asserts that in God's eyes there exists neither Jew nor Greek (Gentile). We have just run into a problem with many contemporary books on prophecy, because some of them say that, spiritually speaking, there is a split between Gentile and Jew, that they are not the same and never can be. That's what Hal Lindsey taught in *The Late, Great Planet Earth*. Several others have presented similar concepts. But here is a Bible verse that declares there is neither Jew nor Greek, neither slave nor free, male nor female—no difference, because we are all one in Christ Jesus.

So we are all one in Christ. That makes sense. He does not care what nation we came from—Israel or otherwise. If we have accepted Him, we are His people!

But what about Hal Lindsey and others arguing that we have to have Israel on one side, the church on the other, and there is no mixing the two? Yet Galatians 3 sounds as if it is saying that God's people, His true Israel, are a mix of Jew and Gentile.

Paul clarifies this in Romans 9:6-8: "It is not that the word of God has taken no effect. For they are not all Israel who are of Israel, nor are they all children because they are the seed of Abraham; but, 'In Isaac your seed shall be called.' That is, those who are the children of the flesh, these are not the children of God; but the children of the promise are counted as the seed." In other words, it's not whether you are an Israelite genetically that matters. According to Paul, what is vital is whether you are spiritually—by faith—an Israelite.

Faith or Genes?

What implication does this have to the book of Revelation and prophecy? To understand God's end-time plan, we must take into account that it does not matter if a person is genetically related, but rather spiritually related. God says that He focuses His attention on those with faith, those who follow His Word.

Think back to the Old Testament. Did you have to be born an Israelite to be one? Not necessarily. Rahab, the prostitute who lived on the wall of Jericho, said she wanted to be on God's side. She ended up in the genealogy of Jesus. That makes her a pretty good Israelite. While she was not genetically an Israelite, she had faith. By faith she comes in! Another woman, Ruth, was from Moab, but she had faith too. She is also in the lineage of Jesus. For a long time God has been letting people into Israel by faith. It is not a new idea. We find many other examples elsewhere in the Old Testament.

"What shall we say then? That Gentiles, who did not pursue righteousness, have attained to righteousness, even the righteousness of faith; but Israel, pursuing the law of righteousness, has not attained to the law of righteousness. Why? Because they did not seek it by faith, but as it were, by the works of the law. For they stumbled at that stumbling stone" (Rom. 9:30-32).

We're never going to make it by our own works, and if we want to push it so far as to reduce it all to genetics, that truly makes salvation "works of the flesh." Can we say, "The way I was born means that I'm in"? Or "By human design, I'm genetically in"? No, it's only and always by faith, God declares. "For there is no distinction between Jew and Greek, for the same Lord over all is rich to all who call upon Him" (Rom. 10:12).

Hal Lindsey claims a spiritual distinction between Jew and Greek, or Gentile, but whenever I am studying any kind of prophetic theory and I find a scripture saying something different from some book that I'm reading, I put the volume down, and I hang on to the scripture. That is a simple plan that I hope you follow also.

In Romans 11 Paul uses the illustration of an olive tree, and I hope this clears it up for you.

"I say then, have they [the Jews] stumbled that they should fall? Certainly not! But through their fall, to provoke them to jealousy, salvation has come to the Gentiles. Now if their [the Jews'] fall is riches for the world, and their failure riches for the Gentiles, how much more their fullness! For I speak to you Gentiles; inasmuch as I am an apostle to the Gentiles, I magnify my ministry, if by any means I may provoke to jealousy those who are my flesh and save some of them" (verses 11-13).

How many genetic Israelites was Paul hoping to save? "Some of them." He did not say "all of them." Keep that in mind, because we are going to find Paul saving "all Israel" before we are out of this chapter. As a result, we need to determine what is "all Israel." Is it genetic Israelites?

Then to the olive tree in verses 16-26:

"For if the firstfruit is holy, the lump is also holy; and if the root is holy, so are the branches. And if some of the branches were broken off, and you [Gentiles], being a wild olive tree, were grafted in among them, and with them became a partaker of the root and fatness of the olive tree, do not boast against the branches [genetic Israelites]. But if you boast, remember that you do not support the root, but the root supports you. You will say then, 'Branches were broken off that I might be grafted in.' Well said. Because of unbelief they were broken off, and you stand by faith. Do not be haughty, but fear. For if God did not spare the natural branches, He may not spare you either" (verses 16-21).

The actions of the Israelite leaders during the time of Jesus' ministry tell the story. They refused to stay attached to the root anymore. When they hardened their hearts and killed Jesus, they were cut off.

"Therefore consider the goodness and severity of God: on those who fell, severity; but toward you, goodness, if you continue in His goodness. Otherwise you also will be cut off. And they also, if they do not continue in unbelief, will be grafted in, for God is able to graft them in again" (verses 22, 23).

Now, did Paul mean that the genetic Israelites were cut off without hope? Had they blown their chance forever? No, he does not state that.

"For if you [Gentiles] were cut out of the olive tree which is wild by nature, and were grafted contrary to nature into a cultivated olive tree, how much more will these [genetic Israelites], who are the natural branches, be grafted into their own olive tree? For I do not desire, brethren, that you should be ignorant of this mystery, lest you should be wise in your own opinion, that hardening in part has happened to Israel until the fullness of the Gentiles has come in. And so all Israel will be saved, as it is written: 'The Deliverer will come out of Zion, and He will turn away ungodliness from Jacob'" (verses 24-26).

Let me explain. Imagine an olive tree, rooted into the ground. It represents the ancient nation of Israel that God established, and the branches are the people. When Jesus came along, did all of the nation have faith in the Messiah? No! A whole bunch of the branches were broken off from the olive tree at that time. Jesus comes to the earth, and only a relatively few Israelites remain as living branches—the disciples, some prostitutes, others who believed in Jesus. They were still connected to the olive tree, contrary to the thoughts of the Pharisees. Those few believed in Jesus. They were being saved by their faith in Him.

Then some Gentiles showed up and believed in Jesus. They are the branches from the wild olive tree. God grafted them into the first olive tree. So here we find a Gentile branch and a Jewish branch on the same tree. Then all kinds of Gentile branches got inserted. Some of the Jews noticed and said, "How is it that they, the Gentiles, are grafted into the tree? Why are we Jews, as branches, lying on the ground, having been broken off?"

Some of the Israelites reconsidered and accepted Jesus as Lord and Savior, and then God picked them up and reunited them with the olive tree of Israel. They graft back in easily, according to the illustration. But do all the genetic Israelites get put back? No! You have a tree with some "wild" olive branches and some "tame" olive branches, and they are all now on the same tree. But they are all God's people, His Israel.

Paul looked at the olive tree and said, "And so all Israel will be saved." Was he talking about the broken-off branches on the ground—the genetic

Israelites? No, rather he said that "all Israel" are those grafted into the tree, both Jew and Gentile.

Now, catch the meaning of that. Israel consists of both Jew and Gentile. What's the definition of the church? The same thing! In the Old Testament, Israel was God's people of faith. In the New Testament, God's people of faith are Israel. They are one and the same from His viewpoint. Keep that definition of Israel in mind when you think about prophecy. It is not a human definition but a biblical one.

Paul said pointedly that it is not genetic Israel that anyone should be looking at now, but the Israel of faith. Unfortunately, most prophecy students today are still focused on genetic Israel, not the Israel of faith that the Bible points to. Thus "all Israel will be saved" means not that every Jewish Israelite will be saved, but rather that everyone who has accepted Jesus Christ will be. All Israel consists of those who are forgiven.

Somebody might protest, "That's replacement theology." No, it's not! God's true people have always been His people of faith—they just have different names. The early church was the continuation of Israel.

If you doubt that, go to Revelation 12 and read about the symbolic woman. She comes along before the time of Christ and gives birth to the child Jesus, and the dragon attempts to kill Him. Then He is taken to heaven to be with God after His death and resurrection. The woman goes and hides in the wilderness, because she is being persecuted. It's the same symbol before and after the time of Jesus—the pure woman, God's faithful people. It is those who were true to Him in Israel before the birth of Jesus, all the way through to those who were true to Him after Jesus goes back to heaven, Jew and Gentile together.

God uses the same symbols through time. He employs the imagery of a bride for Old Testament Israel (Eze. 16:8-14) as well as for New Testament Israel (Eph. 5:23, 25). The symbol of a harlot in the Old Testament represents His people when they were not true to Him (Eze. 16:15, 32), and He uses a harlot for the New Testament believers when they are not faithful to Him (Rev. 12:14—starts out pure and becomes a harlot in Rev. 17:1-6). In the Old Testament God employs the symbol of a "remnant" for those who remained faithful when the rest fell away (Micah 2:12). And He uses the "remnant" imagery in the New Testament for those who stay true to Him when the majority falls away (Rev. 12:11). From God's point of view, each symbol represents the same group throughout human history, not two separate ones in the Old and New Testaments.

Heard and Then Seen

Going back to Revelation 7, can we say that the 144,000 is a literal group of genetic Israelites? Or is it a symbolic one made up of God's people from all over the world? The book of Revelation demonstrates that it is a symbolic group, comprising people from every nation, tribe, and language. Here is how it works.

John announces, "I heard the number of those who were sealed" (verse 4). Next comes the list of tribes, and then John adds, "After these things I looked, and behold, a great multitude which no one could number, of all nations, tribes, peoples, and tongues, standing before the throne and before the Lamb, clothed with white robes, with palm branches in their hands" (verse 9). John is in vision, and he hears something. He does not see anything at this point, but he hears someone proclaim the list of tribes and the 144,000. And then he turns and observes a huge group of people from every nation, tribe, and people. I believe the list of the 144,000 that John hears and the vast group of people he sees are one and the same.

How do we know these two groups are identical? Revelation 7:13: "Then one of the elders answered, saying to me, 'Who are these arrayed in white robes?'" The elder is asking about the great multitude from every nation, tongue, and people. (Notice they wear white robes. They are pure, spotless, clothed with the righteousness of Jesus Christ. All who believe, according to Paul, have the righteousness of Christ and are His Israel.) Where did the multitude come from? the elder inquires.

"And I said to him, 'Sir, you know.' " In other words, John says, "You tell me."

"So he said to me, 'These are the ones who come out of the great tribulation, and washed their robes and made them white in the blood of the Lamb' " (verse 14). That matches what Paul says about the Israel of faith. The vast group of people is following the Lamb.

"Therefore they are before the throne of God, and serve Him day and night in His temple. And He who sits on the throne will dwell among them. They shall neither hunger anymore nor thirst anymore; the sun shall not strike them, nor any heat; for the Lamb who is in the midst of the throne will shepherd them and lead them to living fountains of waters. And God will wipe away every tear from their eyes" (verses 15-17).

Revelation 14:3 declares that "no one could learn that song [that they sang before the throne of God] except the hundred and forty-four thousand who were redeemed from the earth. These are the ones who were not defiled with women, for they are virgins." The group from every nation, tribe, and people are wearing white robes. That matches the "not defiled, purity, virgin" language, doesn't it? But that's not all. The great multitude is following the Lamb wherever He goes. It's the same group. So I am sure that the 144,000 are actually a great multitude from every nation, people, and tongue—Jew and Gentile—who have accepted Jesus Christ, and they are God's true Israel.

You may be thinking, *I'm not so sure about this.* I understand why, because many prophecy "experts" have said that God's Old Testament prophecies to Israel, such as the grand restoration described in Ezekiel, are history written in advance. Therefore, since some of those prophecies have not yet come to pass, they will be brought about for geopolitical Israel in the future. But the "history written in advance" idea, in which every detail of prophecy for the nation of Israel will be fulfilled no matter what, is actually contrary to Old Testament teaching. Let me show you how.

Prophecy Says "If"

God set conditions on the nation of Israel concerning whether or not they would receive the blessings He promised. Deuteronomy 28:1, 2, 15 declares:

"Now it shall come to pass, if you diligently obey the voice of the Lord your God, to observe carefully all His commandments which I command you today, that the Lord your God will set you high above all nations of the earth. And all these blessings shall come upon you and overtake you, because you obey the voice of the Lord your God" (verses 1, 2).

"But it shall come to pass, if you do not obey the voice of the Lord your God, to observe carefully all His commandments and His statutes which I command you today, that all these curses will come upon you and overtake you" (verse 15).

God did not say that no matter what Israel did, He was going to fulfill the promises. Many so-called experts argue that no matter what happens, God will bring to pass His prophecies about the nation of Israel. But God Himself said that was not true—that the nation had a choice about its destiny. The people could either follow Him and receive the blessings or disobey and get the curses. That is why the nation of Israel went into captivity in Babylon. They came under the curses because they rebelled against Him. And that is why pagan Rome destroyed Jerusalem in A.D. 70—because the nation of Israel did not follow God! So there was no fulfillment of the blessings for them.

That is not the only time in Old Testament prophecy when history was not written and set in advance. Jeremiah 18:6-10 states:

"'O house of Israel, can I not do with you as this potter?' says the Lord. 'Look, as the clay is in the potter's hand, so are you in My hand, O house of Israel! The instant I speak concerning a nation and concerning a kingdom, to pluck up, to pull down, and to destroy it, if that nation against whom I have spoken turns from its evil, I will relent of the disaster that I thought to bring upon it.'"

Think about Jonah. He did not want to go to Nineveh and preach, because if he did and told the people that in 40 days they would be destroyed by fire, they might ask God to forgive them, and the Lord would. Jonah wanted Nineveh to be toast. The prophet did not like the Ninevites. So God had to get Jonah's attention. Three days in the belly of the fish would capture my attention! It spit him out on the shore, and he got up and walked the hundreds of miles to Nineveh. Finally he reached the city and began announcing, "Forty days and you're toast!" "Thirty-nine days and you're toast!"

And the Ninevites responded, "Lord, forgive us. We have really blown it."

On the fortieth day Jonah leaves the city and waits for the fire from heaven. Did it come? No. Because the people had repented.

God's prophecies are not unchangeable history written in advance. They are conditional on obedience. If the conditions are met, then the prophecy does become history written in advance. But if they are not met, the promised event does not happen. It's that simple.

God told Jeremiah, "The instant I speak concerning a nation and concerning a kingdom, to build and to plant it, if it does evil in My sight so that it does not obey My voice, then I will relent concerning the good with which I said I would benefit it" (Jer. 18:9, 10). Remember that God started by saying, "Can't I do with you, Israel, like the potter does? Israel, if you don't do what I say, you're not going to get the blessing that I promised." According to God Himself, His promises to Israel are not unchangeable history presented in advance.

What about Daniel 9? Remember the 70-weeks prophecy that we went over in the first chapter, ranging from the decree to rebuild Jerusalem in 457 B.C. down to the time of Christ? It declared that the children of Israel had 490 years either to accept or reject the Messiah. Do you think there were any prophetic implications for their ultimate decision? Oh, yes, some big ones.

Let us consider an incident during Jesus' life on earth. "Then Peter came to Him and said, 'Lord, how often shall my brother sin against me, and I forgive him? Up to seven times?' Jesus said to him, 'I do not say to you, up to seven times, but up to seventy times seven'" (Matt. 18:21, 22). Where might Jesus have gotten that number of 70 times seven? From Daniel 9! In that chapter the prophet was concerned about his people, and God said, "I'm giving them some extra time to accept Me. I'm willing to forgive. I'm willing to give them another chance even after Babylon." Now, according to Jesus, if you can forgive your fellow human beings for 490 years, you are doing well. Since you are not going to live that long, it means, in essence, that you cannot stop forgiving during your lifetime. But there was an end to the forgiveness of Israel—the end of the 490 years in A.D. 34. That was when the branches of the nation of Israel were broken off and the Gentiles added in.

Jesus lived His ministry based on Daniel 9. In Matthew 26:18, when He entered Jerusalem, He said, "My time is at hand." Think for a moment about His triumphal entry into Jerusalem. Everybody was saying to Him, "Hey, Jesus, we want to make You king! Hosanna to the son of David. We're going to make You king."

He replied, "I've come here to die."

How did He know that? Three and a half years into His ministry, He realized that according to Daniel 9 He was going to be "cut off." In spite of the fact that the crowds were proclaiming that they wanted to make Him king, He said, "No, I'm going to Jerusalem to die."

Earlier, when Jesus had visited Jerusalem, His disciples feared that He would be killed there, but He said to them that His time was not yet (John 11:7-16). How did He know that? He had not reached the middle of the seven-year time period. Jesus knew when He was going to die, based on His knowledge of Daniel 9. He knew He would not be killed any earlier.

When Jesus left the earth, He told His disciples, "Go first to Jerusalem, then Judea, then Samaria, then to the uttermost parts of the world" (see Acts 1:8). He said it because they still had three and a half years to work in Jerusalem and Judea, to see if the leadership there would accept Jesus as their Messiah. How well did it work? Large numbers of converts came into the faith, but after a few years the Sanhedrin met and had Stephen put to death. Such an official act of the Sanhedrin was in essence a statement from the leadership of the nation of Israel, declaring, "We reject Jesus Christ and those who follow Him."

Then the Israelite officials sent Saul out to the world to persecute believers. On the road to Damascus God knocked him down and transformed Saul into Paul and commissioned him as an apostle to the Gentiles. That marked the end of the "seventy times seven" for the nation of Israel, and it was time to start grafting the Gentiles into the true Israel.

The Temple of God

As we noticed before, most contemporary prophecy teachers have been saying that Israel and the church are spiritually separate. But in God's Word they are one and the same. Consider how Acts 13 views it.

"And when the Jews went out of the synagogue, the Gentiles begged that these words might be preached to them the next Sabbath. Now when the congregation had broken up, many of the Jews and devout proselytes followed Paul and Barnabas, who, speaking to them, persuaded them to continue in the grace of God. And the next Sabbath almost the whole city [Jew and Gentile] came together to hear the word of God.

"But when the Jews saw the multitudes, they were filled with envy; and contradicting and blaspheming, they opposed the things spoken by Paul. Then Paul and Barnabas grew bold and said, 'It was necessary that the word of God should be spoken to you [the Jews] first; but since you reject it, and judge yourselves unworthy of everlasting life, behold, we turn to the Gentiles'" (verses 42-46).

The incident clearly illustrates Paul's imagery of some branches being cut off and some new ones grafted in. The olive tree model of Israel as a mix of those Jews and Gentiles who accept Christ thus appears all the way through the New Testament.

It is a concept that actually begins in the Old Testament. For example, consider what God says about the status of some of those outside ethnic Israel: "Do not let the son of the foreigner who has joined himself to the Lord speak, saying, 'The Lord has utterly separated me from His people'; nor let the eunuch say, 'Here I am, a dry tree.' For thus says the Lord: 'To the eunuchs who keep My Sabbaths, and choose what pleases Me, and hold fast My covenant, even to them I will give in My house and within My walls a place and a name better than that of sons and daughters; I will give them an everlasting name that shall not be cut off'" (Isa. 56:3-5).

That is significant in light of the olive tree illustration. God said that if any will trust in Jesus Christ, whether Jew or Gentile, foreigner or eunuch, as long as they do so they will become a part of true Israel. It is not just Paul's idea in the New Testament.

"'Also the sons of the foreigner who join themselves to the Lord, to serve Him, and to love the name of the Lord, to be His servants—everyone who keeps from defiling the Sabbath, and holds fast My covenant—even them I will bring to My holy mountain, and make them joyful in My house of prayer. Their burnt offerings and their sacrifices will be accepted on My altar; for My house shall be called a house of prayer for all nations.' The Lord God, who gathers the outcasts of Israel, says, 'Yet I will gather to him others besides those who are gathered to him'" (verses 6-8).

The multitude of people that John saw in Revelation came from every nation, tribe, and people. It is important that we not limit God's desire to save just to the physical, genetic Israelites. He has a lot more people in mind. Jesus shed light on this by what He said about the house of God.

"Then Jesus went into the temple of God and drove out all those who bought and sold in the temple, and overturned the tables of the money changers and the seats of those who sold doves. And He said to them, 'It is written, "My house shall be called a house of prayer," but you have made it a "den of thieves.'" Then the blind and the lame came to Him in the temple, and He healed them. But when the chief priests and scribes saw the wonderful things that He did, and the children crying out in the temple and saying, 'Hosanna to the Son of David!' they were indignant" (Matt. 21:12-15).

Upset at the people getting healed and praising the Lord, the religious leaders were clearly mentally sick! But notice that Jesus, standing in the house of the Lord, calls it His house, and He is referring to Isaiah 56:3-8, which describes it as "a house of prayer for all people."

Later in Matthew 21 Jesus tells a story about Himself. "There was a certain landowner who planted a vineyard and set a hedge around it, dug a winepress in it and built a tower. And he leased it to vinedressers and went into a far country. Now when vintage-time drew near, he sent his servants to the vinedressers, that they might receive its fruit. And the vinedressers took his servants, beat one, killed one, and stoned another. Again he sent other servants, more than the first, and they did likewise to them. Then last of all he sent his son to them, saying, 'They will respect my son.' But when the vinedressers saw the son, they said among themselves, 'This is the heir. Come, let us kill him and seize his inheritance.' And they caught him, and cast him out of the vineyard, and killed him. Therefore, when the owner of the vineyard comes, what will he do to those vinedressers?" (verses 33-40).

The leaders should have stopped and carefully thought through how they replied, but it seemed such an easy question that they answered it off the cuff, and in so doing they passed their own sentence on themselves. "They said to Him, 'He will destroy those wicked men miserably, and lease his vineyard to other vinedressers who will render to him the fruits in their seasons'" (verse 41). Since the men were already planning to kill Jesus, they should have been more cautious in their response.

"Jesus said to them, 'Did you never read in the Scriptures: "The stone which the builders rejected has become the chief cornerstone. This was the Lord's doing, and it is marvelous in our eyes"?'" (verse 42). They were preparing to reject Jesus, but He is the Chief Cornerstone. "'Therefore I say to you, the kingdom of God will be taken from you and given to a nation bearing the fruits of it. And whoever falls on this stone will be broken; but on whomever it falls, it will grind him to powder'" (verse 43).

When you fall on Jesus and ask for forgiveness, you are broken, but you are also saved. Remember that Jesus is the Stone cut out in Daniel 2. When He comes, He grinds to powder everyone who does not follow Him. The imagery is clear. Those who are of faith will be saved. But those who are not of faith will be destroyed.

So which Israel is important to God—the one of faith, or the one involving genetics? The one of faith is far more vital. While the geopolitical nation or land of Israel still has some significance, the people who are the Israel of faith is the primary matter in God's eyes.

A few days later Jesus spoke about the Temple again. Previously He had called it "My house" (Matt. 21:13). Now He says, "'O Jerusalem, Jerusalem, the one who kills the prophets and stones those who are sent to her! How often I wanted to gather your children together, as a hen gathers her chicks under her wings, but you were not willing! See! Your house is left to you desolate" (Matt. 23:37, 38).

Earlier He had spoken of it as "My house," but now the Temple is "Your house," and it is "desolate." It is empty without Him. "'For I say to you, you shall see Me no more till you say, *Blessed is He who comes in the name of the Lord!*'"" (verse 39). It was His house, and then it was not. The Israel of the flesh was losing out rapidly.

Paul's writings also address the house of the Lord. In Ephesians 2:11-13 he declares, "Therefore remember that you, once Gentiles in the flesh—who are called Uncircumcision by what is called the Circumcision made in the flesh by hands—that at that time you were without Christ, being aliens from the commonwealth of Israel and strangers from the covenants of promise, having no hope and without God in the world. But now in Christ Jesus you who once were far off have been made near by the blood of Christ."

He states that we were "once strangers to the commonwealth of Israel," implying that we are now Israel in Jesus Christ. "Now, therefore, you are no longer strangers and foreigners, but *fellow citizens with the saints and members of the household of God*, having been built on the foundation of the apostles and prophets, Jesus Christ Himself being the chief cornerstone, in whom the whole building, being joined together, grows into a holy temple in the Lord" (verses 19-21).

According to this verse, all believers, both Jew and Gentile, are the citizens of Israel! What is the temple now? The people of faith are God's new temple. We call it the church. When Jesus talks about knowing that you are the temple of God and that you should take care of your body (1 Cor. 6:19, 20), He means that we ourselves are His temple. Together as believers, we comprise His temple. He is not focused on a literal Temple in Jerusalem. Rather, the New Testament temple is all who believe in Him.

Bigger and Better

I said before that the promises to the nation of Israel were not history written in advance, but rather that they were conditional on the people's obedience. But God now does something really awesome. "If the nation of Israel doesn't agree with Me or believe in Me or keep My commandments," He in essence announces, "then I will make the promises and prophecies bigger and better for the true people of Israel, the Israel of faith." That is, for those who believe in Him and keep His commandments.

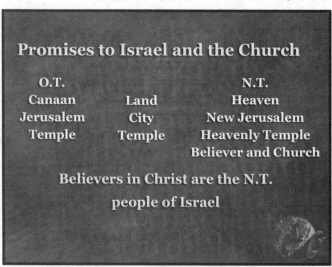

Promises to Israel and the Church

O.T.		N.T.
Canaan	Land	Heaven
Jerusalem	City	New Jerusalem
Temple	Temple	Heavenly Temple
		Believer and Church

Believers in Christ are the N.T.

people of Israel

Note the comparisons in the table above. Old Testament Israel received the Promised Land of Canaan. The New Testament believers have the promise of heaven and a wholly restored earth. Old Testament Israel had Jerusalem for a city. The New Testament promises us the New Jerusalem, first in heaven, then on earth. That's a lot better, isn't it? Old Testament Israel had a temple building in Jerusalem, but the temple in the New Testament is a heavenly temple (Heb. 9:11-28), the believer's own body (1 Cor. 6:19), and also the church (Eph. 2:11-22). Everything gets bigger and better for the New Testament believer. If the Old Testament believer did not accept what God was giving, and God was not able to fulfill the promise, He makes it bigger and better and reapplies it in the New Testament for the believer in Christ—Jew or Gentile.

Some of the popular books on prophecy today claim that in the Old Testament people were saved by works, and that in the New Testament people are saved by faith. But the Bible tells me that it is never "of works, lest anyone should boast" (Eph. 2:8). In Hebrews 11, the faith chapter, the faithful people listed there are all Old Testament individuals who were saved by faith. We are all saved by faith, both in the Old Testament and the New Testament. No one is ever saved by works. So the idea that there is a difference between Old Testament Israel and the New Testament church does not hold up either. The Bible declares that the redeemed have always been saved by faith.

Beautiful Bride

Then we have the theme of God's people as the bride. "At midnight a cry was heard: 'Behold, the bridegroom is coming; go out to meet him!'" (Matt. 25:6). We know that Jesus is talking about the church here. The woman image of Revelation 12 overlaps the Old and the New Testaments: it is God's people dressed in white. The Old Testament book of Ezekiel calls God's people the bride (Eze. 16) as does the New Testament book of Ephesians (see Eph. 5).

Scripture calls God's people a remnant. In the Old Testament Micah 2:12 describes God's faithful as a remnant of the nation. Revelation 12:17 also presents God's faithful as a remnant. They "keep the commandments of God, and have the testimony of Jesus."

The New Covenant

Revelation 7:1-4 speaks of "those who were sealed." In Deuteronomy 11:18 the people had the "seal of God" in their forehead. "Therefore you shall lay up these words of mine in your heart and in your soul," God said to the Israelites, "and bind them as a sign on your hand, and they shall be as frontlets between your eyes." Today God is still waiting for His people to store up His Word and live by it, before He lets the end-time events begin. That is what those four angels are waiting for. God wants His people to put His Word into their minds and into their hearts, not to be saved by works, but because of love for God.

Some claim the new covenant is what the New Testament church has. But do you know where you find the new covenant? In the Old Testament—in Jeremiah 31:31-33:

"Behold, the days are coming, says the Lord, when I will make a new covenant with the house of Israel and with the house of Judah—not according to the covenant that I made with their fathers in the day that I took them by the hand to lead them out of the land of Egypt, My covenant which they broke, though I was a husband to them, says the Lord. But this is the covenant that I will make with the house of Israel after those days, says the Lord: I will put My law in their minds, and write it on their hearts; and I will be their God, and they shall be My people."

Where does God write it? On their minds and in their hearts. Because of their love for Jesus, they follow what they know of God's law. That is the new covenant. He inscribes it in our lives.

In the same terms, John says in Revelation that we hear God's message and do it (Rev. 1:3), because we love Jesus. While He was on earth Jesus said, "If you love Me, keep My commandments" (John 14:15). God's last-day people from all nations are trusting Christ and obeying Him, a reality echoed in Revelation 12:17, which speaks of those "who keep the commandments of God and have the testimony of Jesus Christ." Again, Revelation 14 is the chapter where we began with the 144,000, and verse 12 states: "Here is the patience of the saints; here are those who keep the commandments of God and the faith of Jesus." Do you see how that keeps playing out? We are getting God's word directly in our minds. No one is saved by works, but only by faith in Jesus. And if you have faith in Him, you do what He says. If you claim to have faith in Him and don't do what He says, you are not His.

The Israel of Our Time

In the Old Testament the concept of Israel had more of a geopolitical definition. But in the New Testament it acquires a more spiritual definition—the people of faith, both Jew and Gentile. This matches what happened to the king of the north, which went from more politically defined as pagan Rome to more religious as papal Rome. Jesus' death on the cross changed everything for Israel.

90

Daniel 11 talks about "the Glorious Land," which is geographical. But notice that it does not speak about the people—only about the land. In Daniel 11 the geopolitical depicts real events, and after we go past the time of the cross, the localized struggles represent a worldwide spiritual conflict as well. Events will still happen in Jerusalem or the land of Israel, but God's people (the citizens of Israel in Ephesians 2) are those who are the true Israelites by faith. Everyone from around the world can choose to be a part of God's true Israel. As Jesus taught in Matthew 21, the vineyard is the same but the people have changed.

Notice this intriguing trend in the history and prophecy of Daniel 11. Whenever the king of the north (Papacy) controls literal Jerusalem, it also controls spiritual Jerusalem, the church. During the Crusades, the first conflict between the Papacy and Islam, the Papacy controlled literal Jerusalem and also the church. During the second conflict with Islam (Ottoman Empire), the Papacy never controlled literal Jerusalem, and because of the Reformation it lost control of the church, spiritual Jerusalem. At the time of the end, Daniel 11:40-45, the Papacy once again controls Jerusalem, and Revelation 13:3 says that "all the world . . . followed the beast," indicating that the Papacy will once again have control over the worldwide church. The literal is a parallel to the spiritual. It is not an either/or—it is both literal and spiritual in Daniel 11:40-45.

"Blessed is he who reads and those who hear the words of this prophecy, and keep those things which are written in it; for the time is near" (Rev. 1:3). It is time to listen and do it! You can't just hear God's Word and walk away. You have to put what you learn into practice, or it doesn't do you any good at all. If you don't practice what you learn, it makes you worse off, because now you know what you are missing and you are in rebellion. And so, when you hear these things, live them out in your life.

CHAPTER 7

Islam,
the King of the South

Two Bold Powers

P alestine has a dual application in prophecy. In Daniel 11 the
Glorious Land is geographical Palestine, but religiously or spiritually speaking, Israel is God's people. All who accept Jesus Christ
and thus become heirs of Abraham are God's true Israel worldwide.

The king of the north goes from being primarily geopolitical in nature
during the eras of Greece and Rome to a geopolitical and religious power
as the Papacy. Likewise, the Glorious Land evolves from being primarily
geopolitical to both geopolitical and religious, leading to a worldwide re-
ligious/spiritual struggle. The geographical locations identified in Daniel
11 are a general guideline of where the conflict will take place.

The same principles hold true for the king of the south. That power,
too, goes through a transition from being geopolitical to both geopolitical
and religious. The geopolitical phase is a model of the religious phase that
will be a worldwide struggle, consistent in all three powers (king of the
north, king of the south, and the Glorious Land) of Daniel 11. In prophetic
interpretation we need to see consistency.

The two powers in Revelation 13 are the beast, which we identified
as the papal system, and the power with lamblike horns that comes up in
Revelation 13:11—the United States. Both are striving for world control.

Malachi Martin, in his book about Pope John Paul II, *The Keys of This
Blood,* observes: "He would endow his [John Paul's] papacy with an international profile and, as pope, move around among world leaders and
nations, vindicating a position for himself as a special leader among leaders, because in that competition he plans to emerge as the victor."[1]

When John Paul II started his reign, three superpowers held sway in
the world: the United States, the Soviet Union, and the Papacy. By the

time of his death only two remained. The Catholic Church and the United States worked on eliminating the third one, which they pushed to the side. Here's evidence of American intentions at that time: "In a broad new policy statement that is in its final drafting stage, the Defense Department asserts that America's political and military mission in the post-cold war era will be to ensure that no rival superpower is allowed to emerge in Western Europe, Asia, or the territory of the former Soviet Union."[2]

Remember the peace dividend that everyone talked about at the end of the cold war era? People speculated about how much money the United States could save that it would no longer have to spend on military capability. But it's hard not to notice how many wars the United States has had since the cold war ended. Why so many conflicts? Because the country has been serious about making sure that nobody else gains power.

In our time, both the Papacy strives to be number one and the United States strives to be number one. The book of Revelation depicts those two powers ultimately working together side by side. The world may have witnessed this on a smaller scale in the alliance between President Ronald Reagan and the pope.

"Reagan and the pope agreed to undertake a clandestine campaign to hasten the dissolution of the Communist empire. Declares Richard Allen, Reagan's first National Security adviser: 'This was one of the great secret alliances of all time.' . . .

"Step by reluctant step, the Soviets and the Communist government of Poland bowed to the moral, economic, and political pressure imposed by the pope and the president."[3]

The two men supported the labor unions within Poland, building up their power. While the United States continued its arms race that was bankrupting the Soviet Union, the Catholic Church spread through Poland a moral message that sought to undermine Communism. At a time of great social and technological change and the combination of the Catholic Church's support of the labor unions and the military might of the United States, Reagan and the pope possibly transformed the course of history.

As we have seen, Revelation 13 tells us the United States will end up being the military might to help bring people in line with the Papacy. The two powers have already taken advantage of times of change by working together to alter history. It would not be a surprise to have them cooperate again. "If European federalism triumphs, the EC [now European Union] will indeed be an empire. It will lack an emperor; but it will have the pope. It is difficult not to think that Wojtyla [John Paul II] realizes this,"[4] a contemporary newspaper in England, the *Sunday Telegraph,* reported, suggesting that the pope was a kind of emperor for Europe. Some really interesting things happened in the late 1980s and the early 1990s with the Papacy, the Soviet Union, and the United States. Everything was setting up, I believe, for future events.

A Threat From the South

Where does Islam fit into the picture? To begin to answer that question, consider the view of the late Charles Malik, a prominent Lebanese politician and educator. Malik was Greek Orthodox, served as Lebanon's minister of education and arts, and taught at several American universities, including Harvard and Dartmouth. He was even president of the United Nations General Assembly for one session. A lifelong supporter of the Christian cause, Malik had this to say in 1979 about the future role of Islam and how the Christian West and the Christian East should handle Islam:

"The only hope for the Western world lies in an alliance between the Roman Catholic Church, which is the most commonly influential, controlling, unifying element in Europe, and the Eastern Orthodox Church. Rome must unite with Eastern Orthodoxy, because the Eastern Orthodox Church controls the western Middle East, the east end of the Mediterranean. And if they don't solidify that control, Islam will march across Europe. Islam is political. The only hope of the Western world lies in a united Europe under the control of the pope."[5]

Malik was an Eastern Orthodox Christian, and he urged that Eastern Christianity should reunite with the Papacy. The reason that he wanted to see a unified Christian world under the Papacy was the threat from Islam. I don't believe that Malik was studying prophecy, but being from the Middle East, he knew well the potential dangers.

Take a look at Daniel 11:40 again: "At the time of the end the king of the South shall attack him [the king of the north]; and the king of the North shall come against him like a whirlwind, with chariots, horsemen, and with many ships; and he shall enter the countries, overwhelm them, and pass through."

During the Crusades the king of the north was papal-dominated Western Christianity, and Islam was the king of the south. Islam was the powerhouse that came from the south of Jerusalem (see Dan. 11:23-28). Daniel 2, 7, and 8 do not suggest another change in the series of kings from the north until the return of Jesus Christ, nor do we find any indication for a new identity of the king of the south. The king of the north should still be the Papacy until the end of time, and I'm suggesting the king of the south will continue to be Islam.

Charles Malik's statement sounds almost prophetic. I believe that we are looking at something that has not yet been fulfilled but is in the beginning stages. A conflict may be brewing between Islam and Christianity that could metamorphose into a holy war. We have not gone there yet, but I believe, based on this prophecy, that we will. If I am right, it places us at the beginning of the last showdown between Islam and Christianity. Things could go quickly from here.

Continuing with verses 41-43: "He [the king of the north] shall also enter the Glorious Land." This suggests that something will somehow compromise the sovereignty of the geopolitical nation of Israel.

"And many countries shall be overthrown; but these shall escape from his hand: Edom, Moab, and the prominent people of Ammon. He shall stretch out his hand against the countries, and the land of Egypt shall not escape. He shall have power over the treasures of gold and silver, and over all the precious things of Egypt; also the Libyans and Ethiopians shall follow at his heels."

In chapter 1 we saw that Daniel 11:24-39 covers the time period of the Papacy's 1260-year rule, which included both the Crusades against Islam and the Reformation. The king of the south during that period was Islam, and I believe it still is. The king of the south power changed from the political Ptolemaic kingdom, which was its beginning form, to the geopolitical and religious power of Islam.

In the present day we have the king of the north on one side, the king of the south on the other, and God's people in between. Those who accept Jesus Christ truly find themselves stuck in the middle. They are the heirs of Jesus, heirs of Abraham, the true Israel, and they have the faith of Jesus and keep His commandments. As an example of how they are caught between the two powers, consider that the Papacy changed the day of worship from Saturday to Sunday. Islam chose Friday as its day to gather for prayer and public worship. You can see the parallel transformation from a politically based power to a religiously based one.

Jeremiah 1:15 says that a series of kings would come to Jerusalem. From history and prophecy we know that it started with the king of Babylon, then Medo-Persia, then Greece, then Rome. The land invasion route entered Israel from the north.

The power in the south started out as the Ptolemaic kingdom in Egypt, and then the Ptolemies faded away. The new power emerged from along the Red Sea—Mecca and Medina—and thrust up from the south. This is Islam.

Looking at the globe from the point of view of Africa, we note that the shaded area is the nations predominantly controlled by Islam. Israel is the tiny country in the middle. How would you like to live in Israel, when all the countries surrounding it have basically sworn to exterminate you? It would be a rough neighborhood to grow up in!

Similar and Opposite

In 2002 a friend and I were having an e-mail conversation about Islam and the Papacy. He believed that at the time of the end, Islam and the Papacy would unite into one power, an idea he based on Martin Luther calling both Islam and the Papacy the antichrist. Martin Luther identified one leg of the Daniel 2 statue as Rome and the Papacy and the other leg as Islam. As I was reading the e-mail message from my friend, I thought, *They are much alike, yet they are opposites, like polar north and south.* When that thought went through my mind, I thought, *Daniel 11!* I opened my Bible and read it, and suddenly Daniel 11 made sense for the first time in my life. If the Papacy was the beast and was in the north, then the other power should have a point/counterpoint relationship to it. Let's go through the opposites and the correlatives to see if it works.

1. The Papacy emerged from within Rome. Islam spread through the southern territory of the Roman Empire, and papal Rome dominated the northern part.

2. Daniel said that the little horn, the Papacy, would uproot three horns, and it did—the Heruli, the Vandals, and the Ostrogoths. Islam conquered three regions: North Africa, the Middle East, and Turkey.

3. Both powers have a "man at the head"—one the pope, the other Muhammad. Ask a member of the Roman Catholic Church, "Who's the man at the head of your church?" They'll say, the pope. Then ask a Muslim, "Who's the man at the head of your movement?" and they will reply, "Muhammad."

4. They would be "diverse," or different, from previous powers. They both shift from being a political to a religious power. Pagan Rome was political while papal Rome was political and religious. Egypt under the Ptolemies was political. But Islam is both strongly political and religious. The ancient world did not separate governments into religious and politi-

cal spheres. The leader would often be the chief priest of the national religion. But papal Rome and Islam emphasized the religious aspects much more than ancient governments did. They focused primarily on religious conquest.

5. They are characterized as "speaking great words," or blasphemy. Even the term *antichrist* applies. The Greek term translated as antichrist means either in place of Christ or against Christ. The Papacy claims to be ruling in the place of Christ. Islam denies the divinity of Christ.

6. They would "persecute the saints." The Papacy has persecuted Christians and others who did not believe as it does. Islam has persecuted Christians and Jews as well, although at times it could be quite tolerant (as especially happened in Islamic Spain).

7. They would "receive the dragon's seat," or the capital of the Roman Empire. The pagan Roman Empire had two capitals. Emperor Constantine moved the capital from the city of Rome to Constantinople. After he left, the city of Rome became the center of papal power. Constantinople later became Istanbul, capital of the Islamic Turkish Empire for several hundred years. The Papacy got one capital of the Roman Empire and Islam the other.

Some have seen allusions to Islam in Revelation 9:1-12: "Then the fifth angel sounded: And I saw a star fallen from heaven to the earth. To him was given the key to the bottomless pit." Two interpretations here might make sense. One is that the star was Muhammad, beginning as a true prophet of God and then wandering away. The other approach is the one that I lean more toward: the angel that fell from heaven is Satan.

Both the beast we find in Revelation and the power that some believe to be Islam come from the "bottomless pit." The bottomless pit is defined as a lifeless place, a desolate, abysmal area. The Bible commentators[6] who believe that Muhammad has a role in Revelation 9 view the bottomless pit as the Arabian Peninsula, which seemed lifeless. But Satan is the one who brings destruction from either beast. Verse 2 says: "He opened the bottomless pit, and smoke arose out of the pit like the smoke of a great furnace." Smoke often represents the judgments of God, and I think that's what it is here, because by the time we get to verses 20 and 21, the smoke is indeed demonstrating that it was divine judgment:

"And the sun and the air were darkened because of the smoke of the pit. Then out of the smoke locusts came upon the earth. And to them was given power, as the scorpions of the earth have power. They were commanded not to harm the grass of the earth, or any green thing, or any tree, but only those men who do not have the seal of God on their foreheads" (verses 2-4).

When we talked about the "seal of God," we found that it meant getting God's Word into our mind after we made the decision to follow Him, a concept that goes back at least as far as Deuteronomy 11:18. The new covenant in Jeremiah 31:31-33 was the same thing. Don't think that the seal of God pertains only to end-time people. It has applied to His people for a long, long time. Throughout history individuals have accepted God and made a decision to follow Him. At the end of time the same seal of God is in people's foreheads, and He protects them from the plagues to come.

Two Have Passed, One Is Yet to Come

What we just described was the first of three "woes" depicted in Revelation 9. "One woe is past. Behold, still two more woes are coming after these things" (verse 12). Some have interpreted the three "woes" as three historical phases. The first woe might be the Arab phase, the time when Muhammad conquered the Arabian Peninsula. As Islam continued to expand, it seized Egypt, Palestine, and parts of Turkey. Although the Islamic armies tried to take Constantinople, they could not. So in the first 150 years of conflict, that's what Islam was able to conquer. "And they were not given authority to kill them, but to torment them for five months." Those who hold this position regard the five months of prophetic days as 150 years.

Here's another aspect of the first "woe." Revelation 9:3 talks about locusts. The desert locusts come out of the Saudi Arabian desert and spread across North Africa when the wind blows from east to west. Or, if the wind goes from southwest to northeast, it sends the locusts that way. A map of the range of the desert locust shows that it is the same area as covered by the Arab phase of Islam. God could have used the locust as a symbol to describe the spread of Islam in the first historical phase, or the first "woe."

In verses 13-17 comes the second "woe." "Then the sixth angel sounded: And I heard a voice from the four horns of the golden altar which is before God, saying to the sixth angel who had the trumpet, 'Release the four angels who are bound at the great river Euphrates.' So the four angels, who had been prepared for the hour and day and month and year, were released to kill a third of mankind. Now the number of the army of the horsemen was two hundred million, and I heard the number of them. And thus I saw the horses in the vision: those who sat on them had breastplates of fiery red, hyacinth blue, and sulfur yellow; and the heads of the horses were like the heads of lions; and out of their mouths came fire, smoke, and brimstone."

Many old commentaries regard this group as representing the Turks. The Turks came out of what is now Russia, advanced down through Persia, accepted Islam, spread along the area of the Tigris and Euphrates rivers, broke through the region's mountain passes, and reached the area now called Turkey, and as they did they brought in a brand-new phase of Islamic conquest. Capturing Constantinople, they pushed all the way up into Europe. By then they had put a lot of pressure on Western Christianity.

The Ottoman push ultimately enabled the Reformation to take root, because much of Christendom was preoccupied with trying to hold the line against the Islamic Turks. During that time period Martin Luther and other Reformers began to proclaim "the Bible and the Bible only," and the Papacy could not immediately deal with them because of the threat from the Turks. Why would God allow the Islamic invasions? I believe that He used Islam to revitalize Christianity. It gave an opportunity for the Reformation to develop and spread.

Notice something interesting in verse 20: "But the rest of mankind, who were not killed by these plagues, did not repent of the works of their hands, that they should not worship demons, and idols of gold, silver, brass, stone, and wood, which can neither see nor hear nor walk." Both Western and Eastern Christianity increasingly used images and statues in their churches and worship, a practice that upset Muhammad and his followers. During the earlier Arab phase he and his people had left those Christians who were serious about following the Bible alone, but of those who seemed to worship statues, Muhammad's father-in-law, Abu Bakr, said they should "cleave their skulls."[7]

Some see this as God using Islam to attempt to bring Christianity back to truth, but it would not. Verse 21: "And they did not repent of their murders or their sorceries or their sexual immorality or their thefts." What did God use as the symbol of their spiritual falling away? He called them a harlot, a prostitute, just as He did with Old Testament Israel. Also, when Old Testament Israel worshipped idols, God sent in the descendants of Ishmael (Midianites, Ammonites, and Moabites—the children of the East) to punish Israel.

So we see the passing of the first and second woes, which were both "wars" of Islam against Christianity. Daniel 11:25-39 speaks of the first two of three conflicts between Islam and Christianity. As Daniel 11 has three conflicts, so in Revelation there are three woes. Again, I suggest that God was using Islam as a wake-up call to bring His New Testament Israel, or Christians, back to His Word. I believe the same pattern will occur in the end-time—Islam will be a tool in the hand of God to confront the world with His Word.

---

[1] Malachi Martin, *The Keys of This Blood* (New York: Touchstone, 1990), p. 480.

[2] Patrick E. Tyler, "U.S. Strategy Plan Calls for Insuring No Rivals Develop," *New York Times,* Mar. 8, 1992. Available online at http://query.nytimes.com/gst/fullpage.html?res=9E0CE5D61E38F93BA35750C0A964958260.

[3] Carl Bernstein, "The Holy Alliance: Ronald Reagan and John Paul II," *Time,* Feb. 24, 1992. Available online at www.time.com/time/magazine/article/0,9171,974931-1,00.html.

[4] *Sunday Telegraph,* Aug. 25, 1991. Article obtained by e-mail through the syndication office of the *Daily Telegraph,* London, England.

[5] This quote appears on many Web sites, but the best documentation is at www.atuiora/Resources/Sermons/27-08_The-Rise-and-Fall-of-the-World-Part2, where John MacArthur claims to have heard it in person. However, MacArthur gives a summary, not a direct quote.

[6] See the June 1944 *Ministry* magazine article listing views of many Bible commentaries from 1100 to the 1930s in Appendix D, pp. 220, 221.

[7] Edward Gibbon, *The Decline and Fall of the Roman Empire* (New York: Random House, 1932), vol. 5, p. 286.

CHAPTER 8

The Time-of-the-End
Holy War

The Three Conflicts

Daniel 11:29 states: "At the appointed time he shall return and go toward the south; but it shall not be like the former or the latter." The verse apparently describes the second major conflict between Christianity and Islam. The king of the north has headed south for a second round, but it will not be like the "former," nor like the "latter." From this statement we can conclude that general periods of conflict take place between the kings of the south and north in Daniel 11. In Daniel 11 the first two have passed, and the third one begins in verse 40. This leads me to conclude that yet another struggle will take place in the future. That is, another battle between Islam and Christianity is likely.

It suggests, furthermore, still another similarity between the kings of the north and south. A deadly wound would be healed, according to Revelation 13:3. The Papacy was wounded in 1798, but eventually regained its power. What about Islam? Did it go through a time it had great strength, lost it, and got it back again?

One day I decided to graph the

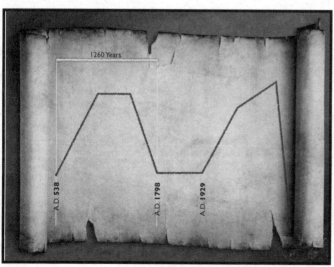

power curve, as I call it, of the Papacy. It rose to prominence in A.D. 538, increased in influence for centuries, had a zenith, and then, after 1260 years of strength, saw its power ended in 1798. Then in 1929 the Papacy began to rise again and, according to the Bible, will expand in strength until Jesus destroys it at the very end.

Then I thought that I would find out what happens if I plot the power curve of Islam over that of the Papacy. Here's what I got.

Wow! It's almost identical. If we re-gard Revelation 9 as portraying the role of Islam and interpret a day for a year (as sug-gested previously), then 150 years ext-ends from A.D. 612 (about the period His followers believe that Muhammad began receiving revelations) to 762. Then we have starting in 1449 the 391 years of the

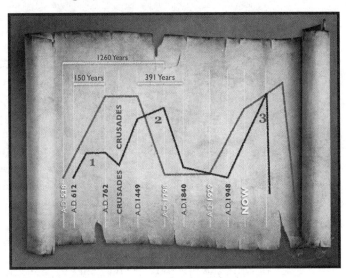

second woe as the period of the Turkish Empire, and that one brings you to 1840 and the change in the Ottoman Empire. From the mid-1800s to the mid-1900s Islam did not have much power at all. It wasn't until about 1948, when Islamic countries acquired a common enemy, that they started drawing back together. The modern state of Israel came into being in 1948. That ral-lied Islamic nations, and instead of fighting each other, they would now turn their guns on Israel. About the same time many of those countries started earning petroleum dollars, so that now they had some money to fight with. In the 1960s the new tool of terrorism appeared. Islam had begun to grow in might.

Here in the graph is the early (with the Crusades), the middle (with the Ottoman Empire), and the latter struggles in Daniel 11. The third one is the one at the time of the end—the period we live in.

When I saw that, I thought, *Wow!* Just think of all the things that hap-pened during the 100 years that these two powers were lying low: Communism sprang up, Darwin and evolution appeared—all kinds of stuff was happening. We are talking about the beginning of the time of the end.

Let's go back through Daniel 11:40. "At the time of the end the king of the South [Islam] shall attack him [the Papacy and its alliance]; and the king of the North [the Papacy] shall come against him [Islam] like a whirlwind." When the third conflict breaks loose, it will become a religious war like the Crusades. We don't have a full-blown holy war yet, but it is looming in the near future.

The Path of Chaos

In an op-ed piece for ynetnews.com, secular commentator Avi Rath wrote about the pope's exoneration of the Jews[1] for killing Jesus. As Rath points out, this act might seem insignificant in today's tumultuous world, but it comes in an era of the resurgence of religion as the defining factor in the world's conflicts.[2] As he outlines the flashpoints in the Middle East in the early twenty-first century, he notes: "This is not just a political dispute over territory or refugee rights. What we have here is a deep religious war between Judaism and Islam, with political arguments only constituting the outer layer of this religious war. Islam's hate for Judaism is in some ways different than its hate for Christianity yet similar in other ways. In Islam's view, both Jews and Christians are infidels and deserve the same fate."

It's no stretch of the imagination to believe that the religious conflict I described in the previous section could happen. But when we know the history, it seems almost inevitable.

Ramzi Yousef is a name you might remember from recent history. He was the terrorist who carried out the first World Trade Center bombing in 1993. That bomb blew a big hole in the parking garage. It filled the twin towers with smoke, and the buildings had to be evacuated. But they didn't come down. Eventually the authorities captured Yousef, and while being flown by the World Trade Center in a helicopter, one of the security agents sitting by his side commented, "Hey, Ramzi, look out the window—it's still standing."

"Not if I had enough time and money," Yousef replied.

I guess he got the last word. The World Trade Center no longer exists.

Ramzi Yousef is in a United States prison after planning another terrorist act. In 1995 he was working on one in the Philippines now called the Bojinka plot. The local authorities stopped it eight days before it was supposed to be carried out.[3] Yousef intended to assassinate Pope John Paul

II. (Interestingly, Daniel 11:40 suggests that the king of the south [Islam] would make war against the king of the north [or the Papacy].) So what happened in the Philippines?

Yousef was building bombs, and he had a small group of al-Qaeda operatives helping him. He planned to dress them as Catholic priests, and they would be wearing suicide bombs underneath the robes. On World Youth Day in January 1995 in Manila, Philippines, the "priests" would approach the motorcade of the pope. When they all got close together, they would detonate simultaneously and blow up the religious leader and those around him. Ramzi Yousef himself would not be one of the suicide bombers, however. That was Phase 1 of the Bojinka plot.

In Phase 2 Yousef and several other operatives would get on separate flights out of the Philippines. During the flight they would reach under the seat and pull out the life vest. They would use the liquid in their shaving kit that wasn't shaving fluid, and the cotton that wasn't cotton, to make a bomb, attach a watch as the timer, put it underneath the seat where the life vest had been, and get off the plane when it landed. Each of the men would do this on three or four flights and then board a plane headed to Pakistan. All of those bombs had timers on them. They were intended to blow up 14 United States airliners simultaneously over the Pacific Ocean, just after the time that the pope was to be assassinated.

But the scheme failed eight days beforehand. As Ramzi Yousef worked in the kitchen of his apartment in Manila, preparing a bomb, he made a mistake. Nothing exploded. It just caused a smoky fire. But the smoke forced him and his accomplices to flee the building. When the fire department arrived, it concluded that it was not a grease fire in the kitchen. They brought in law enforcement.

Police officials were still there when one of the al-Qaeda operatives showed up and said that he needed to get his computer. The police arrested him.

Ramzi Yousef skipped the country and headed back to Pakistan. On the computer investigators found details of the Bojinka plot, including plans to use airliners to crash into the CIA building in Washington, D.C. That was in 1995, six years before 2001. We should have known what was coming. The Bojinka plot brought the world to within eight days of triggering a religious war.

Another possible scenario to consider is that of the twelfth imam, al-Mahdi. Muhammad ibn al-Hasan al-Mahdi, born in A.D. 869, was the twelfth imam of Islam. Shi'a Islam believes that he did not die but that God hid him so that he could reemerge when the right time comes. The twelfth imam is the Mahdi, an Islamic savior of humanity, who will appear with Jesus Christ and bring peace and justice to the world.

The man who is president of Iran as I write this book, Mahmoud Ahmadinejad, believes in the return of the twelfth imam, and that should make us nervous. In his version of the belief, the world must be in chaos before the twelfth imam, the Islamic messiah, will appear. A hadith (a narrative report of what Muhammad or his companions said or did), believed to be authentic, quotes the prophet as saying: "He [the twelfth imam] will then fill the earth with peace and justice as it will have been filled with injustice and tyranny before then."[4] When chaos sweeps the world, al-Mahdi will come, and he will bring Islam to the world, and peace under Islam. All you have to do, if you are a believer in the twelfth imam, is initiate world chaos.

In that light, some of Ahmadinejad's comments make more sense, don't they? He believes in the twelfth imam, and as a leader he is trying to stir up world disorder. If he obtained nuclear weapons, he would be tempted to help fulfill the prophecy. The teaching about the twelfth imam is another reason that I believe the Islamic attack against the Christian West could happen. Notice some of Ahmadinejad's comments about the 2011 Egyptian revolution:

"President Mahmoud Ahmadinejad said . . . that a new Middle East is being created which would be free of the United States and Israel. . . .

"'We will soon see a new Middle East materializing without America and the Zionist regime, and there will be no room for world arrogance [the West] in it,' Ahmadinejad told the cheering crowds. . . .

"In his fiery style, Ahmadinejad showed his messianic beliefs on Friday, saying the world was witnessing a revolution managed by Imam Mehdi, the 12 Shiite imam [sic] who disappeared as a 5-year-old in the tenth century and who Shiites believe would return on the judgment day.

"'The final move has begun. We are in the middle of a world revolution managed by this dear [twelfth imam]. A great awakening is unfolding. One can witness the hand of Imam in managing it,' said Ahmadinejad."[5]

What does biblical prophecy say happens after Islam attacks the Papacy and its allies? The papal alliance counterattacks, fragmenting Islam into three segments. "At the time of the end the king of the South shall attack him; and the king of the North shall come against him like a whirlwind, with chariots, horsemen, and with many ships; and he shall enter the countries, overwhelm them, and pass through" (Dan. 11:40). This sounds like a very rapid conquest of those areas fostering radical Islam. And once you have the Papacy involved, it will become a holy war. Notice how Western leaders try to keep the current situation from becoming an all-out religious confrontation. They often say such things as "This is just a conflict with radical Islam. It is not a 'holy war.'" But, I believe, eventually it will become exactly that.

The Hard, Fast War

In Daniel's description of rapid destruction, the forces will "overwhelm them, and pass through. He [the king of the north, the papal alliance] shall also enter the Glorious Land, and many countries shall be overthrown." Notice that they enter Israel. As I mentioned in chapter 6, that means the Israeli nation's sovereignty is compromised either by the Christian powers or, more likely, the Christian powers are "saving" Israel from radical Islam. Many countries will be overthrown—not just a couple of them, but many. The whole of the Middle East will be in turmoil.

"But these shall escape from his hand: Edom, Moab, and the prominent people of Ammon. He shall stretch out his hand against the countries, and the land of Egypt shall not escape. He shall have power over the treasures of gold and silver, and over all the precious things of Egypt; also the Libyans and Ethiopians shall follow at his [the king of the north's] heels" (verses 41-43).

The overwhelming attack from the north causes a three-way breakup of Islam:

    1. Those who escape the king of the north

    2. Those who are overthrown by the king of the north

    3. Those who follow after the king of the north

First look at those who escape. Daniel 12:1 mentions the people recorded in the book and rescued by Jesus. Revelation 17:8 reports that all the world follows the beast, except those whose names are written in the Lamb's book of life. Hebrews 2:3, 4 asks: "How shall we escape if we neglect so great a salvation, which at the first began to be spoken by the Lord, and was confirmed to us by those who heard Him . . . ?" Concerning the time of Christ's return we find the following in 1 Thessalonians 5:2, 3: "For you yourselves know perfectly that the day of the Lord so comes as a thief in the night. For when they say, 'Peace and safety!' then sudden destruction comes upon them, as labor pains upon a pregnant woman. And they shall not escape." Repeatedly the Bible says that those who survive the coming of Christ are those who trust in Jesus, and so I interpret "escape" in Daniel 11:41 as referring to those who trust in Jesus. The Hebrew word translated as "escape" in Daniel 11:41 is the same word translated as "delivered" in Daniel 12:1. This gives added credibility to understanding these two groups as linked. The groups listed as "escaping" this third holy war—Edom, Moab, and the prominent people of Ammon—were called the "people of the East" in Bible times (Isa. 11:14). They were heirs of Abraham through his son Ishmael. Could any of them be people of the Book, or Bible-believing Christians? Before the time of David, God used the people of the East to chastise Israel for its idolatry and disobedience. Later, during the reign of David, their territory formed part of the Davidic kingdom. In a similar way as in the past, after using Islam to chastise modern Israel (Christians), God rescues those who refuse to follow the Papacy and accept Jesus instead, and He includes them as a part of Jesus' restored

THE DAVIDIC
KINGDOM

ISRAEL

JERUSALEM

AMMON

JUDAH

MOAB

EGYPT

EDOM

"Davidic" kingdom.

While Scripture focuses on the blessing given Isaac, we must not forget that God also blessed Ishmael (Gen. 21:13, 18). And if Gentiles can be sons of Abraham by being grafted in, why can't a Muslim person become a true "son of Abraham" also?

Within Islam today there is a growing movement of people who accept Jesus Christ as the Messiah, as their Savior. They believe in Him as their judge and that He is coming back to rescue them. In fact, they are willing to die for Him and trust Him with their lives. I believe that among Muslims, this group that believes in Jesus is the "Edom, Moab, and the sons of Ammon" in Daniel 11. After the overthrow of radical Islam a short window of time will open to lead Muslims to Jesus, the true Savior.

Consider one more thing about those who escape. Daniel 12:1 tells us: "At that time your people shall be delivered, every one who is found written in the book." According to Revelation 17:8: "Those who dwell on the earth will marvel, whose names are not written in the Book of Life . . . when they see the beast." All the world follows the beast except those who are included in the book of life. We just learned that when the beast power, the king of the north, wipes out Islam with its counterattack, a group from within Islam will escape. In Revelation you either follow the Lamb or follow the beast. The ones who escape the beast must be following the Lamb. That applies to Muslims as much as anyone else. Christians should not look down their noses at Islamic people. We should share Jesus with them—should love them, not hate them. If we did that on both sides, we could really do some good and might lead many to become our brothers and sisters in Christ.

The big problem is that Satan, the power from the bottomless pit, has stirred up the majorities on both sides, and he is causing havoc in the world. God's people get caught in the middle—between the north and the south. His people always find themselves in that position and often get hit from both sides of the worldwide spiritual battle.

The other two groups in the breakup of Islam are those that were overthrown—Egypt and many others—and Libya and Ethiopia, those that follow after the king of the north, the papal beast power. Revelation 13:3 declares that "the world marveled and followed the beast." In Daniel 11 part of Islam "follows at his heels," which is the same idea.

One of the three categories of fragmented Islam consists of the radicals fighting against Christianity, maybe trying to bring chaos for the emergence of the twelfth imam. That group gets destroyed by the counterattack. In a second group you have those in more secular Islam who really would rather not die for their beliefs. When it comes right down to it, they will bow and follow after the Papacy. They say, "Hey, we're not all that serious. We'll go along with you to save our lives." Anytime there's a conquest, many, if not most, will submit to the victor. They look out for their own good. But in this case it eventually leads to their own destruction, because it's not a good idea to follow the beast. The secular Muslim people will go along with the king of the north/beast power. And finally, as I said above, the third group is the one that escapes the king of the north—those who accept Jesus Christ.

While the Smoke Rises

The Papacy and its allies (possibly NATO) eventually overthrow Islam, and that leaves the Papacy and the United States in control. What will be next? We have not yet gotten to the end of Daniel 11.

My understanding of Islam is that God will use it as a counterweight against the problems of Christianity. The showdown between the various powers will bring people within Islam to a decision point. Will they go with the radicals? Will they choose the example of secular Islam and support the Papacy? Or will they accept Jesus Christ and truly follow Him?

Likewise, those within the Christian world, by getting caught in between, will have to decide whether they will join those who follow the Papacy or obey God's Word in the Bible. At that time a core group of people will gather from both Christianity and Islam, one that holds true to Jesus Christ. Stuck between north and south, they will suffer abuse from both sides at the time of the end. Are you ready to stand for Jesus when everyone else is following a counterfeit?

---

[1] "Pope Exonerates Jews," New York *Times*, Mar. 2, 2011. Available online at www.nytimes.com/2011/03/03/world/europe/03pope.html.

[2] Avi Rath, "Prepare for Holy Wars," ynetnews.com, Mar. 8, 2011. Available at www.ynetnews.com/articles/0,7340,L-4039081,00.html.

[3] For an in-depth history of the Bojinka plot, see Peter Lance's book *1,000 Years for Revenge: International Terrorism and the FBI—The Untold Story* (Harper Paperbacks, 2004).

[4] *Sahih Tirmidhi*, 2:86; 9:74, 75.

[5] "U.S., Israel Will Soon Exit Middle East: Ahmadinejad," *France* 24 (Feb. 11, 2011). Available at www.france24.com/en/20110211-us-israel-will-soon-exit-middle-east-ahmadinejad.

CHAPTER 9

Tidings From the East
and the Mark of the Beast

News From the East

Daniel 11:44, 45 describes the final moments of the beast power, the little horn—the king of the north. What does it do in the last little bit of time? When armies are going downhill and about to lose, typically their commanders throw everything they have into one last-ditch effort. That is what Satan and his followers try.

"News from the east and the north shall trouble him; therefore he shall go out with great fury to destroy and annihilate many. And he shall plant the tents of his palace between the seas and the glorious holy mountain; yet he shall come to his end, and no one will help him" (Dan. 11:44, 45). What is the news from the east? I can think of all kinds of bad news it might be, but the Bible spells out the news from the east. First we go to Ezekiel 43:1-9 and a voice from heaven:

"Afterward he brought me to the gate, the gate that faces toward the east. And behold, the glory of the God of Israel came from the way of the east. His voice was like the sound of many waters; and the earth shone with His glory. It was like the appearance of the vision which I saw—like the vision which I saw when I came to destroy the city. The visions were like the vision which I saw by the River Chebar; and I fell on my face. And the glory of the Lord came into the temple by way of the gate which faces toward the east" (verses 1-4).

So far, the news from the east is the glory of God and His very loud voice.

"The Spirit lifted me up and brought me into the inner court; and behold, the glory of the Lord filled the temple. Then I heard Him speaking to me from the temple, while a man stood beside me. And He said to me, 'Son of man, this is the place of My throne and the place of the soles of My feet, where I will dwell in the midst of the children of Israel forever.

No more shall the house of Israel defile My holy name, they nor their kings, by their harlotry or with the carcasses of their kings on their high places. When they set their threshold by My threshold, and their doorpost by My doorpost, with a wall between them and Me, they defiled My holy name by the abominations which they committed; therefore I have consumed them in My anger. Now let them put their harlotry and the carcasses of their kings far away from Me, and I will dwell in their midst forever'" (verses 5-9).

The news is that God is planning to live in His house and has had enough of the sins of His people. He wants to get rid of the abominations committed there, so that He can move into a clean place.

Consider in Revelation 7:2, 3 that the sealing arrives from the east. God's messages keep coming from the east. "Then I saw another angel ascending from the east, having the seal of the living God. And he cried with a loud voice to the four angels to whom it was granted to harm the earth and the sea, saying, 'Do not harm the earth, the sea, or the trees till we have sealed the servants of our God on their foreheads.'" Right before the end of time, the angel will finish up his sealing ministry. Those who are sealed have made their decision to follow God and His Word—the Bible—in all that they do. That means getting rid of the abominations, the sins of rebellion and disobedience. And the message comes from the east. It matches the call to clean up the abominations that we found in Ezekiel.

How about the direction of Jesus' return? Matthew 24:27 reports: "For as the lightning comes from the east and flashes to the west, so also will the coming of the Son of Man be." Jesus' return to earth is seen coming from the east. What could be better tidings from the east than a message to "clear up your abominations, get right with God, because Jesus is coming"? This is great news for a Christian!

In our day the Eastern Gate of Jerusalem, the one described by Ezekiel, has an interesting problem. You cannot walk through it. Centuries ago the Muslims walled up the gate. It is solid stone. Why? Because of these prophecies! They said to themselves, "We're not going to have any Jewish or Christian Messiah arriving from the east. Ha! They will not get through this gate!"

If that were not enough, just beyond the walled-in eastern gate in the city wall lies a Muslim cemetery, spreading all over the hill on the outside. Why? Because no Jewish religious leader can go near a Gentile's grave without becoming unclean. So the Muslims thought to themselves, *That will keep out the Jewish Messiah. He can't come in from the east!*

But they forgot something about Jesus. He resurrects the dead. And if Jesus comes in the clouds of heaven, what wall can stop Him?

Revelation 18:1-8 is John's account of that message from the east, and it is a repeat of Revelation 14. It is the last warning to the world to get ready for the appearance of Jesus. The powerful message fills the earth with light and glory. But it is not a new message. God has presented it often over time. However, this time heaven repeats it with great power, signified by the whole earth being illuminated by the glory of the angel.

Get Rid of Abominations

"After these things I saw another angel coming down from heaven, having great authority, and the earth was illuminated with his glory. And he cried mightily with a loud voice, saying, 'Babylon the great is fallen, is fallen, and has become a dwelling place of demons, a prison for every foul spirit, and a cage for every unclean and hated bird! For all the nations have drunk of the wine of the wrath of her fornication, the kings of the earth have committed fornication with her, and the merchants of the earth have become rich through the abundance of her luxury.'

"And I heard another voice from heaven saying, 'Come out of her, my people, lest you share in her sins, and lest you receive of her plagues'" (Rev. 18:4).

The plagues strike just before the very end, so this message also occurs just before the Second Coming. The plagues attack the king of the north/ little horn (the beast, the antichrist power) and destroy it. So in the chronology of Daniel 11 these tidings from the east happen shortly before the plagues but after the third battle with Islam. God wants His followers to flee the beast power and get away from it.

"For her sins have reached to heaven, and God has remembered her iniquities. Render to her just as she rendered to you, and repay her double according to her works; in the cup which she has mixed, mix for her double. In the measure that she glorified herself and lived luxuriously, in the same measure give her torment and sorrow; for she says in her heart, 'I sit as queen, and am no widow, and will not see sorrow.' Therefore her plagues will come in one day—death and mourning and famine. And she will be utterly burned with fire, for strong is the Lord God who judges her" (verses 5-8).

Just before the destruction of the king of the north, or the beast and its allies, God sends His final warning message: get rid of abominations and separate from them. Right before the plagues, the message declares,

"Come out of Babylon, the false church, and don't have anything to do with her."

I have said before that I believe countless people within the Catholic Church (or any entity supporting it) are true Christians. But according to this verse, that is not where God desires for them to stay. He actually wants them to get out in the open and follow His Word. The Lord wants you and me to be serious about honoring His Word and being a Christian. Those who do not become so will end up following the beast right into the plagues—and that would be fatal. But those who trust God are sealed and will spend eternity with Jesus. And that will be wonderful!

News From the North

In Ezekiel 44:4-6 we find a warning and judgment against abomination. It echoes the loud cry we read about in Revelation 18, which was a repeat of Revelation 14.

"Then He brought me by way of the north gate to the front of the temple; so I looked, and behold, the glory of the Lord filled the house of the Lord; and I fell on my face. And the Lord said to me, 'Son of man, mark well, see with your eyes and hear with your ears, all that I say to you concerning all the ordinances of the house of the Lord and all its laws. Mark well who may enter the house and all who go out from the sanctuary.

"'Now say to the rebellious, to the house of Israel, "Thus says the Lord God: 'O house of Israel, let us have no more of all your abominations'"'" (verses 4-6).

This applies not just to Old Testament Israel. Remember that the New Testament calls anyone who follows Jesus Christ an Israelite. God is saying to Israel—Old Testament Israel, New Testament Israel, either one—"I am tired of your abominations. Get rid of them, or you're in trouble." Eliminate the false teachings and follow the Bible and the Bible only.

Satan is a usurper, because God is the true king of the north. The north was always His cosmic direction. Look at what Isaiah 14 says.

"How you are fallen from heaven, O Lucifer, son of the morning! How you are cut down to the ground, you who weakened the nations! For you have said in your heart:

"'I will ascend into heaven, I will exalt my throne above the stars of God; I will also sit on the mount of the congregation on the farthest sides of the north; I will ascend above the heights of the clouds, I will be like the Most High.' Yet you shall be brought down to Sheol, to the lowest depths of the Pit" (verses 12-15).

The news from the east (the direction of Jesus' coming) is all the messages that say to get rid of abominations, or sins. The tidings from the north, from the real King of the north, is the message that Jesus is right, that Satan is wrong, and that it is time to get rid of anything that comes between us and God.

A Furious Fight

The news brings the dark truth about the devil and the beast powers into the open. What do you think is Satan's response? We've already read in Daniel 11:44, 45 that he seeks to annihilate all that he can. As Revelation 12:12 puts it: "For the devil has come down to you, having great wrath, because he knows that he has a short time." When Satan realizes that he has at last run out of time, his side will make their last-ditch effort, their final stand. They will fight furiously to eradicate God's people.

Revelation 13:11-17 describes the devastation committed by that second beast that we found to be the United States. "Then I saw another beast coming up out of the earth, and he had two horns like a lamb and spoke like a dragon. And he exercises all the authority of the first beast in his presence, and causes the earth and those who dwell in it to worship the first beast, whose deadly wound was healed. He performs great signs, so that he even makes fire come down from heaven on the earth in the sight of men. And he deceives those who dwell on the earth by those signs which he was granted to do in the sight of the beast, telling those who dwell on the earth to make an image to the beast who was wounded by the sword and lived. He was granted power to give breath to the image of the beast, that the image of the beast should both speak and cause as many as would not worship the image of the beast to be killed. And he causes all, both small and great, rich and poor, free and slave, to receive a mark on their right hand or on their foreheads, and that no one may buy or sell except one who has the mark or the name of the beast, or the number of his name."

Daniel 11 depicts the king of the north as authorizing the destruction. The book of Revelation shows how that power gets its authority from the beast and denies people the opportunity to buy or sell. If you are not allowed to buy or sell, that would destroy you financially. Daniel's beast destroys or annihilates or kills, and the Revelation beast does not allow buying and selling and kills if you do not go along with it. So the seal or mark of the beast is put on those who follow it. Both Daniel and Revelation present the same idea from slightly different perspectives.

Here is the choice all people face at that time. In the short term, you can go along with the beast and acknowledge its authority, so that you avoid persecution, but you end up lost forever. The other option is that you accept God's seal, and while you might be persecuted or die in the short term, you're going to end up living forever. Everyone is going to be in difficulty one way or another. But you have to choose. Would you rather be in trouble with human beings or with God? I have made my decision, and I hope I stay true to that decision. I would rather face the wrath of fallen humanity than God. Why? Because He gives some extreme warnings about following the beast power.

A Warning About the Mark

"And another angel followed, saying, 'Babylon is fallen, is fallen, that great city, because she has made all nations drink of the wine of the wrath of her fornication.' Then a third angel followed them, saying with a loud voice, 'If anyone worships the beast and his image, and receives his mark on his forehead or on his hand, he himself shall also drink of the wine of the wrath of God, which is poured out full strength into the cup of His indignation. And he shall be tormented with fire and brimstone in the presence of the holy angels and in the presence of the Lamb. And the smoke of their torment ascends forever and ever; and they have no rest day or night, who worship the beast and his image, and whoever receives the mark of his name'" (Rev. 14:8-11).

The book of Revelation speaks of a seal and a mark. You want God's sign—the seal—not the beast's sign, the mark. Would any sane person want to receive the mark? God is pretty emphatic with that warning. The people with the seal are following Jesus, because they love Him. "Here are those who keep the commandments of God and the faith of Jesus," says verse 12.

The pressure builds in Revelation 18:1-5. "After these things I saw another angel coming down from heaven, having great authority, and the earth was illuminated with his glory. And he cried mightily with a loud voice, saying, 'Babylon the great is fallen, is fallen, and has become a habitation of demons, a prison for every foul spirit, and a cage for every unclean and hated bird! For all the nations have drunk of the wine of the wrath of her fornication, the kings of the earth have committed fornication with her, and the merchants of the earth have become rich through the abundance of her luxury.'

"And I heard another voice from heaven saying, 'Come out of her, my people, lest you share in her sins, and lest you receive of her plagues. For her sins have reached to heaven, and God has remembered her iniquities.'"

The book of Revelation follows more of a cyclic rather than chronological pattern, and so we find the plagues described earlier in Revelation 16:2. "The first [angel] went and poured out his bowl upon the earth, and a foul and loathsome sore came upon the men who had the mark of the beast and those who worshiped his image." The ones targeted by the plague are those who have the mark of the beast. The mark is a lot more than a number. It shows whom you are worshipping. Are you ultimately worshipping God, or are you worshipping human traditions and thus in effect worshipping Satan?

The Sign of Worship

In the chapter on Israel in Bible prophecy we found that worship of the true God is the seal which shows that the Israel of faith—those who trust in Jesus Christ—are heirs of Abraham. We find that group of people described in Revelation 7:1-3 and 9.

"After these things I saw four angels standing at the four corners of the earth, holding the four winds of the earth, that the wind should not blow on the earth, on the sea, or on any tree. Then I saw another angel ascending from the east, having the seal of the living God. And he cried with a loud voice to the four angels to whom it was granted to harm the earth and the sea, saying, 'Do not harm the earth, the sea, or the trees till we have sealed the servants of our God on their foreheads'" (verses 1-3).

"After these things I looked, and behold, a great multitude which no one could number, of all nations, tribes, peoples, and tongues, standing before the throne and before the Lamb, clothed with white robes" (verse 9).

Here we see God's people, His true Israel, at the end of time. They are the ones who survive the great tribulation. But they are not pure by their own works. Rather, they are forgiven because Jesus died to save them from their sins. As a result, they are saved by being washed by the blood of Jesus.

In Deuteronomy 11:18 God urges His people to bring His words into their minds as though they were a frontlet on their forehead. Some of the Jews actually hung a little piece of Scripture in a leather box on their forehead between the eyes. But that is not what God meant. He was talking about having us put His Word into our mind and living by it. At the end of time, God's people are keeping His commandments from their mind and heart and following the faith of Jesus.

Likewise, the new covenant that we found in Jeremiah 31:31–33 was God's law being written in our hearts and our minds. Remember that the new covenant comes in the Old Testament, and it is about worship. We worship the Creator God who is the judge of all, or we worship the beast and ultimately Satan, who is behind the beast. So the seal of God on one hand or the mark of the beast on the other ultimately indicates whom you are worshipping.

Someday we will come to a showdown over how serious we are about God's Word. On God's side are those who worship Him who made heaven and earth, worship in spirit and in truth, keep the commandments of God and have the faith of Jesus, have the seal on their forehead, and have the Father's name in their forehead. On the beast's side are those who worship the beast and the beast's images, ascribe to the commandments and traditions of men, follow the teachings of Babylon, and have the mark of the beast in their forehead and the beast's name in their forehead. In this showdown everyone chooses a side.

Deuteronomy and Revelation thus speak of the same thing: God's people observing His commandments and having the faith of Jesus. Similarly, 1 John 5:3 declares: "This is the love of God, that we keep His commandments. And His commandments are not burdensome." That is not an Old Testament text but a New Testament one.

The Sign of the Sabbath

Ezekiel 20:12 identifies the sign that we are God's and that He is ours. "I also gave them My Sabbaths, to be a sign between them and Me, that they might know that I am the Lord who sanctifies them." He said that His sign or mark is the Sabbath.

We saw earlier that the king of the north shifted the day of the Sabbath from Saturday to Sunday, and that the king of the south established his day of public assembly and worship on Friday. Satan is pulling the Sabbath off the mark. Notice the words God announces in Exodus 31:13: "Surely My Sabbaths you shall keep, for it is a sign between Me and you throughout your generations, that you may know that I am the Lord who sanctifies you."

Some claim that by observing the Sabbath we try to make ourselves holy, but exactly the opposite is true. God said that keeping the Sabbath is a reminder that it is He who renders us holy. It's interesting how human beings get that twisted around. We do it on a fairly regular basis.

In ancient times one form of a seal was an inscribed signet ring. The signer of an agreement would press the ring into wax or clay to authenticate a document.

One of my professors in seminary came back after a summer of archaeological digging in Jordan, and he was excited because of his big find. He had excavated the signet ring of a king whose existence had never been confirmed outside of the Bible before. It was not an Israelite king, but still someone mentioned in the Bible. My professor proved that the king had actually lived. He could bring home only a picture of it, however, because the ring stayed in a museum in Jordan.

The seal of a king would show the name of the person, his title, and his territory. If you look through God's law—the Ten Commandments—you find that only one part of it has the seal of God in it. Read it in Exodus 20:8-11: "Remember the Sabbath day, to keep it holy. Six days you shall labor and do all your work, but the seventh day is the Sabbath of the Lord your God." This identifies who God is. "In it you shall do no work: you, nor your son, nor your daughter, nor your manservant, nor your maidservant, nor your cattle, nor your stranger who is within your gates. For in six days the Lord made the heavens and the earth, the sea, and all that is in them, and rested the seventh day. Therefore the Lord blessed the Sabbath day and hallowed it." What is God's territory? He is the Creator of all and has "Lord God" as His title. And the Lord blessed the Sabbath day and hallowed it. There you have His seal in the fourth commandment.

Only one of the commandments starts out with the word "remember." If you had children and were giving them directions, and you wanted them to follow them carefully and were concerned lest they forget one of them, you would put the word "remember" in front of the one you thought that they might forget. Isn't it interesting that the one commandment God said to remember, the king of the north went away from one way, and the king of the south wandered from another way? Neither of them remembered it, and it is the commandment that most of the world has also forgotten.

Revelation 12:17: "The dragon was enraged with the woman, and he went to make war with the rest of her offspring, who keep the commandments of God and have the testimony of Jesus Christ." What does Satan especially target at the end? The seventh-day Sabbath. It is the one commandment that God said was His sign. It was His seal placed within the totality of the commandments.

The king of the north went to Sunday, the king of the south to Friday, and God's people—His true Israel—as they honor His Word find themselves worshipping on the Saturday Sabbath, between the two days. "Here is the patience of the saints; here are those who keep the commandments of God and the faith of Jesus" (Rev. 14:12). The people of God have to be patient while they are in a way caught in the middle. They have to hang on to Jesus even though the going gets tough for a while.

When Revelation 14 warns about not receiving the mark of the beast, it declares that Satan's people do receive the mark while God's followers keep the commandments. It also says: "Fear God and give glory to Him, for the hour of His judgment has come; and worship Him who made heaven and earth, the sea and springs of water" (verse 7). Does that last sentence sound familiar? It is a quote from Exodus 20, the fourth commandment! Here is God's seal once again. When the apostle John cites the Old Testament, he always does it for a reason, and he does it a lot. He intends for you to realize, "Oh! The fourth commandment is an issue. God's people keep His commandments, and the fourth commandment, the seal of God, is a sticking point."

The Status of the Sabbath

In the beginning God created the earth and then rested on the seventh day, and He blessed and sanctified that day (see Gen. 2:2, 3). When He brought Israel out of Egypt, He caused manna to fall six days a week, but on the seventh day, the Sabbath, it did not come. God put His approval on the seventh-day Sabbath at the beginning of the world, and He has never changed it.

People ask me, "If the Sabbath is God's seal, didn't He change it to Sunday in the New Testament?" Remember, a number of catechisms claim that the Roman Catholic Church had the authority to change the day of worship. But that is not what the New Testament presents. For example: "And when the Jews went out of the synagogue, the Gentiles begged that these words might be preached to them the next Sabbath" (Acts 13:42). Many years after Jesus died and went back to heaven, the apostle Paul meets with Jew and Gentile on which day of the week? The seventh-day Saturday Sabbath. If the Sabbath had shifted to Sunday after Jesus died, then the New Testament church would have known about it. But here they are meeting on the seventh-day Sabbath.

What happened the next week? "When the congregation had broken up, many of the Jews and devout proselytes followed Paul and Barnabas, who, speaking to them, persuaded them to continue in the grace of God. And on the next Sabbath almost the whole city came together to hear the word of God" (verses 43, 44). Paul and Barnabas did not say to the Gentiles, "Uh, you guys come back on Sunday. We will meet with the Jews next Saturday, and we'll meet with Gentile Christians on Sunday." No, they all gathered again on the seventh-day Sabbath.

This was not an isolated occurrence. "He reasoned in the synagogue every Sabbath, and persuaded both Jews and Greeks" (Acts 18:4). Paul met with the people "every Sabbath." Seven verses later verse 11 comments: "He continued there a year and six months, teaching the word of God among them." Meeting every Sabbath for a year and a half indicates Paul's normal practice with Jew and Gentile. We find no alteration of Sabbath in the New Testament.

The most important clue to the status of the Sabbath comes from the example of Christ Himself while He lived on earth. All we have to do is go back to the practice of Jesus to decide if Sabbath is still the seventh day of the week or not. It is really pretty easy. He worshipped every week on the Sabbath (see Luke 4:16), so He put His seal of approval on the seventh day in His time.

Some of the confusion about the Sabbath comes from the days around Jesus' death. At the time of His death, the Jewish council member Joseph of Arimathea "went to Pilate and asked for the body of Jesus. Then he took it down, wrapped it in linen, and laid it in a tomb that was hewn out of the rock, where no one had ever lain before" (Luke 23:52, 53). He removed the body because Jesus had just died on the cross on a Friday.

"That day was the Preparation [day], and the Sabbath drew near. And the women who had come with Him from Galilee followed after, and they observed the tomb and how His body was laid. Then they returned and prepared spices and fragrant oils. And they rested on the Sabbath according to the commandment.

"Now on the first day of the week, very early in the morning, they, and certain other women with them, came to the tomb bringing the spices which they had prepared. But they found the stone rolled away from the tomb" (Luke 23:54–24:2).

The stone no longer sealed the tomb because Jesus was not in it anymore. He had been resurrected.

Luke was not a Jew by birth. He was a Gentile physician, an educated man. If Jesus had changed the day of rest to Sunday, right here would have been a wonderful chance for the Gospel writer to point out that the seventh-day Sabbath was the day that the Jews kept holy but that Christians would not be doing that anymore. But Luke does not say any such thing, and neither do the other New Testament writers.

Instead, Luke announces that Jesus died on the preparation day, the day most people today call Good Friday. Then the Sabbath came. The word is *Sábado* in Spanish. How did Spanish get the name Sábado for the seventh day? More than 100 different languages have a form of the term "Sabbath" for the name of the seventh day of the week. Is that an accident? I don't think so. And then Jesus was resurrected on the first day of the week, today commonly called Easter Sunday. Luke does not say anything about a change of the Sabbath to that day.

The Jews have not lost track of the seventh day of the week, and they still say it is Saturday. Nor has God made any decree since the time of Jesus to transfer the holy day of God. We can be certain that Saturday is the biblical seventh day, which is the sign that we are God's and He is ours and that He sanctifies us.

As mentioned before, some people argue that if you honor the seventh-day Sabbath, you are trying to get to heaven by works. But the Bible says it is a sign of sanctification—that it is God that actually makes you holy. "He [God] has spoken in a certain place of the seventh day in this way: 'And God rested on the seventh day from all His works'" (Heb. 4:4). "There remains therefore a rest for the people of God. For he who has entered His rest has himself also ceased from his works as God did from His" (verses 9, 10). Sabbathkeeping is a sign that we stop our own works and trust in God's.

At Creation God made the world and then rested on the seventh day. When Jesus came to save us and to remake us, He died on the sixth day, rested in the tomb on the Sabbath, and then started working for us again on the first day of the week. So on both the Sabbath at Creation and the Sabbath at our redemption, He rested. The rest is now a symbol of the completed sacrifice of Jesus Christ. We don't do it on our own! He does it for us.

The Sabbath is not a sign of works but rather of righteousness by faith and resting in His works. Some people have probably tried to work their way to heaven by observing Sabbath, but they have twisted what the Bible says. The Bible says that the Sabbath is a representation of trusting God for our salvation.

False Claims

The conflict raging on earth has only two sides. God's side worships Him who made heaven and earth. Serious about all of God's commandments, including the fourth, they follow the faith of Jesus, have the seal of God in their forehead, and have been forgiven and cleansed by God.

Then there is the beast's side of the conflict. As described in Daniel 7:25, the little horn would intend to change times and laws, an act that ultimately becomes the mark of the beast and its claim of authority over Scripture. Repeatedly the Papacy has offered this as the power and symbol of its religious sovereignty.

"The Pope is of so great authority and power that he is able to modify, declare, or interpret even divine laws. The Pope can modify divine law, since his power is not of man but of God, and he acts as vicegerent of God upon earth with most ample power of binding and loosing his sheep."[1]

"What is the Third Commandment? Remember that thou keep holy the Sabbath day. Which is the Sabbath day? Saturday is the Sabbath day. Why do we observe Sunday instead of Saturday? We observe Sunday instead of Saturday because the Catholic Church transferred the solemnity from Saturday to Sunday."[2]

The church claims that it did that at the council of Laodicea in A.D. 360. That sure wasn't the time of Jesus, was it?

Notice the following quote from a Roman Catholic church newsletter.

"Perhaps the boldest thing, the most revolutionary change the Church ever did, happened in the first century. The holy day, the Sabbath, was changed from Saturday to Sunday. 'The Day of the Lord' (*dies Dominica*) was chosen, not from any directions noted in the Scriptures, but from the Church's sense of its own power. The day of the resurrection, the day of Pentecost, 50 days later, came on the first day of the week. So this would be the new Sabbath. People who think that the Scriptures should be the sole authority should logically become Seventh-day Adventists and keep Saturday holy."[3]

Here a Roman Catholic writer is saying that if you want to follow the Bible only, you should keep the Saturday Sabbath. I completely agree with the author. Again and again the Catholic Church has made such statements. They don't hide from it. The church claims to have the right to change God's Word.

The *Catholic Record* states bluntly: "The Church is above the Bible; and this transference of Sabbath observance from Saturday to Sunday is proof of that fact."[4]

In the late 1930s John O'Brien wrote a book called *The Faith of Millions*. In it he observed:

"But since Saturday, not Sunday, is specified in the Bible, isn't it curious that non-Catholics who profess to take their religion directly from the Bible and not from the Church, observe Sunday instead of Saturday?

Yes, of course, it is inconsistent; but this change was made about 15 centuries before Protestantism was born. . . . They have continued the custom, even though it rests upon the authority of the Catholic Church and not upon an explicit text in the Bible. That observance remains as a reminder of the Mother Church from which non-Catholic sects broke away—like a boy running away from home but still carrying in his pocket a picture of his mother or a lock of her hair."[5]

When Islam attacks the Papacy in Daniel 11:40, and the Papacy and its allies conquer Islam or overturn Islam, the Papacy and its allies are in control. I'm suggesting that Sunday worship will be the sign of allegiance to the papal brand of Christianity. Islam splits three ways, with some surviving Muslim people who trust Jesus Christ, some overthrown by the recent defeat, and those who follow after the beast/king of the north. For the latter, what better sign of their new allegiance to the Papacy and the papal alliance than to show it by changing their day of worship from Friday to Sunday? Just as the king of the south is gone, so is Friday as a day of worship.

Some have pointed out to me that Islam really does not observe Friday as a holy day. That is true. However, Friday in practice is the special time for sermon and prayers. Muslims don't keep the whole day as holy. But then neither do most Christians fully honor Sunday, either. They go to worship for an hour and then afterward do whatever they want. There's not much difference between Christian and Muslim worship times—it is just observing an hour or two as holy, not a day. Keeping the first day of the week holy would be a good sign of allegiance to the beast power.

Would the papal alliance try to enforce Sunday observance on the world? Yes, it would do that. The most recent Catholic catechism was written during the time of Pope John Paul II. The person in charge of putting it together was Joseph Cardinal Ratzinger. As I write this, Cardinal Ratzinger is Pope Benedict, so this catechism should have some current authority in the Catholic Church. Here's what it says. "In respecting religious liberty and the common good of all, Christians should seek recognition of Sundays and the Church's holy days as legal holidays."[6] The church would like to have civil laws to enforce its rules. I do not believe I am stretching things when I say I expect it to be a worldwide showdown between God's day and the one that the church says it wants laws to enforce. In the European Union religious leaders are already working to get their wish. Sunday laws are starting to happen there.

Jesus said in the Bible, "In vain they worship Me, teaching as doctrines the commandments of men" (Matt. 15:9; Mark 7:7). So if you are following human teachings, how good is your worship? It is in vain. Ultimately, if you are following after the beast, that goes back to the dragon, Satan. You may not be worshipping quite the one you thought you were.

Not a Seventh-day Adventist Doctrine

Is this just a Seventh-day Adventist thing? No, we can find lots of statements by others about the Sunday Sabbath as the mark of the beast. The concept did not originate with Seventh-day Adventists. The furthest back that I can find Sundaykeeping explained as the mark of the beast is more than 200 years before any Seventh-day Adventists existed. In 1657 Thomas Tillman, a Protestant, wrote a book entitled *The Seventh-Day Sabbath Sought out and celebrated. Or, The Saints last Design upon the man of sin, with their advance of Gods first institution to its primitive perfection, being a clear discovery of that black character in the head of the little Horn, Dan. 7.25. The Change of Times & Laws. With the Christians glorious Conquest over that mark of the Beast, and recovery of the long-slighted seventh day, to its antient [sic] glory, wherein Mr. Aspinwal, may receive full answer to his late piece against the SAB-BATH.* Right on the title page Tillman describes the little horn in Daniel 7 and the change of times and laws. The Papacy's claim is thus not a new

discovery. It has been one that it has been making for a long time. With the Christian's glorious conquest over the mark of the beast outlined right on the cover of the book, Tillman identified Sundaykeeping as the mark of the beast

in 1657. The Catholic-owned Notre Dame University library has a copy of the book. (You can also find it on my Web site, www.islamvs christianity.org.)

Remember that I said I would go back to the Reformers a lot? This is another example. What did the Reformers get for printing messages like this? Many of them suffered death for what they said. You could get killed either by Islam or the Papacy (it didn't much matter), but you actually had a better chance of survival with Islam than you had with the Papacy if you preached these ideas.

The coin from the Vatican pictured on page 46 shows a woman holding a cup. Coming out of the cup is a sunburst. The Catholic Church says that it took as a new day of worship one that the pagan world regarded as the day of the sun. Church artists put halos around the heads of the saints, which is the solar-disk imagery familiar to those who worshipped the sun. Christians employed the trappings of the cult of Mithras, a religion that included elements of sun worship.[7] Yet Scripture regarded sun worship as an abomination (see Eze. 8:15-18). What did Revelation 18 say? To get rid of the abominations and separate from them, lest you partake of the plagues. It is an important message to remember in light of Ezekiel 20:12: "I also gave them My Sabbaths, to be a sign between them and Me, that they might know that I am the Lord who sanctifies them."

The Real Spirit

God's law is a test of love and loyalty. Jesus said, "If you love Me, keep My commandments" (John 14:15). He did not say observe the commandments so you can be good enough to go to heaven, but rather, "If you really believe in Me, if you really love Me, keep My commandments." Then He went on: "I will pray the Father, and He will give you another Helper, that He may abide with you forever" (verse 16). The prerequisite for getting the real Holy Spirit was loving Jesus and honoring His commandments. "The Spirit of truth, whom the world cannot receive, because it neither sees Him nor knows Him; but you know Him, for He dwells with you and will be in you" (verse 17). Notice that the beast had a counterfeit of the Holy Spirit: the fire from heaven that worked signs and miracles and deceived the whole world. Scripture calls the second beast in Revelation 13 the false prophet, because it has the wrong spirit. That power has its own traditions—human laws. If you follow them, you get the counterfeit spirit. But if you obey God's law because you love Him, you receive the real Spirit.

What about people who unknowingly worship on the wrong day? "Truly, these times of ignorance God overlooked, but now commands all men everywhere to repent, because He has appointed a day on which He will judge the world in righteousness by the Man whom He has ordained. He has given assurance of this to all by raising Him from the dead" (Acts 17:30, 31). Jesus, the one raised from the dead, is the judge. God takes into account ignorance (the King James Version says that He winks at it), so for those people who do not understand, He forgives it. The context of Acts

17 is that God was overlooking the Gentiles' worship of idols when they did not understand that it was the wrong thing to do, even though it was breaking one of His commandments. The Bible explains that if you break one, you have violated them all (James 2:10-12). So which commandment we break does not matter. But when we disobey the commandment out of ignorance, God understands why. If we love Him, and we are following Him according to what we know, He will accept that. But He does not want to leave us ignorant. He wants us to come to Him and to understand the truth before the judgment takes place—before the end.

"The lawless one will be revealed, whom the Lord will consume with the breath of His mouth and destroy with the brightness of His coming. The coming of the lawless one is according to the working of Satan, with all power, signs, and lying wonders, and with all unrighteous deception among those who perish, because they did not receive the love of the truth, that they might be saved. And for this reason God will send them strong delusion, that they should believe the lie, that they all may be condemned who did not believe the truth but had pleasure in unrighteousness" (2 Thess. 2:8-12).

What is God saying here? At the end, each one of us will either be following His Word because we love it, or, if we don't, we are on the way to destruction. If we decide to be willingly ignorant, we have chosen to be led into deception and condemnation. Scripture gives a strong warning— a life-and-death warning. The simple question is Whom do we choose to follow: God or human traditions?

Revelation 18:4, 5 tells us where we really need to be. "And I heard another voice from heaven saying, 'Come out of her, my people, lest you share in her sins, and lest you receive of her plagues. For her sins have reached to heaven, and God has remembered her iniquities.'" Before the final destruction, I encourage you to separate from anything that is not biblical.

Surrounded by Support

As you get closer to Jesus, you need a supportive fellowship to keep you true to God's Word. "Let us consider one another in order to stir up love and good works, not forsaking the assembling of ourselves together, as is the manner of some, but exhorting one another, and so much the more as you see the Day approaching" (Heb. 10:24, 25). But do you want to belong to a community that downplays biblical teaching and instead emphasizes human tradition? Beware of that! You need to surround yourself with those who will encourage you to follow all of God's Word and not just part of it. And do not continue in known, willful sin. "For if we sin willfully after we have received the knowledge of the truth, there no longer remains a sacrifice for sins" (verse 26).

Humanity will divide into those loyal to God, and those who align themselves with fallen humanity. Those who follow the dragon, and those who follow Jesus Christ. Which side do you choose? Your actions speak louder than your words. Such love for God—to obey His commandments—is not burdensome. Choose well, because it is right after this that the king of the north—the little horn, the man of sin, the beast—is destroyed. You don't want to perish with it. I encourage you to follow God. Follow His Word—all of it.

---

[1] Translated from the Latin in F. Lucius Ferraris, "Papa, Articulus II," *Prompta Bibliotheca: Canonica, Juridica, Moralis, Theologica, Ascetica, Polemica, Rubristica, Historica* (Paris: J. P. Migne, 1858), vol. 5, pp. 25-29. Retrieved from www.aloha.net/~mikesch/prompta.htm.

[2] See Peter Geiermann, *The Convert's Catechism of Catholic Doctrine* (St. Louis: Herder Book Co., 1946), p. 50.

[3] St. Catherines Catholic Church *Sentinel*, May 21, 1995, p. 1.

[4] *The Catholic Record*, Sept. 1, 1923.

[5] John A. O'Brien, *The Faith of Millions* (Huntington, Ind.: Our Sunday Visitor, 1974), pp. 400, 401.

[6] *Catechism of the Catholic Church*, 2nd ed. (Doubleday, 1995), p. 585.

[7] The cult of Mithras appeared in the century before Jesus was born and remained strong in Roman society, especially among the civil service and military, into the fourth century A.D. The god Mithra was the sun, and the emperor his representative on earth. Franz Cumont, in *The Mysteries of Mithras* (1903), wrote: "They [worshippers of Mithras] also held Sunday sacred, and celebrated the birth of the Sun on the 25th of December" (p. 119). And: "Sunday, over which the Sun presided, was especially holy" (p. 105). *The History of Christianity in the Light of Modern Knowledge* (1929), notes: "It had so much acceptance that it was able to impose on the Christian world its own Sun-Day in place of the Sabbath, its Sun's birthday, 25th December, as the birthday of Jesus; its Magi and its Shepherds hailing the divine star, and various of its Easter celebrations" (pp. 73, 74).

CHAPTER 10

When Michael Stands Up

The Rescue Begins

We have seen how Satan has been working in the world and how God's people found themselves caught between the kings of the north and south. Then, at the end of Daniel 11, the king of the south gets wiped out. The king of north—the papal beast power—claims all authority, and when his power is challenged, he will destroy and annihilate many. The mark of the beast—a criteria that allows people to buy or sell—comes into play, and people face death unless they have the mark. Finally, God annihilates the beast power—the king of the north. As we get past the last moments of the beast power, we begin to see in Daniel 12 the rescue and reward of God's people.

One time I was stranded in floodwaters for close to 20 hours. My group of eight people, including three of my kids, had been on a hike in a national park, and we needed rescuing. When I finally saw a ranger from the search party looking for us, I was happy to have every one of my group alive. Although I had broken into a historic cabin in the national park to survive, thus committing a felony, I was never happier to see someone in uniform. The cabin had no heat, but at least we were out of the rain and snow for many hours. And then to see somebody with that uniform and think, *We're going to make it!* I felt overwhelming joy.

However, glimpsing Park Ranger Bill Strobel is nothing compared to seeing Jesus when He comes to rescue His people from earth. I'm looking forward to that rescue as well. Daniel 12 gives the picture of how it will happen.

"At that time Michael shall stand up" (Dan. 12:1). Daniel 10, 11, and 12 repeatedly mention Michael, the prince of the covenant, the great prince. Martin Luther and the Reformers, as well as the early church, taught that Michael is Jesus Christ, and I agree with them.[1] How do we know this is true?

The name Michael means "who is like God?" or "one who is like God," but does that mean Michael is God? Scripture also calls Michael the archangel (Jude 9), but "archangel" does not require that He be a created being. Rather, He is commander of the angels. When Joshua was outside the Israelite camp, he met someone who said that He was the commander of the Lord's host (see Joshua 5). Joshua fell down and worshipped Him, and the Being accepted his worship. Earlier the Angel of the Lord had spoken to Moses from the burning bush. Moses asked, "Who are you?" and the Angel said, "I AM" (see Ex. 3). Read these passages carefully. Both in Hebrew and Greek the word translated "angel" has a dual meaning, and here it does not mean a created being, but rather God's message or messenger. Martin Luther was clear in his belief that Jesus was, in this instance, called an angel, and I agree with Luther. Michael the Archangel is Jesus Christ, the Son of God, the second person of the Trinity, the one who has always been God. If we understand Michael the Archangel, the great prince, to be Jesus Christ, then we see Jesus in Daniel 11 and 12. Pope Gregory the Great, who died in A.D. 604, first brought into the church the teaching that Michael was not Jesus.[2]

"And there shall be a time of trouble, such as never was since there was a nation, even to that time. And at that time your people shall be delivered, every one who is found written in the book" (Dan. 12:1). God sent 10 plagues when He delivered ancient Israel from Egypt. That was a time of great trouble. But because of the plagues, God's people were delivered. The book of Revelation describes the time of trouble near the end of the world, and it likewise involves plagues.

Verse 2: "Many of those who sleep in the dust of the earth shall awake, some to everlasting life, some to shame and everlasting contempt." Jesus comes to earth, and He resurrects those who died trusting in Him. "Those who are wise shall shine like the brightness of the firmament, and those who turn many to righteousness like the stars forever and ever" (verse 3). After their rescue God's people live and reign with Him forever!

"But you, Daniel, shut up the words, and seal the book until the time of the end; many shall run to and fro, and knowledge shall increase" (verse 4). We have seen that the last showdown is between the kings of the north and south. But it was a prophecy that would be grasped only at the time of the end. In our day everything should be fitting together, and we can begin to interpret the prophecy. When verses 40 and following happen (and they have been unfolding during the past several years), the understanding comes.

Two Happenings at Once

Have you ever tried to explain two things occurring at the same time? Since you can really explain only one at a time, eventually you find yourself having to say, "This one happens, but then this other thing happens at the same time." I have previously shown how Daniel 11:1–12:3 is chronological, but we find an exception in the last verse of chapter 11 and the first verse of Daniel 12. As I have studied them, I came to the conclusion that Daniel 12:1 overlaps with Daniel 11:45. That is why Daniel starts out chapter 12 by saying, "At that time." The last segment was verse 45, which is the period after the third Islam versus Christianity conflict. At that same time, God starts to deliver His people, and the deliverance begins with Michael standing up.

As you can see in the table below, at the time of the tidings from the east the king of the north goes out to annihilate as many as possible, and then he himself is destroyed in verses 44 and 45.

Immediately after Michael stands up, we have that time of trouble—the tribulation and the plagues. Revelation 16 ties the destruction of the beast power (the little horn, the king of the north) to the events right at the end of the plagues.

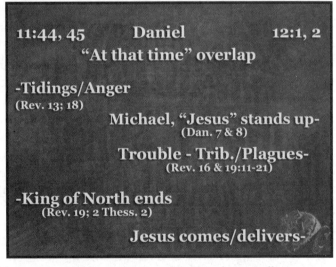

11:44, 45   **Daniel**   12:1, 2

"At that time" overlap

-Tidings/Anger
(Rev. 13; 18)

       Michael, "Jesus" stands up-
           (Dan. 7 & 8)

    Trouble - Trib./Plagues-
      (Rev. 16 & 19:11-21)

-King of North ends
(Rev. 19; 2 Thess. 2)

      Jesus comes/delivers-

In Daniel 11:45 the king of the north reaches its end. Revelation tells us this is at the conclusion of the plagues, so Michael's standing up occurs just before the king of the north ceases to be in verse 45. I have said all along that the Daniel 11 prophecy is chronologically sequenced, and it is, except for those events that happen simultaneously and are pointed out as such by Daniel himself.

Why Michael Stands Up

Why does Daniel 12:1 say that Michael "stands up"? Think back over the prophecies. Did Jesus ever sit down at some previous time? If He sat down before, then we know when He started something. Now, when He stands up, we know that whatever He started to do when He sat down has been completed.

Consider some reasons that you might stand up. If you have been eating a meal, it means you are finished. But I can think of one especially relevant here. One time during seventh grade I was in study hall, and we had a student teacher in charge. He should not have been a teacher. Becoming angry and losing his self-control, he picked up a young seventh grader by the neck and lifted him off the ground—not the right move for a teacher to make. My best friend was sitting beside me, and on the other side was the teacher hoisting this kid by the neck. The friend was already more than six feet tall by the seventh grade. Standing up, he said, "Put him down."

The teacher looked at him. "What?"

"I said, 'Put him down!'"

The college student finally got a little sense into his head, and he lowered the student. Fortunately, my friend did not get into trouble for standing up and telling the teacher to release the boy.

At the end of Daniel 11 God's people face annihilation by the beast power. And if you are Jesus, you might be tempted to stand up and put an end to it. He says, "That's enough!" Jesus apparently did something similar at the stoning of Stephen in Acts 7:56,[3] which was the end of the 70 weeks for the nation of Israel. At the end of the time of judgment Jesus stands up for His people.

Now we turn to Daniel 7, which helps us to see what has been happening since Jesus went back to heaven. The beast power is on the earth, doing what the prophecy predicted. "After this I saw in the night visions, and behold, a fourth beast, dreadful and terrible, exceedingly strong. It had huge iron teeth; it was devouring, breaking in pieces, and trampling the residue with its feet. It was different from all the beasts that were before it, and it had ten horns" (verse 7). Rome's pagan aspect was about to metamorphose into a religious form, the Papacy. Verses 8 and 9: "I was considering the horns, and there was another horn, a little one, coming up among them, before whom three of the first horns were plucked out by the roots. And there, in this horn, were eyes like the eyes of a man, and a mouth speaking pompous words."

We have heard before about the beast and the pompous words. While he is in the world uttering his blasphemous words and thinking he is really something when he's not, then come verses 9 and 10: "I watched till thrones were put in place, and the Ancient of Days was seated." The little-horn beast thinks he is someone really special, but while he's thinking that, something is going on in heaven, and it does not bode well for the beast. Somebody is being seated. But who is it?

The Ancient of Days is God the Father. "His garment was white as snow, and the hair of His head was like pure wool. His throne was a fiery flame, its wheels a burning fire; a fiery stream issued and came forth from before Him. A thousand thousands ministered to Him; ten thousand times ten thousand stood before Him. The court was seated, and the books were opened" (Dan. 7:9, 10). The little horn is about to be judged.

"The books were opened" refers to the kind of judgment book mentioned in Daniel 12:1, which speaks about those inscribed in the book. Likewise, in Revelation it is the Lamb's book that God will consult to make judgment.

Notice that while this is going on in heaven, the beast power is still on earth doing its evil deeds. "I watched then because of the sound of the pompous words which the horn was speaking" (verse 11). It does not know that its days are numbered. The beast power is being judged and found wanting, just like the king of Babylon at the end of the Babylonian Empire. Then "I watched till the beast was slain, and its body destroyed and given to the burning flame" (verse 11). That is the same description as we find at the end of Daniel 11.

"As for the rest of the beasts, they had their dominion taken away, yet their lives were prolonged for a season and a time" (verse 12). Every one of the previous beasts, when its power ended, continued on in some form. We still have Greece today, Babylon in the form of Iraq, and Persia as Iran. They still existed in some form after the end of their prophetic kingdoms. But when the beast power ends, it will completely cease to exist. For the little horn, when it's over, it's over.

Verses 13 and 14: "I was watching in the night visions, and behold, One like the Son of Man, coming with the clouds of heaven! He came to the Ancient of Days, and they brought Him near before Him." Jesus enters the judgment chamber to meet the Father, and He arrives on clouds. This tells me the heavenly courtroom is huge! Millions of angels stand in it. The courtroom is set up, Jesus arrives, and He sits down on the judgment throne and joins the judicial session.

"Then to Him was given dominion and glory and a kingdom, that all peoples, nations, and languages should serve Him. His dominion is an everlasting dominion, which shall not pass away, and His kingdom the one which shall not be destroyed" (verse 14). Jesus, the King of kings, receives His kingdom in heaven before He comes to claim it on earth.

Daniel 7:26, 27 repeat the sequence for explanation and emphasis. "But the court shall be seated, and they shall take away his [the beast's] dominion, to consume and destroy it forever. Then the kingdom and dominion, and the greatness of the kingdoms under the whole heaven, shall be given to the people, the saints of the Most High. His kingdom is an everlasting kingdom, and all dominions shall serve and obey Him." Here are the people whom Jesus delivers when He stands up. When Jesus comes, He presents the kingdom to His people. He has not given it yet, because not everybody on earth is serving and obeying God. In fact, most people are not.

At a particular time, then, a judgment was set up, or "seated," in heaven. Near the end of time it will take place simultaneously in heaven and on earth while the beast is causing havoc. I'm suggesting to you that, as Daniel 12:1 indicates, when the judgment concludes Jesus stands up. He comes to rescue His people and bring them the dominion and power that He just received from His Father. When that happens, it is all over for the little horn, because his destruction quickly follows. We do not know its exact time, but it accompanies the little horn's last stand (as we learn from Daniel 7 and from further details in Daniel 8). This is the really neat thing about Daniel 11. It gives us the framework, and then we find the details in other chapters of Daniel and Revelation that add to the file system or the framework.

Destruction of the Little Horn

Daniel 8 reveals the path and behavior of the little horn power from its inception to the final days of its destruction. This passage must match the Daniel 11 scenario to be valid. "And out of one of them came a little horn which grew exceedingly great toward the south, toward the east, and toward the Glorious Land" (Dan. 8:9).

Some people argue that one of the Seleucid kings, Antiochus Epiphanes IV, is the little-horn power. However, Antiochus' kingdom shrank during his reign and did not grow as described in the verses, so he cannot be the little horn.

"And it [the little horn] grew up to the host of heaven; and it cast down some of the host and some of the stars to the ground, and trampled them. He even exalted himself as high as the Prince of the host" (verses 10, 11). The Prince of the host is Jesus, the commander of the host who accepted worship from Joshua (Joshua 5:14). "And by him [the little horn] the daily sacrifices were taken away" (Dan. 8:11). The sacrifice of Jesus that is available to us every day was subverted by the teaching that a sinner must come to the Catholic Church to be forgiven. The Papacy claims to control who is a saint in heaven—who makes it and who does not. It asserts that it has authority over the powers of heaven. "He cast truth down to the ground. He did all this and prospered" (verse 12).

The End of the 2300 Days

"Then I heard a holy one speaking; and another holy one said to that certain one who was speaking, 'How long will the vision be, concerning the daily sacrifices and the transgression of desolation, the giving of both the sanctuary and the host to be trampled underfoot?'

"And he said to me, 'For two thousand three hundred days [evenings and mornings in the Hebrew, meaning it is one of those symbolic situations, not one of the terms for normal days]; then the sanctuary shall be cleansed.'

"Now it happened, when I, Daniel, had seen the vision and was seeking the meaning, that suddenly there stood before me one having the appearance of a man. And I heard a man's voice between the banks of the Ulai, who called, and said, 'Gabriel, make this man understand the vision.' So he came near where I stood, and when he came I was afraid and fell on my face; but he said to me, 'Understand, son of man, that the vision refers to the time of the end'" (Dan. 8:13-17).

At the end of Daniel 8 the prophet has literally become sick because he does not understand what the 2300 days means. He has heard a time prophecy without a beginning point, and he desperately seeks to find out what it means.

He is also thinking about another time prophecy, given when he was a young man, that the exiled Israelites would remain in Babylonian captivity for 70 years. At the end of the 70 years they would be able to go back to Jerusalem. Now Daniel is an old man, and he knows it is time to return. But he hears something about 2300 days and then the sanctuary will be cleansed. Does that mean it will be 2300 days/years before the Israelites get their Temple back? That thought overwhelms him.

In Daniel 9:24 and following he receives an answer. "I've come to give you an understanding of the vision," an angel announces. He will reassure the prophet that the 70-year prophecy would be fulfilled as promised and provide Daniel with understanding of both the 70-weeks prophecy and the 2300-day prophecy. The angel begins to explain that 70 weeks, or 490 years, had been designated for the time after the 70 years in exile. The 70 weeks, or 490 years, are set for the Israelites to make an end of sin and bring in everlasting righteousness. The angel dates the 70 weeks, or 490 years, from the decree that would order the restoration of Jerusalem following the 70 years of exile. Daniel has just received the key to both the 70-week and 2300-day prophecies: they have the same starting date. The Daniel 9 prophecy was cut off from (meaning simultaneous with) the longer one of Daniel 8. The starting point for both is the decree to restore Jerusalem in 457 B.C. (see Ezra 7).

The prophecy declares that after 2300 days, or years, the sanctuary will be cleansed. What does that mean? To understand the cleansing of the sanctuary, we must read about the Day of Atonement in Leviticus 16:30-33.

"On that day the priest shall make atonement for you, to cleanse you, that you may be clean from all your sins before the Lord. It is a sabbath of solemn rest for you, and you shall afflict your souls. It is a statute forever. And the priest, who is anointed and consecrated to minister as priest in his father's place, shall make atonement, and put on the linen clothes, the holy garments; then he shall make atonement for the Holy Sanctuary, and he shall make atonement for the tabernacle of meeting and for the altar, and he shall make atonement for the priests and for all the people of the congregation."

In ancient Israel the Day of Atonement was a time of judgment. It was a day on which sins were either cleansed and erased or left on the record. The Day of Atonement was one day a year when the high priest made a cleansing atonement, not just for one person's sin, but for all the people and for the Temple, or sanctuary, itself. It was a symbol of how salvation works. Although the priests offered animal sacrifices back then, the sacrifice is really Jesus. The high priest is also Jesus. This is how Jesus cleanses us from sin.

On any other day of the year, when an Israelite had sinned, they approached the door of the sanctuary with an animal sacrifice. They would place their hands on the animal and confess their sins, then the lamb representing Jesus would die for the sin, and the person was forgiven through the blood of the sacrifice. The sacrifice symbolized Jesus Christ dying on the cross.

The blood of the sacrifice depicted sins being brought to God for Him to deal with in heaven, where Jesus is our high priest. To understand better how this works, read the book of Hebrews. The whole book is about Jesus acting as our high priest in the heavenly tabernacle. The earthly tabernacle was only a model of what God showed Moses of the heavenly one (see Ex. 25). Moses viewed the heavenly reality, and when he built the tabernacle he was making a representation of the real thing in heaven.

The individual Israelite's record of sin had been placed on the sacrificial animal and transferred to the sanctuary. The guilt of the sin was taken on into the sanctuary and deposited in the holy place, where the smoke symbolizing the prayers goes over into the Most Holy Place, thereby taking the record of sin—the guilt of sin—and stacking it up for God to deal with. The Israelite at the entrance walked away free, because the sin was now God's problem, not his. By faith the Israelite was forgiven.

On the once-a-year Day of Atonement the high priest entered the holy place, the second room in the tabernacle. He took all of the sins of the year and symbolically placed them on a goat called the "scapegoat." That act would cleanse the tabernacle of sin and make it clean again. Someone would take the scapegoat far away from the Israelite camp so that it could never return. It symbolized God's forgiveness for the sin and cleansing of the sin from the tabernacle. God held that sin, and all the others presented to Him, until Jesus Christ Himself deals with it as our sacrifice and high priest.

When Jesus died and rose again and went back to heaven, He said that He was going to sit down at the right hand of the Father. In the illustration of

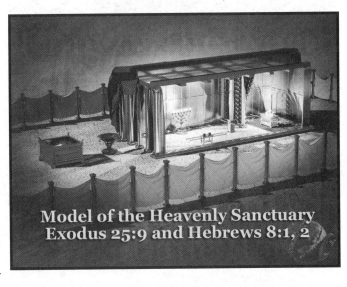

Model of the Heavenly Sanctuary Exodus 25:9 and Hebrews 8:1, 2

the sanctuary above notice the table of showbread, two stacks of bread, six in each. I suggest to you that the table of showbread represents the throne of God. After all, Jesus said, "If you've seen Me, you've seen the Father" (see John 14:9). There are two piles of bread there, and they are seated side by side on the throne, a fitting symbol of the throne room in heaven.

Revelation 4 pictures Jesus in a room in the sanctuary, and He is on the throne with the Father. But which room is it? Before the throne is a seven-branched candlestick (verse 5). That tells us He is in the outer room of the sanctuary. Here are the Father and the Son, sitting together, and here is the Holy Spirit, depicted by the fire. On the day of atonement— the day of judgment—they move into the Most Holy Place, to the mercy seat. In Daniel 7 the Ancient of Days, the Father, sits down, showing that they have advanced to the next phase of salvation ministry. And Jesus joins Him.

The high priest entered the holy place only on the Day of Atonement, the day of cleansing. The prophecy given to Daniel said, "For two thousand three hundred days; then the sanctuary shall be cleansed" (Dan. 8:14). This indicates when the special time of cleansing begins in the heavenly sanctuary as the Father and Son sit down. And remember, this happens while the little horn is still active on earth.

Here we have the 70-weeks prophecy starting in 457 B.C.: 457 (the date of the decree to rebuild Jerusalem in Ezra 7) + 70 weeks = A.D. 34, and 457 + 69 weeks = A.D. 27. The latter calculation brought us from the decree to rebuild Jerusalem in 457 B.C. to Jesus' baptism in A.D. 27. Jesus was cut off in the middle of the last week (A.D. 31). The end of the time period for the exclusivity of the Jewish nation was A.D. 34. That explains the 490 years given in the prophecy.

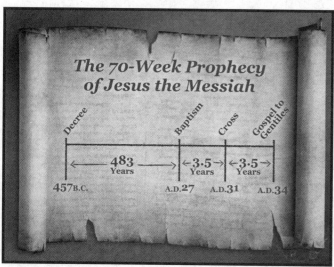

What about the 2300-day period we saw earlier that begins at the same time? If we add 2300 days (years) to 457 B.C., it brings us to A.D. 1844.

What was supposed to happen in 1844? Would it be something taking place on earth that year? No, because the prophecy says that the cleansing takes place in the heavenly judgment room/Most Holy Place, while the beast is still active on earth. He continues to run around exercising his power before and after the judgment, so the judgment is not taking place on earth.

You recall that when Jesus died the veil of the earthly Temple that shielded the Most Holy Place tore in two from top to bottom. Because of His death, the animal sacrifices on earth no longer applied—were no longer

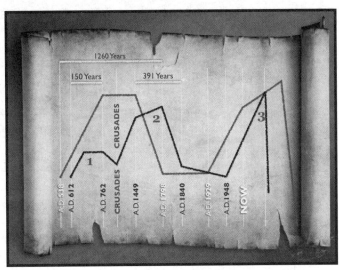

needed. From that we know that Daniel's prophecy of the 2300 days indicates a heavenly sacrifice. Jesus died for us as the Lamb of God, and He went to be that heavenly sacrifice as both priest and sacrifice. It is His blood that cleanses our sins, and He is ministering, or applying, it for us in the heavenly sanctuary.

When Jesus left this earth, He told the Jews: "See! Your house is left to you desolate" (Matt. 23:38). In Daniel 9:27 He said that He would make it desolate even to the "consummation," and I believe that the consummation is the time that He returns for His people. As far as God is concerned, there will be no more sacrifices that He will honor in an earthly temple. For us to offer such sacrifices would be blasphemy, because it would mean denying that Jesus Christ was the sacrifice! It would be right up the beast's alley, though, to claim something false like that. I do not know if there ever will be another Temple in Jerusalem, as some are planning on. But it will never be God's temple, because He said that He was going to leave it desolate until the consummation. While the Dome of the Rock and the Mosque of Omar occupy the site of the former Temple, it is desolate from the viewpoint of the descendants of Abraham through Isaac (whether Jewish or Christian).

According to Daniel 8:17, the prophecy that begins with the decree to rebuild Jerusalem after the Exile will extend to "the time of the end." Look what happens when we graph the power of the Papacy and the power of Islam (see chart on page 139). I call it their political power curve.

In Daniel 7 and 8 the beast acts with power both before and during the judgment. Now on the political power curve chart the judgment commences right in the valley between the second conflict and the third and final conflict, at or during the time of the end. The judgment starts, and the little-horn/king of the north power regains its power and causes havoc simultaneously with the judgment taking place in heaven.

When Jesus came to the Ancient of Days, it was not to this earth. He went to where the Father was—the next part of that heavenly sanctuary. Just think of everything that sprang up on earth during this time period, however. It saw the emergence of Communism, the theory of evolution, Mormonism, and countless other movements. One in particular called the Millerite movement preached that Jesus would return to earth in 1844, the natural end of the 2300-year prophecy. But they were not alone. Sir Isaac Newton, a scientist fascinated with eschatology, believed that too! Also, the Reformers taught that something connected with the last days might happen during the mid-1800s.

How did the Millerites and others misunderstand the relationship of Daniel 8 and the second advent of Jesus? They saw, in Daniel 7:13, Jesus coming to the Ancient of Days with clouds and assumed that since Christ arrives with clouds when He returns to earth, therefore that verse must indicate the Second Coming. They missed in Daniel 7 and 8 that while He was going in to the Ancient of Days in the clouds, the little-horn power was still actively doing its thing on the earth. And so the Millerites, and others before them, misinterpreted what the prophecy was pointing to.

The Millerites were historicists, which means that they believed prophecy is in a process of fulfillment from the time it was written to the final end of the age, and they were following the methods of the Reformers. Unfortunately, Protestants soon began looking for a different way of viewing prophecy, and they went to futurism, which believes that all or most of prophecy represents an end-time fulfillment, with little applying now, and thus they ignored historicism. But you don't have to follow what the Millerites taught about the Second Coming in 1844 to be a historicist. You can believe that Jesus actually started the judgment in heaven at that time.

We can see, then, that according to Daniel 7 and 8 the judgment in heaven and the time of the end started in 1844, at the end of the 2300 years, when the court was seated to judge the little-horn beast and to cleanse the sanctuary from sin. The judgment and the "time of the end" concludes when Jesus stands up in Daniel 12. We have a beginning date of 1844 that inaugurates the time of the end, and we have an ending time, a date not known by anyone, when Jesus stands up and finally rescues His people by bringing the kingdom and power to them. That is exactly what Daniel 7 says the judgment is for.

Now we need to see if we can find the same thing in the New Testament. Is there any evidence there of a judgment taking place before Jesus' second coming? Consider Revelation 14:6, 7:

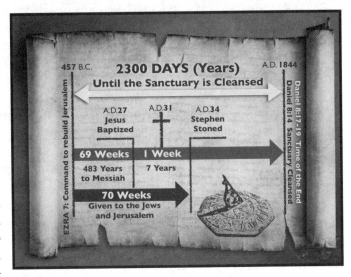

"Then I saw another angel flying in the midst of heaven, having the everlasting gospel to preach to those who dwell on the earth—to every nation, tribe, tongue, and people—saying with a loud voice, 'Fear God and give glory to Him, for the hour of His judgment has come; and worship Him who made heaven and earth, the sea and springs of water.'"

Clearly there is a time on earth when Jesus' judgment is already in process before He returns. "And another angel followed, saying, 'Babylon is fallen, is fallen, that great city, because she has made all nations drink of the wine of the wrath of her fornication'" (verse 8). What is the result of the judgment in heaven? Just as in Daniel 7 and 8, it deals with the little horn/the beast/the Papacy, here symbolized by Babylon. "Then a third angel followed them, saying with a loud voice, 'If anyone worships the beast and his image, and receives his mark on his forehead or on his hand, he himself shall also drink of the wine of the wrath of God'" (verses 9, 10). That's what the judgment involved—pronouncing and implementing the divine verdict against the beast and those who followed it. So there we have the same thing in the New Testament.

Who is the judge? Again in the New Testament, John 5:22 says: "The

Father judges no one, but has committed all judgment to the Son." Ultimately, the judge is Jesus. Entering the presence of the Ancient of Days, He joins the tribunal, and the Father lets Him do the judging.

Acts 17:30, 31 confirms it: "Truly, these times of ignorance God overlooked, but now commands all men everywhere to repent, because He has appointed a day on which He will judge the world in righteousness by the Man whom He has ordained." Again, who is the judge? Jesus. And again it says that He has appointed a day on which He will judge the world. Daniel 8:14 designates when judgment will begin, which starts the time-of-the-end scenario. After that time, both Islam and the Papacy commence their climb back up from the deep hole/loss of political power they fell into. They think they are doing really well, but the judgment announces that their days are numbered. Right at the end of those days, as the judgment in heaven winds down, the last message from the east goes out: "Come out of her, my people" (Rev. 18:4)—get away from Babylon, flee from the beast/king of the north power. Satan knows his time is running out, and he tries to annihilate all that he can because he realizes that the judgment is almost finished.

If God is our judge in the heavenly investigation, then who seeks to prosecute us? Revelation 12:10 says: "Then I heard a loud voice saying in heaven, 'Now salvation, and strength, and the kingdom of our God, and the power of His Christ have come, for the accuser of our brethren [called the devil and Satan in verse 9], who accused them before our God day and night, has been cast down.'" Up in the heavenly court Satan has thrown his charges against us. "Hey, that Pastor Tim, I got him to sin," Satan declares. And he gives a list of the sins. Satan is the accuser.

In every court case the defendant finds himself or herself standing before the judge, awaiting the verdict. But we have some good news here. It will either be us or Jesus as the defendant when our cases come up. We get to choose which one goes on trial. "We must all appear before the judgment seat of Christ, that each one may receive the things done in the body, according to what he has done, whether good or bad" (2 Cor. 5:10). We are not saved by works, but the verse tells us that we stand judged according to our deeds. If we have one sin on our record, the heavenly court may not be a good thing for us unless—and here comes that good news again. Yet before we get to that we need to focus on the reality that all of us will face judgment.

I have heard people say that if you are a believer in Christ, you are not under judgment. But that is not what the apostle Peter said. "The time has come for judgment to begin at the house of God" (1 Peter 4:17). God's house is His Israel, the Old and New Testament people of faith, so the judgment starts with the believers. But that is a good thing if you really understand it.

Since the judgment "begins with us first, what will be the end of those who do not obey the gospel of God? Now 'if the righteous one is scarcely saved, where will the ungodly and the sinner appear?' Therefore let those who suffer according to the will of God commit their souls to Him in doing good, as to a faithful Creator" (verse 19). God will be faithful to get you through the judgment.

Romans 8:1: "There is therefore now no condemnation to those who are in Christ Jesus, who do not walk according to the flesh, but according to the Spirit." While God's people will undergo judgment first, they do not find themselves condemned. The phrase "in Christ" is very important. Remember the saved people in Revelation who are wearing a white robe? Jesus offers us His righteousness when we ask for forgiveness, and He cleanses us and gives us His righteousness. His life covers our life when we ask Him to take our place. It is no longer I but Christ living in me, as Paul puts it.

So here's the key. We ask Jesus to take control of our lives, and then it is no longer us but Christ living in us. When our case is called in the judgment, it is not our record but His that appears there. As long as we let Him take our case, we win! Now we can begin to see how the court is set up in our favor. That is really good news.

Finally, who is the defense attorney in the courtroom? "My little children, these things I write to you, that you may not sin. And if anyone sins, we have an Advocate with the Father, Jesus Christ the righteous" (1 John 2:1). An advocate means a defense attorney. Ours is Jesus Christ Himself.

Let's review the lineup in the celestial courtroom. The judge is Jesus, the accuser is Satan, the defendant is either me or Jesus, and the defense attorney is Jesus if I let Him take my case.

What kind of law operates in the divine court? The New Testament tells us that clearly it is the Ten Commandments. "For whoever shall keep the whole law, and yet stumble in one point, he is guilty of all. For He who said, 'Do not commit adultery,' also said, 'Do not murder.' Now if you do not commit adultery, but you do murder, you have become a transgressor of the law. So speak and so do as those who will be judged by the law of liberty" (James 2:10-12). John 14:15-17 reminds us: "If you love Me, keep My commandments. And I will pray the Father, and He will give you another Helper, that He may abide with you forever, even the Spirit of truth." The commandments mentioned there are the Ten Commandments—do not kill, don't commit adultery. In other words, all of them. That is the foundation. So we know which law is being applied in the heavenly court.

Are the Ten Commandments really a law of liberty? Yes, they are. Imagine what life would be like if everyone followed the Ten Commandments. Have you ever locked your keys in the house or the car and could not retrieve them? One time as I left the church office the door locked behind me as I closed it. Turning, I looked through the window in the door and could see my keys lying on the desk. I could not get to them. Why do I have to use keys? Because some people are not following God's law. That is why, for example, you have a car key and not just a push button. If you had only a push button and you parked your car and went away, when you came back it would be gone.

You are not at liberty to believe everything you are told. Nor are you at liberty to walk any street at any hour of the day or night. People do not follow God's law. If they did, you could safely go on any street at any time, believe everything that you're told, and not need a key or a lock. That would be heaven.

And you can be sure that God's laws will be practiced in heaven. His people will obey every one of them, including the Sabbath commandment. "And it shall come to pass that from one New Moon to another, and from one Sabbath to another, all flesh shall come to worship before Me, says the Lord" (Isa. 66:23). In the new heaven and the new earth the Sabbath commandment still applies.

What is the result of the judgment—reward or punishment? Jesus said: "Behold, I am coming quickly, and My reward is with Me, to give to every one according to his work" (Rev. 22:12). There it is again! In some way we are rewarded according to what we do. But what kind of works or deeds is it?

Hebrews 10:26, 27 tells us that "if we sin willfully after we have received the knowledge of the truth, there no longer remains a sacrifice for sins, but a certain fearful expectation of judgment, and fiery indignation which will devour the adversaries." Remember the Day of Atonement? If an Israelite had, earlier in the year, offered a sacrifice for a sin and afterward they no longer cared about the law and disobeyed it, on the Day of Atonement their guilt went back on them. If you accept Jesus Christ as your Lord and Savior, but deliberately reject part of God's law and continue to live in sin, your guilt is still with you. Hebrews says that if I ask for forgiveness and then I later stubbornly persist in deliberate sin, I lose my forgiveness, the sacrifice for sins. Jesus will not cover willful sin. He will cover ignorant sin, as seen in the continuous sacrifice given for those who did not know they were sinning, but He cannot overlook deliberate sin in the judgment. Each person will receive reward or punishment: reward if they are trusting and obeying Jesus, punishment if they willfully refuse to trust and obey Him. The reality is that when Jesus rewards His people, He is rewarding them for His (Jesus') perfect life in place of ours, and He is rewarding us for all the good that the Holy Spirit has done through us. The reward is all about Jesus doing it all for us.

The Judgment Ends

Right now the judgment is still going on in heaven. According to the 2300-day prophecy, the judgment in heaven began in 1844, and it does not stop until just before the plagues. How do I know that it ends then? Daniel 12 tells us that immediately before the time of trouble, Michael stands up. The book of Revelation presents the same events. Look at Revelation 14:7; 22:11; 15:8; and 16.

"For the hour of his judgment has come" (Rev. 14:7). The judgment has been going on in heaven, and then Revelation 22:10, 11 describes how the process reaches an end. "Do not seal the words of the prophecy of this book, for the time is at hand. He who is unjust, let him be unjust still; he who is filthy, let him be filthy still; he who is righteous, let him be righteous still; he who is holy, let him be holy still." A decree comes from heaven that the judgment is over. Everyone has made up his or her mind. With all people having made their final choices, Jesus stands up.

When does that decision to end the judgment happen? It is not during the time of the tidings from the east, because the loud cry urges, "Come out of her, my people." During the period of the loud cry God is still offering forgiveness to any who want it. So the end of the judgment occurs after that point.

In Revelation 15:8 we find that "the temple was filled with smoke from the glory of God and from His power, and no one was able to enter the temple till the seven plagues of the seven angels were completed." Right now our forgiveness is taking place in the heavenly sanctuary, the temple in heaven. At the beginning of the plagues we will no longer be able to come to Jesus to ask for salvation. Why? Because Jesus has finished His work there. He has stood up, because all the decisions have been made and His ministry is complete. It happens right before the plagues in Revelation 15:8.

We know that the judgment has closed in heaven just before the plagues because Revelation 16 says the plagues are poured out on those who have the mark of the beast, and no one changes his or her mind at that time. Instead of confessing their sins, the wicked curse God. During the plagues both the righteous and the filthy remain as they were before.

Strange as it may seem, this fact is really good news for us. If I am a sinner, and I am, I'm a forgiven one. When my case goes to the court in heaven, Jesus is the judge. Satan makes an accusation against me. He knows what sins I have done because he tempted me to do them, and as soon as I do them, he runs to God like a tattletale and says, "Did you see what Pastor Tim just did?" At this point I have a choice. I can defend myself and my record, or I can say, "Jesus, how about putting Your record in place of mine?" It is no longer me but Christ in me. I say to Him, "Jesus, You're in charge." And now Christ's record is the one on trial. How many sins does Jesus have in His record? None! I am going to be OK!

But it gets even better. The defense attorney is Jesus. How would you feel about going into a courtroom if your defense attorney was also the judge? The deck is stacked in your favor. You are not going to get a hung jury here—there is no jury. The judge rules in this courtroom.

What happens if I decide to represent myself and present my own case? In that situation Jesus is still the judge. Satan accuses me, and he has a strong case against me. I have to be the defense attorney and defend myself, because I have rejected Jesus Christ. The law is the Ten Commandments, and it says that I am guilty. And the wages of sin is death! The result for me is punishment.

The person who accepts Jesus Christ as His attorney and lets Him be the defendant comes out of the judgment sentenced to eternal life with Jesus. I love the judgment! It sets me free from Satan, and it frees me from the little-horn/king of the north/beast that thinks he is ruling the world right now. Although I believe I'm going to be sentenced to live with Jesus forever, I'm willing to accept that verdict!

Thus the judgment is not a bad thing. It is good news for everyone who is written in the Lamb's book of life. Everyone who continues to love and serve Jesus Christ and has allegiance to Him has their name included in the Lamb's book of life.

It's important to note that the judgment has a definite time period. Twice the New Testament tells us that a date was set for the judgment to begin, and the prophecy fixing the date appears in Daniel 8. The end of the 2300 years from the decree to rebuild Jerusalem brings us to 1844, and that date inaugurates the time of the end. According to that prediction, the judgment would go on until just before the plagues. That is when Jesus stands up. The smoke of God's presence fills the heavenly sanctuary, and the righteous and the wicked have made their final and permanent choice of what they will always be. Jesus has been waiting until the very last moment, hoping for a chance to cleanse your record and mine.

Then, when He stands up, He is not saying arbitrarily, "Time's up!" He has given every warning message He could, and He has let the world get into all kinds of trouble to allow people time to decide, and finally the last individuals have made their decision. Then He can declare, "That's it! There is no point in waiting anymore—it's done! I'm getting up, and I'm coming to rescue My people."

---

[1] For a helpful discussion, see www.dr-fnlee.org/docs/witaotl/witaotl.pdf.

[2] *Ibid.*

[3] Stephen said: "Look! I see the heavens opened and the Son of Man standing at the right hand of God!" (Acts 7:56).

CHAPTER 11

The Worst-ever
Time of Trouble

We saw in the previous chapter that a judgment convenes in heaven and that the court is in session. When Michael stands up, just before the time of trouble, the judgment is over. The heavenly temple is the place in which Jesus Christ has been working out our salvation, and when He is finished there, He declares, "Let the righteous be righteous still, and the filthy be filthy still" (see Rev. 22:11). With that, it is over with. We have all made our choices, one way or the other. "After these things I looked, and behold, the temple of the tabernacle of the testimony in heaven was opened. And out of the temple came the seven angels having the seven plagues. . . . Then one of the four living creatures gave to the seven angels seven golden bowls full of the wrath of God who lives forever and ever. The temple was filled with smoke from the glory of God and from His power, and no one was able to enter the temple till the seven plagues of the seven angels were completed" (Rev. 15:5-8).

The plagues begin to fall. When they do, no one changes sides. The wicked get only more angry at the God they refuse to follow, and God's people dig in deeper and hang on.

The time of the plagues is parallel to Daniel's time of trouble and will be worse than anything the world has ever experienced. Once it has passed, we will be able to look back and see that it was the most terrible period of earth's history.

Daniel 12:1 describes it as "a time of trouble such as never was," but it is followed by deliverance. It is part of God's process for rescuing His people. "At that time Michael shall stand up, the great prince who stands watch over the sons of your people; and there shall be a time of trouble, such as never was since there was a nation, even to that time. And at that time your people shall be delivered, every one who is found written in the book." I want to be deliberate about being found in God's book. Don't you?

The Bible talks about the time of trouble in a variety of places, and we will look at them in this chapter. We need to see how the Bible sheds light on this tumultuous period.

Exodus and Revelation both speak about plagues followed by deliverance. When God's people were in Egypt, 10 plagues befell the Egyptians, and then deliverance came. The book of Revelation presents a series of seven plagues and then deliverance. In Exodus 5:5 Moses summons the Israelites to worship God and rest. Pharaoh protests: "You make them rest from their labor!" As slaves, they had been forced to work seven days a week. Pharaoh was not going to let them off work. When Moses assumed the leadership of Israel, he got them back into the "rest mode," back into a Sabbath cycle. Then in Revelation God summons people to worship the Creator: "Worship Him who made heaven and earth, the sea and springs of water" (Rev. 14:7). That is a quote from the Sabbath commandment. So we have a call to worship and rest in both Exodus and Revelation.

God instructs Moses: "Go to Pharaoh and say to him, '. . . Let My people go, that they may serve Me'" (Ex. 8:1). God called His people out of Egypt. In Revelation 14 and 18:4 He summons His people out of Babylon. "Come out of her, my people, lest you share in her sins, and lest you receive of her plagues" (Rev. 18:4). The call out of Babylon is just like the call out of Egypt. Do you see the similarities?

Here is another parallel. In Exodus 11:4-7 we find a "death warning" before the deliverance. Revelation 14:9-11 also has a "death warning" before deliverance. Both were not for God's people but rather for those who opposed them. Exodus 11 says: "Then Moses said, 'Thus says the Lord: "About midnight I will go out into the midst of Egypt; and all the firstborn in the land of Egypt shall die. . . . But against none of the children of Israel shall a dog move its tongue, against man or beast, that you may know that the Lord does make a difference between the Egyptians and Israel"'" (verses 4-7).

Similarly, we find a death warning right before deliverance in Revelation 14: "Then a third angel followed them, saying with a loud voice, 'If anyone worships the beast and his image, and receives his mark on his forehead or on his hand, he himself shall also drink of the wine of the wrath of God, which is poured out full strength into the cup of His indignation. And he shall be tormented with fire and brimstone in the presence of the holy angels and in the presence of the Lamb'" (verses 9, 10).

149

The firstborn in Egypt perished, and at the end of time anybody who has the mark of the beast likewise faces a death penalty or worse—fire-and-brimstone punishment.

The last seven plagues in Egypt targeted particular people, and the seven plagues in Revelation focus on certain people also. While the first three Egyptian plagues affected both Israelites and Egyptians, during the last seven only Egyptians suffered, not the Israelites. For example, Exodus 8:22 announces: "And in that day I will set apart the land of Goshen, in which My people dwell, that no swarms of flies shall be there." The differentiation was so that the Egyptians would recognize that the Lord was the God of Israel. When Moses pronounced a death penalty, it would hit only the Egyptians, so that they would understand that the Israelites were following the Lord God.

We find a similar parallel with Revelation's seven last plagues. Revelation 16:2 portrays the first plague: "So the first went and poured out his bowl upon the earth, and a foul and loathsome sore came upon the men who had the mark of the beast and those who worshiped his image." It targeted those who had the mark of the beast. If you want to be delivered from the plagues, don't follow the beast and get his mark.

The psalmist David wrote about God's people going through this very difficult time in Psalm 91. He points out that we will see the result of what happens to the wicked, but the plagues will not afflict us.
"He who dwells in the secret place of the Most High
    Shall abide under the shadow of the Almighty.
I will say of the Lord, 'He is my refuge and my fortress;
    My God, in Him I will trust.' . . .
A thousand may fall at your side,
    And ten thousand at your right hand;
    But it shall not come near you.
Only with your eyes shall you look,
    And see the reward of the wicked.
Because you have made the Lord, who is my refuge,
    Even the Most High, your habitation,
    No evil shall befall you,
    Nor shall any plague come near your dwelling;
For He shall give His angels charge over you,
    To keep you in all your ways" (verses 1-11).
Many have taught that God would remove His people from the earth at this time, because, surely, they could not remain here, lest they would

suffer the plagues. Hal Lindsey taught this in *The Late, Great Planet Earth* years ago. Here is the important question, though. Were God's people living in Egypt during the time of the plagues? Yes. Did they suffer the last seven of those plagues? No, because God has good aim! Likewise, at the end of time, in the book of Revelation, God has good aim. He targets only those who have the mark of the beast. Psalm 91 tells us that God's people, His Israel of faith, will see the results of the plagues, but the plagues will not come near them.

So what does this tell us? That God has perfect aim, and that He will not remove His people from this world before the plagues. After the model of the plagues in Egypt, the end-time plagues in the terrible time of trouble are part of the setup to deliver God's people. They are aspects of the deliverance process.

What about the conditions that God's people will endure as they go through this? It will not be easy for them. Jeremiah 30:7 talks about "Jacob's trouble." Remember, anyone who has faith in Jesus is an heir of Abraham and thus part of the Israel of faith. If you belong to God's Israel, then you are a son of Jacob. Jeremiah 30:5-7 describes the experience that His people will go through.

"For thus says the Lord:
'We have heard a voice of trembling,
   Of fear, and not of peace.
Ask now, and see,
   Whether a man is ever in labor with child?
So why do I see every man with his hands on his loins
   Like a woman in labor,
   And all faces turned pale?
Alas! For that day is great,
   So that none is like it;
   And it is the time of Jacob's trouble,
   But he shall be saved out of it.'"

Jeremiah explains that after the period of trouble, God will save or deliver His people. Guess what happens right after the trouble in Daniel 11? God's people are delivered! Continuing in Jeremiah 30:

"'For it shall come to pass in that day,'
   Says the Lord of hosts,
'That I will break his yoke from your neck,
   And will burst your bonds;
   Foreigners shall no more enslave them.

But they shall serve the Lord their God,
>   And David their king,
>   Whom I will raise up for them'" (verses 8, 9).

Who is "David their king" whom God raises up for us? Jesus Christ, the son of David.

Why are the people of God living through such a terrible time of trouble? Two reasons: One, the king of the north is furious, and he seeks to destroy anyone who refuses to receive his mark. If people are trying to kill you, would it be just a little bit stressful for you? Satan's people are trying to annihilate God's people. Just as it was in Egypt for the Israelites, it is a difficult time right before the deliverance.

A second reason that God's people go through the time of trouble is the questions that it raises. Once the plagues start being poured out, and you realize that everything has been settled in heaven, one of the first questions that will come to my mind (and I bet to yours too) is "Have I made everything right with God?" At that time it would be too late to change. It is crucial that we confess our sins now and trust Jesus for forgiveness now. We also need to practice placing our assurance in God and not in ourselves. God's people will then be relying completely on the Holy Spirit.

What's really interesting is that during this time God's people are filled with the Spirit and living by His power, and they know that it is vital to do so. On the other hand, Satan's people have totally rejected the Spirit. The two groups have become polar opposites.

Notice that God's people are not on their own at this time. But instead of cleansing them from sin, Jesus is now cleansing them from sinning by the indwelling Spirit, because He has ended the judgment in heaven.

Revelation 16:1 declares: "Then I heard a loud voice from the temple saying to the seven angels, 'Go and pour out the bowls of the wrath of God on the earth.'" Let's take a look at the various plagues. Each one strikes at some different aspect of the beast power, or false worship.

The first plague: "So the first went and poured out his bowl upon the earth, and a foul and loathsome sore came upon the men who had the mark of the beast and those who worshiped his image" (verse 2). We have already gone past the time of the "tidings from the east and the north." The king of the north has already become infuriated and inflicted death and destruction upon those who are resisting. Now, suddenly, those following the beast are getting nasty, horrible sores all over them. We don't know at this point if it is a worldwide plague of sores, but toward the end of the plagues people still continue to suffer from them.

The second plague: "Then the second angel poured out his bowl on the sea, and it became blood as of a dead man; and every living creature in the sea died" (verse 3). Suppose that you are on a cruise ship, and when you wake up in the morning, you look out to find yourself sailing in a sea of coagulated blood. What a horrible end to a cruise. Or, if you are at the beach, the waves turn from clear water into bloody ones and begin to stink as dead fish float to the surface. That would get people's attention, wouldn't it?

The third plague: "Then the third angel poured out his bowl on the rivers and springs of water, and they became blood" (verse 4). Somebody opens the tap in the morning to get a drink of water, and they fill their glass with blood.

Notice verses 5-7:

"And I heard the angel of the waters saying:

'You are righteous, O Lord,

The One who is and who was and who is to be,

Because You have judged these things.

For they have shed the blood of saints and prophets,

And You have given them blood to drink.

For it is their just due.'

And I heard another from the altar saying, 'Even so, Lord God Almighty, true and righteous are Your judgments.'"

"You've been killing My people, shedding their blood!" God reminds them. In the past the king of the north/beast power, the Papacy, was a persecuting power for more than 1,000 years. At the end of time the beast is a persecuting agency again. And God says, "You are bloodthirsty? OK, drink blood. Get what you want. You say you are out to get the blood of My people? Have some blood to drink." And the angels say, "God, that is fair."

Do the people with the mark of the beast change their minds once the plagues strike? No, not at all. Jesus has already announced, "Let the righteous be righteous still, and the filthy be filthy still" (see Rev. 22:11). Jesus stood up from the judgment seat, and everybody's case has been decided.

The fourth plague: "Then the fourth angel poured out his bowl on the sun, and power was given to him to scorch men with fire. And men were scorched with great heat, and they blasphemed the name of God who has power over these plagues; and they did not repent and give Him glory" (verses 8, 9). This fourth plague causes the people of the beast to get burned by the sun. Remember, they were enforcing a death penalty on anyone who would not worship on the "day of the sun." God says, "You want the sun? OK, I'll turn up the heat. I'll give you a little more sun!"

The fifth plague: "Then the fifth angel poured out his bowl on the throne of the beast."

Where's the throne of the beast? It could be the Vatican. But remember that in Daniel 11, right at the end, before the beast's destruction, he moves to the "Glorious Land." It could be that this means only military forces invade the Glorious Land, but it could also imply setting up the king of the north's headquarters there. So his throne could be situated in either Israel or the Vatican. I'm not sure which it will be.

"Then the fifth angel poured out his bowl on the throne of the beast, and his kingdom became full of darkness" (verse 10). The people have been complaining, "We're tired of the burning sun!" God says, "OK, no more sun." And this marks where the problem is. Spiritual darkness is what the Papacy has given the world. God turns that spot dark, wherever that headquarters is.

"And they gnawed their tongues because of the pain. And they blasphemed the God of heaven because of their pains and their sores, and did not repent of their deeds" (verse 11). They still have their sores here at the fifth plague. I don't know how long the plagues take, but I don't want to be suffering the pain during that time. I would rather be one of God's people during this period.

The sixth plague: "Then the sixth angel poured out his bowl on the great river Euphrates, and its water was dried up, so that the way of the kings from the east might be prepared" (verse 12). The United States military crossed the river Euphrates a few times during different battles in Iraq. Is the river Euphrates a major challenge for a modern-day military operation? No, not at all. I suggest that this is probably symbolic at the end of time, especially when you consider that Babylon sits on the Euphrates River, and Babylon in Revelation is a spiritual power.

There's historical background to the waters drying up in Babylon. Note the comparisons between the experiences of ancient Israel and spiritual Israel.

- The book of Jeremiah tells us that Babylon oppressed God's ancient people. In Revelation 17 Babylon also persecutes God's people.
- In Daniel 3 God's ancient people were forced to worship an image. In the end-time God's people also find themselves compelled to worship an image.
- In Daniel 4:30 Nebuchadnezzar refers to his empire of Babylon (the

enemy of God's people) as "great." Revelation 17:5, at the end of time, calls the final enemy of God's people "Babylon the Great."

- In the Old Testament Babylon "sits on many waters" (Jer. 51:12, 13). In Revelation, at the end of time, Babylon "sits on many waters" (see Rev. 17:15). (Remember, we suggested earlier that water in the Bible may represent peoples and nations [see Rev. 13]).
- In Isaiah 44 in the Old Testament God rescues His people by the drying up of the Euphrates River. Revelation 16:12 also tells us that God will rescue His people by the drying up of the river Euphrates.
- In Jeremiah 51 God summons His people out of Babylon. In Revelation 18:4 they are called to "come out of her" (Babylon) at the end of time.
- In the Old Testament Isaiah 45 calls Cyrus the anointed one when it predicted his rescue of ancient Israel. Daniel 9 refers to the coming New Testament divine rescuer as the Messiah, the anointed one. Jesus the Messiah is the rescuer who comes at the end as well.
- In Isaiah 45 both rescuers emerge from the east. Cyrus came from the east in the Old Testament. In the New Testament Jesus comes from the east for the final rescue.

Continuing in Revelation 16: "And its water was dried up, so that the way of the kings from the east might be prepared. And I saw three unclean spirits like frogs coming out of the mouth of the dragon" (verses 12, 13). We have a lot of symbols running through this particular plague. The dragon is a symbol for Satan, the beast is the symbol of the papal system, and the false prophet, we discovered, is the United States in prophecy. "For they are spirits of demons, performing signs, which go out to the kings of the earth and of the whole world, to gather them to the battle of that great day of God Almighty" (verse 14).

Verse 15 announces something very significant: "Behold, I am *coming as a thief.* Blessed is he who watches, and keeps his garments, lest he walk naked and they see his shame." The reason I emphasize "coming as a thief" is that we are going to talk about the timing in that statement. Many prophecy students today talk about Jesus coming "as a thief" before the time of tribulation and the plagues. But right there between the sixth and seventh plagues, Jesus says He is coming as a thief. That is not past tense. It means He is about to come as a thief. It is a very important distinction we need to make.

What happens next? Revelation 16:16 explains: "And they gathered them together to the place called in Hebrew, Armageddon." Satan's people—God's enemies—were starting to lose their cohesiveness, and Satan has to reassemble his forces because they are all suffering from those plagues. They are starting to get tired of listening to the beast and the dragon and enduring the plagues. Now they come together for a final battle at a place called Armageddon.

Have you heard the idea that the final battle will take place on the Plain of Megiddo? I have visited it. The place is rather small for a major worldwide battle. And if we are to expect a battle on the Plain of Megiddo, should we not be able to find the Plain of Megiddo mentioned in the Bible? But Scripture does not name it. Verse 16 says "Har Megeddon," which means the Mountain of Megiddo. That is not the Plain of Megiddo. But guess what? A mountain sits right alongside the Plain of Megiddo, and it is called Mount Carmel. Actually, it is a mountain range that goes from right above Megiddo all the way over to the Mediterranean Sea. That is where a showdown took place between the prophets of Baal and the prophet Elijah—and the God of heaven won.

What did we just see in Revelation 16? That Satan's forces have gathered for a showdown with God. At issue is: Who is the real God? Who is the real power? The struggle is for the divine throne. Satan says, "I am going to take God's place." "For you [Satan] have said in your heart: 'I will ascend into heaven, I will exalt my throne above the stars of God; I will also sit on the *mount of the congregation* . . . I will be like the Most High'" (Isa. 14:13, 14). It is Satan's last-ditch effort, because he is starting to lose.

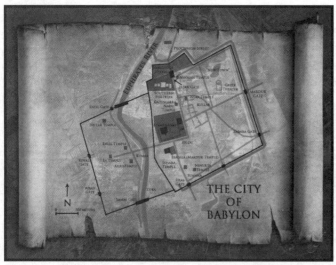

The plagues are not going well for his side. This is a battle for the throne just before Jesus comes, a struggle between the true Trinity and the false trinity.

Go back to the fall of ancient Babylon for a moment. Babylon was located on the Euphrates River, and the river went right through the city.

The city had a moat around it and walls next to the river on the inside, with little gated bridges across it. If you were an enemy army, would you want to get underneath these walls and come up in the river and be a sitting duck, literally, with arrows raining down on you in the water? You would have to climb up the wall while soldiers were shooting at you. It was not a good deal to break in alongside that river.

When the Medes and the Persians besieged the city of Babylon, the ruler of Babylon decided to show his contempt for them by hosting a feast. As a part of the feast, he had the sacred cups and bowls from God's Temple in Jerusalem brought out for his guests to drink wine from. Suddenly a disembodied hand wrote on the wall, "MENE, MENE, TEKEL, UPHARSIN" (Dan. 5:25). Nobody could read it. The ruler brought in Daniel, and the prophet interpreted the inscription: "You have been weighed in the balances and found wanting. This night your kingdom will be taken from you" (see verses 26-28).

As Daniel spoke, the armies of the Persians, led by a general named Cyrus, encircled the city. Now, Daniel was no dummy. He must have known that Isaiah had predicted that someone named Cyrus would attack Babylon and conquer it (see Isa. 45). Just as Daniel knew the prophecies, we need to know the prophecies too, or we will be blindsided, as the people in Babylon were.

Daniel said to the king, "This night your kingdom will be taken from you." Tradition tells us that Cyrus diverted the river through a canal he excavated. He then sent his army marching right under those gates that were over the river, and they got inside. The Persian army marched into the palace and killed the ruler of Babylon.

The nation of Babylon fell because of the drying up of the river Euphrates. At the time of the end spiritual Babylon falls because of a drying up of the river Euphrates. The people who had supported the false trinity now abandon it. Satan has to reorganize everything and rehype everything to get his people to gather together for a final struggle with God.

And finally the seventh plague:

"And the seventh angel poured out his vial into the air; and there came a great voice out of the temple of heaven, from the throne, saying, It is done. And there were voices, and thunders, and lightnings; and there was a great earthquake, such as was not since men were upon the earth, so mighty an earthquake, and so great.

"And the great city was divided into three parts, and the cities of the nations fell: and great Babylon came in remembrance before God, to give unto her the cup of the wine of the fierceness of his wrath. And every island fled away, and the mountains were not found.

"And there fell upon men a great hail out of heaven, every stone about the weight of a talent: and men blasphemed God because of the plague of the hail; for the plague thereof was exceeding great" (Rev. 16:17-21, KJV).

God's wrath is being poured out as hailstones weighing 100 pounds each. They would come crashing through the roof, right through you, and right on down to crack the floor—if you happen to have the mark of the beast. But if you don't have the mark of the beast, they smash into something beside you and do not hit you. I do not want to have the mark of the beast in that kind of hailstorm.

I believe that the seventh plague is the beginning of Christ's return. You find descriptions of His return in Revelation 6 and 19, and both of them reveal that Jesus Christ Himself finishes pouring out the wrath of God. What are the plagues? The wrath of God. Revelation 6:14, describing God's response to the slain martyrs' plea for justice, tells us: "Then the sky receded as a scroll when it is rolled up, and every mountain and island was moved out of its place." It is part of a description of the Second Coming (see verse 17). During the seventh plague in Revelation 16 we also see islands and mountains moving around as Jesus is about to make His grand appearance.

CHAPTER 12

The False Prophet Exposed

Picture the armies of Satan massed together to fight against God. "The kings of the earth, the great men, the rich men, the commanders, the mighty men" (Rev. 6:15) have gathered to fight, and here comes Jesus. He arrives to enforce God's plan. Are you ready for a showdown? He's ready to take it on! The armies on the earth have all the military might of the world ready to fight against Jesus and His host of angels. Revelation 19:11 depicts Him riding a white horse.

I can imagine NASA getting a signal that something unidentified is approaching earth through space—Jesus and His millions of angels. I can picture the military leaders of the world planning the redirection of their nuclear weapons, no longer aimed at each other but at whatever this phenomena in space is. If they did launch a nuclear weapon, the lead angel would just laugh. He grabs the little nuclear missile, turns it around, and throws it back. Terror spreads among the wicked when they see Jesus coming closer. See what it is like for them:

"The kings of the earth, the great men, the rich men, the commanders, the mighty men, every slave and every free man, hid themselves in the caves and in the rocks of the mountains, and said to the mountains and rocks, 'Fall on us and hide us from the face of Him who sits on the throne and from the wrath of the Lamb! For the great day of His wrath has come, and who is able to stand?'" (Rev. 6:15-17).

Remember what is happening during the seventh plague and while Jesus is coming? The mountains rise and collapse and islands shift out of their place. The people scream, "Let the rocks and mountains fall on us," and God says, "You get your wish." Revelation 19 says that all those mighty men and all the slaves and everyone else end up dead.

Jesus' coming is the worst thing that the wicked could face, and it is the best thing that God's people could hope for. It depends on whether you are 100 percent filled with the Holy Spirit or have nothing of Him.

People ask me, "Pastor, will Jesus' return happen before the time of tribulation (worst-ever time of trouble), in the middle of the tribulation, or after the tribulation?" You may be thinking, "Huh? I didn't know there was a discussion on that topic." But some believe in Jesus' arrival before the time of trouble, and some believe that He will appear after the tribulation. I get questions about this all the time. We are going to answer that here and now. Does Jesus make His appearance before, during, or after the plagues and the time of tribulation?

The members of the early Christian church knew that an antichrist would arise. Paul said it was already starting in his day. A time of tribulation and plagues would come, but it would be of an indefinite duration. They did not have a time set for it, and they did not apply the last seven years of the 70-week prophecy to the tribulation, as some do today. During those early years Christians believed that members of the church would be present on earth during the plagues and tribulation. The time of trouble would end with the second coming of Christ at the time of the seventh plague. That is when Jesus would show up. His arrival would be visible to all, a resurrection of the saved would take place, and His coming would start the millennium, the 1,000 years for God's people to be with Him in heaven. A variety of early church teachers taught much of this during the first and second century.[1]

Then during the Protestant Reformation the Reformers taught almost the same thing, but with one change. Calvin, Luther, Wesley, Wycliffe, and others not only preached about the antichrist but also identified it as the Papacy. They had no question that the antichrist, the beast power, was the Roman Catholic papal system. Again, we must remember that it is not the Catholic people but the Roman Catholic papal structure. "In calling the pope the 'antichrist,' the early Lutherans stood in a tradition that reached back into the eleventh century. Not only dissidents and heretics but even saints had called the bishop of Rome the 'antichrist' when they wished to castigate his abuse of power."[2] In other words, Martin Luther was teaching what the early church had presented in the past. It was during the time of ecumenical dialogue a couple decades ago that Pope John Paul II pulled Martin Luther out of hell, because an earlier pope had consigned him there—that is, if you believe the Roman Catholic Church has the power to put people in and out of hell. But I don't think Martin Luther was too worried about that.

Here is what we have today.

Up at the top, you can see the part I have labeled A. It is the historicists' viewpoint, and it shows what I have been sharing with you. It matches what the Reformers taught, and it is also what I find in Daniel 11—a chronological, step-by-step presentation.

The Counter-Reformation was the time from 1560 to 1648, when the Roman Catholic Church instituted a series of reforms in response to the views and influence of the Reformers. During the Counter-Reformation the Catholic Church introduced the view called futurism. If you go into a Christian bookstore, you will find that almost every book on prophecy operates on that concept. I have labeled the futurist view as commonly presented today as B. I discovered, when I started checking into the Bible, that what they present and what the Bible teaches do not match. However, what the Reformers taught does reflect what the Bible says.

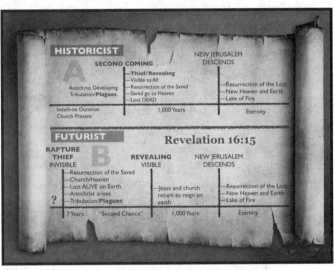

Remember that Revelation 16:15 said that between the sixth and seventh plague Jesus was about to "come as a thief" (KJV). The basic question is, as we look at the table above, Which side, A or B, matches this verse? Does it agree with what the Reformers taught or with what most people proclaim today? Let's see which one of those has Jesus arriving as a thief, right after the plagues, matching the description of Revelation 16:15.

The historicists and the Reformers taught that the plagues come first, and then Jesus would show up. That is a match. But those on the B side claim that Jesus comes as a thief, and then seven years later, right at the end . . . did the Bible get this wrong, or is it more likely that the people writing the popular prophecy books did? So far, that tells me that A is right, and not B.

Second Thessalonians 2:1 and 2 declares: "Now, brethren, concerning the coming of our Lord Jesus Christ and our gathering together to Him, we ask you, not to be soon shaken in mind or troubled, either by spirit or by word or by letter, as if from us, as though the day of Christ had come." The word "come" used here is a translation of the Greek word *parousia,* which futurists say is the invisible return of Christ at the beginning of a seven-year time of trouble/tribulation. At that time, futurists claim, the antichrist rises in power. For three and a half years he is friendly to the Jews, but then he receives the "deadly wound," comes back to life, and emerges as an enemy against Israel for three and a half years. The plagues happen during those last three and a half years. But, the futurists say, the seven years started with the Parousia, the coming of Christ.

Let's keep reading. Verse 3: "Let no one deceive you by any means; for that Day"—the Second Coming, the Parousia—"will not come unless the falling away comes first, and the man of sin is revealed, the son of perdition." The antichrist power will manifest himself before Jesus arrives in His parousia.

Look at the chart and find out which one, A or B, matches this verse. The A side has the emergence and unveiling of the antichrist, and then Jesus is revealed at His parousia. But on the B side the Parousia occurs in what futurists call the secret rapture, and then the antichrist gains his ascendancy. They have the order reversed. This should be setting off all kinds of alarm bells in your head, because Satan is up to something. I'm going to show you part of his scheme. I don't think I'm smart enough to know it all, but I've got part of it.

Our next verse is 2 Thessalonians 2:8. "And then the lawless one will be revealed, whom the Lord will consume with the breath of His mouth and destroy with the brightness of His coming." Again, the word for coming is *parousia,* which the futurists want to say is the secret rapture or the invisible return of Christ, as well as the beginning of the seven years. That Parousia should consume or destroy the antichrist power. Let's take a look at the chart. On the A side, according to the Reformation teachers, the antichrist would develop, and then when Jesus returns, He would destroy the antichrist. So that's a match! But the B side has the Parousia before the antichrist arises. In other words, according to what the futurists are teaching, the power vacuum created when Jesus snatches all the believers away will lead to the rise of the antichrist. Again they have the order backwards. The Bible says that Jesus' parousia destroys the antichrist rather than setting him up in power. So, again, A matches the Bible verse and B does not.

Now let's consider 2 Peter 3:10: "But the day of the Lord will come as a thief in the night, in which the heavens will pass away with a great noise, and the elements will melt with fervent heat; both the earth and the works that are in it will be burned up."

If the chair you are sitting on melts from under you, what is it going to be like? Will there be many survivors? No. I had a friend who worked in a steel mill, and one of the guys that he knew was discouraged and going through a hard time, and he took a running jump into a furnace. He was gone before he hit the molten steel. When the heat is enough to melt elements, you don't survive long in that kind of fire. Jesus said that He was going to destroy the beast and those who follow him by the "brightness of His coming" (2 Thess. 2:8).

According to 2 Peter 3:10, when Jesus comes as a thief, the lost are dead. But when the futurists talk about Jesus' returning as a thief, they write a whole series of books that say the lost are wandering around on earth, saying, "Where'd everybody go? What happened?" Did you notice that they got almost everything wrong? Don't trust the novels and the films. Put your confidence in God's Word.

What about Matthew 24 and Luke 17? The Reformers taught that the "coming as a thief" and the "revealing" were different terms for the same event. The futurists say the "thief" and the "revealing" are separate terms for separate events. Let's allow the Bible to describe for itself whether it involves one event or two. We will put Matthew 24 and Luke 17 side by side.

Matthew 24:27: "For as the lightning comes from the east and flashes to the west, so also will the coming of the Son of Man be." Luke 17:24: "For as the lightning that flashes out of one part under heaven shines to the other part under heaven, so also the Son of Man will be in His day." Definitely seems as if they have the same event in mind.

Matthew 24:37-39: "But as the days of Noah were, so also will the coming of the Son of Man be. For as in the days before the flood, they were eating and drinking, marrying and giving in marriage, until the day that Noah entered the ark, and did not know until the flood came and took them all away, so also will the coming of the Son of Man be." Luke 17:26: "And as it was in the days of Noah, so it will be also in the days of the Son of Man." Does it sound as if we are hearing the same sermon that Jesus is giving about the same event?

Matthew 24:40: "Then two men will be in the field: one will be taken and the other left." This verse is the whole basis for Tim LaHaye's understanding of prophecy in the Left Behind series—that one would be snatched into heaven and the other remain on earth. Compare Luke 17:35, 36: "Two women will be grinding together: the one will be taken and the other left. Two men will be in the field: the one will be taken and the other left." The two verses parallel passages in Matthew and Luke and have basically the same order within the chapters. The problem for the futurist is that Matthew calls it the *parousia* (futurists say "rapture"), but Luke labels the same event as the "revealing" (see Luke 17:30).

Do these passages describe one event with two different names, or do we hear about two separate events? Clearly they are one event, with slightly different words used to present the same thing.

Does God use different ways to describe the same thing in other parts of the Scriptures? What about the Lamb slain on the throne, and the Lion of Judah? They are the same person (Jesus) under different names. They are not two separate Saviors. "Lord of lords and King of kings" is another name for Him. The Bible often employs two or more terms to refer to the same thing. What we have here is that the Reformers were right again. Do you see a trend?

Another assertion of the futurists is that the lost continue to wander around on the earth, wondering what happened. The historicists have said, "No, they are destroyed by the brightness of Jesus' coming at the very end." The people killed by the Flood did not wonder where Noah went. They were dead! Matthew 24:38, 39: "For as in the days before the flood . . . [they] did not know until the flood came and took them all away, so also will the coming of the Son of Man be." How many kinds of people were there in Noah's day? Those who got on the ark and lived, and those who didn't and died.

Luke says the same thing, and he adds a reference to Sodom and Gomorrah. "On the day that Lot went out of Sodom it rained fire and brimstone from heaven and destroyed them all. Even so will it be in the day when the Son of Man is revealed" (Luke 17:29, 30). Again, how many kinds of people were there in Sodom and Gomorrah? Those who got out when God said to, and they lived; and those who didn't, and they died.

Now, look at Luke 17:35-37: "One will be taken and the other left. And they answered and said to Him, 'Where, Lord?' So He said to them, 'Wherever the body is, there the eagles will be gathered together.'" The eagles gather where the dead bodies lie. God's people who are rescued will not be dead at that time. So who is dead here? The wicked! Those who refuse to trust Jesus! Are the wicked going to be left wandering around on the earth for seven years, puzzled at what happened to the rest? No! They are dead. Jesus was very clear. So side A in our diagram works, and the B side does not.

What about New Testament Israel? The authors of the Left Behind series, *The Late, Great Planet Earth,* and other books believe that all Bible prophecies for ancient Israel will literally be fulfilled to the Jews, and they ignore the conditional aspect of the prophecies. They say that God's New Testament people (the church) and His Old Testament people (Israel) are not the same, even though the New Testament declares that God's Old Testament and New Testament people are indeed the same and that there is no line of distinction between Jew and Gentile. Anyone who has accepted Christ is an heir of Abraham and a part of the commonwealth of Israel. So which one is right, A or B? Side A matches on that one too.

What about the seven years? The futurists get it from Daniel 9. Remember, when we studied Daniel 9, we looked at the historicists' or Reformers' viewpoint that 70 weeks equals 490 years. The last week, or the last seven years, started in A.D. 27 when the Messiah would be anointed. Jesus was anointed at His baptism in A.D. 27. In the middle of the week, after three and a half years, the Messiah would die. He would be "cut off" and bring an "end to sacrifices." When Jesus died, it did terminate the significance of animal sacrifices. You don't offer a lamb as a sacrifice whenever you sin now. And then the gospel goes to the Gentiles in A.D. 34. So that seventh week—those seven years—has already happened way back then. And Jesus is the center of those seven years!

But the futurist says, "Oh, no, it's not! We're going to rip out the seven years from the prophecy, and we're going to throw them a couple of thousand years into the future, and instead of it being about Jesus, we're going to have this long gap, and we're going to start the prophetic time clock again by the secret rapture, when Jesus comes." And they say nobody will see Him at that time. Then, in the middle of the week, the antichrist will receive a deadly wound, and finally Jesus Himself will visibly show up at the end of the seven years. But in this scenario, who is the center of the prophecy after three and a half years? The antichrist.

Remember that Satan said he wanted to take the place of God? He does exactly that in the futurists' version of prophecy! You saw that the whole futurist view of prophecy, when we went through the whole string of comparisons, does not match Scripture. If it doesn't match Scripture, and it puts Satan in the center of the prophecy instead of Jesus, do you think there is a problem here? A huge one! Satan is deceiving people!

You recall that the Roman Catholic Jesuit priest Francisco Ribera in the sixteenth century employed futurism to take the heat off the Papacy. The Reformers were studying the antichrist power, the beast, the little horn, and they concluded, "The antichrist is the papal system." But Ribera said, "No, Daniel and Revelation and the antichrist are all in the future. The prophecy has nothing to do with the Papacy." So he threw it out into the future, and now almost every Protestant has adopted futurism. And you know, it had to happen, because Revelation says that all the world would end up following the beast.

Protestant futurism came by way of Samuel Maitland, who in the 1820s wrote that the descriptions of the antichrist do not fit the pope. Edward Irving, in the 1840s, began to be a futurist. Margaret McDonald, a woman in his congregation, had a "tongues" vision, and when she came out of the vision she said, "There are going to be two comings of Christ, separated by a time period, and that's when the antichrist will be active." Until Margaret McDonald in the 1840s, the church had never had the concept of two comings of Christ, separating the "coming as a thief" from the coming as the "revealing." Up until then it was known as one event only. Remember that Revelation promised there would be signs, wonders, and miracles to deceive people, and this new idea came from a "tongues" vision. I believe in tongues, and I believe in visions, but I also believe there are counterfeits, because God's Word said counterfeits would surface to deceive people.

John Nelson Darby picked up futurism from there and created dispensationalism in 1848. By this time he was teaching that the Jews in the Old Testament were saved by works, contrary to Hebrews 11, which declares that they were all saved by faith.

Futurism went into the *Scofield Reference Bible* about 1909, and Hal Lindsey picked it up in the 1970s in his book *The Late, Great Planet Earth*. Then came religious films such as *Years of the Beast* and *A Thief in the Night*. Once people have seen the film, they "know" what is going to happen, so why should they read the Bible? As a result, many Christians, especially in North America, believe in a seven-year tribulation, or worst-ever time of trouble. Now you know how this belief came to be. It resulted, not from careful Bible study, but rather a vision. One commentator that I read recently, who believes in the seven-year tribulation, admitted that you could not find the seven-year tribulation in Scripture if you didn't already know about it. And the only way they knew about it was through Margaret McDonald's vision.

Does it really matter what you believe on this topic? Yes! I have heard people say, "Well, if I miss the first coming of Jesus (when He arrives as a thief), I'll have to go through seven years of really troubled times, but I can be ready for when He returns at the 'revealing.'" What if there is no second chance? Wouldn't Satan like for us to assume that we have an additional opportunity, and we can wait to make our decision for God? But the Lord says that now is the day to accept Him. Don't put it off.

What about preparation for the time of tribulation? Those who believe and follow God and are still alive during that time of trouble on earth, although they know they will be protected by God, realize that it is still going to be tough to get through, and they will have to hang on for however long it takes. They understand that they have got to be making spiritual preparation, which is being filled with the Holy Spirit. We can do that only by digging into God's Word and following what it says in every aspect of our lives.

Others, who believe they are going to get raptured out of this world and taken away at the beginning of the seven years, assume that they don't need to be ready for hard times. Do you remember the parable of the 10 virgins who wanted to get into the wedding? Five were prepared, and five were not. The first five made it through, while the latter five did not. That's important to keep in mind.

Those who believe they will be raptured also get blindsided by the antichrist. Here's the problem. Suppose a deaf person is standing on a railroad track. "Keep alert for the antichrist out that way," someone tells him or her. "He's going to come in the future." So the deaf individual remains on the railroad track, waiting for the train, watching for it, because he or she does not want to get run over by this train. But in reality the antichrist is coming the other way, from behind, and it is already a part of history. It has already had a 1260-year run. Sure, it stopped for a little bit, but it is picking up steam and barreling ahead at a furious pace. The deaf person stands on the tracks, looking into the future, not knowing what is looming from behind. What's going to happen to him or her? What awaits many Christians all over the world?

Whom do many Christians accept as a worldwide leader of the Christian church? Both Protestants and Roman Catholics acknowledge the pope as a major figure in Christianity. The Bible says that all the world would follow after him. They are watching for him, not as the antichrist, but rather as someone to oppose the antichrist.

When we talked about the United States in prophecy, we found that the country starts out as a lamblike beast, or beast with lamblike horns, and ends up being the false prophet. Do you know which region of the world most pushes prophetic futurism? (I'm talking about the seven-year tribulation, getting Israel back in charge of the Temple Mount, building the third temple, and all the rest of the package that is dispensationalism and futurism.) The United States.

God does not require that the Jerusalem Temple be rebuilt. First of all, if the Temple were rebuilt and sacrifices started again, that would be blasphemy. From God's perspective, sacrifices ended at the death of Jesus, for He was the true sacrifice, the Lamb of God. Also, Daniel 9:26, 27 announces that the Temple would be desolate until the confirmation. Jesus called it "desolate" when He left it for the last time. And it will remain that way until the return of Christ. If the Temple is rebuilt, it will be a part of Satan's counterfeit.

I know that what I'm saying may not be the same as what you often find in a Christian bookstore. Revelation 18:4 says: "Come out of her, my people." It's important to know that you are following what the Bible says, and not what anybody else is teaching. It is vital to surrender to Jesus Christ and to His Word.

---

[1] I recommend that you read George Eldon Ladd's *The Blessed Hope* (Grand Rapids: Eerdmans, 1990), which details the history of the teachings about Christ's return through the Christian Era.

[2] Joseph A. Burgess and Jeffrey Gros, eds., *Building Unity: Ecumenical Dialogues With Roman Catholic Participation in the United States* (Mahwah, N.J.: Paulist Press, 1989), p. 140.

CHAPTER 13

Jesus Rescues His People

The Rock

We've gone over the overlap in Daniel 11:44, 45 and Daniel 12:1. The tidings of the final warning have gone out, and then the anger of the beast power dominates. Jesus finishes the judgment, and the time of trouble begins. The king of the north meets his end, and Jesus rescues God's people when He returns.

Now we will focus on Jesus delivering His people. In the Daniel 2 vision of the statue, Nebuchadnezzar sees the head of gold, Babylon, then Persia, Greece, Rome, and divided Europe, and then it ends with a rock, cut out without hands, that strikes the statue, destroys it completely, and takes over the world. That rock is Jesus, the King of kings and Lord of lords.

One of my favorite promises about the coming of Jesus is John 14:1-3.

"Let not your heart be troubled; you believe in God, believe also in Me. In My Father's house are many mansions; if it were not so, I would have told you. I go to prepare a place for you. And if I go and prepare a place for you, I will come again and receive you to Myself; that where I am, there you may be also."

Jesus promised that He is going to pick us up and take us to our "mansions" in heaven. A special place in heaven has your name on it. You don't want to miss out on that.

What do we know about Christ's coming? Here are five facts.

Number 1: *It will be literal.* I know pastors who claim that the Second Advent is spiritual, and that He will never physically return to earth. They say that Jesus comes back every time someone accepts Him into their heart, but that He will not appear in the clouds to bring an end to sin and suffering. How depressing is that! But is it true?

In Acts 1:9-11 the Bible tells us:

"Now when He had spoken these things, while they watched, He was taken up, and a cloud received Him out of their sight. And while they looked steadfastly toward heaven as He went up, behold, two men stood by them in white apparel, who also said, 'Men of Galilee, why do you stand gazing up into heaven? This same Jesus, who was taken up from you into heaven, will so come in like manner as you saw Him go into heaven.'"

Jesus was a tangible human being when He left. The disciple Thomas doubted the reality of the resurrected Savior, and Jesus said to him, "Come touch Me. Check Me out. Give Me something to eat and watch Me eat it. I'm no ghost." When Jesus departed in a cloud, all of the disciples watched Him leave. If He was a physical being when He left earth, then when He comes back He will also be a physical being. We will be able to see Him. The people who teach an invisible return of Christ cannot be correct. When Jesus appears at the Second Advent, He arrives in the clouds, and He is seen just as He was when He left.

Number 2: *Jesus at His coming will be visible to every living person on earth.* Revelation 1:7 declares: "Behold, He is coming with clouds, and every eye will see Him, and they also who pierced Him. And all the tribes of the earth will mourn because of Him." Will only His followers be aware of Him? No! Every eye will witness His arrival.

Matthew makes it clear that if someone appears on earth and claims to be Jesus Christ, they are lying. "For false christs and false prophets will arise and show great signs and wonders, so as to deceive, if possible, even the elect. See, I have told you beforehand. Therefore if they say to you, 'Look, He is in the desert!' do not go out; or 'Look, He is in the inner rooms!' do not believe it" (Matt. 24:24-26). If someone announces that they are the Messiah and walks around on the earth, and only a few people are seeing them, you know they are not Jesus Christ. When Jesus returns, every eye sees Him.

You say, "How is that possible?" I have one possible explanation. If you have ever used a timing light on a flywheel, you know that it is a strobe light and that it flashes at the same speed as that wheel rotates. It makes a moving flywheel appear as though it is standing still, although it's turning very fast. All Jesus has to do is travel very fast around the world and have a strobe-like appearance, as the verse says, like lightning. To everyone in the world, it would appear as though He's just standing there. But He must have a lot of ways to be visible everywhere. If I can come up with one, then there are a lot more. One way or another, everyone in the world will see Him.

Number 3: *His coming will be audible.* "For the Lord Himself will descend from heaven with a shout, with the voice of an archangel, and with the trumpet of God" (1 Thess. 4:16). Not only will you see the coming of Jesus, but you will also hear it loud and clear.

Number 4: *It will be spectacular.* "For the Son of Man will come in the glory of His Father with His angels, and then He will reward each according to his works" (Matt. 16:27). When Jesus was resurrected, one angel showed up and gave a little burst of glory. What happened to the soldiers guarding the tomb? They fell down as dead men. Imagine what it will be like when Jesus arrives in His full glory. He comes with the Father's glory and with the radiance of millions of angels. Who is going to miss that? In the last chapter we saw the rebellious ones calling for rocks and mountains to fall on them to hide them from the brightness. When Jesus returns, it will be the worst thing in the world for those who don't trust in Him, and it's the best thing for those who do.

How will the antichrist, the little-horn beast, perish? "And then the lawless one will be revealed, whom the Lord will consume with the breath of His mouth and destroy with the brightness of His coming" (2 Thess. 2:8). God's glory is a consuming fire to sin and wickedness.

"It is a righteous thing with God to repay with tribulation those who trouble you, and to give you who are troubled rest with us when the Lord Jesus is revealed from heaven with His mighty angels, in flaming fire taking vengeance on those who do not know God, and on those who do not obey the gospel of our Lord Jesus Christ. These shall be punished with everlasting destruction from the presence of the Lord and from the glory of His power" (2 Thess. 1:6-9).

The glory of God can be destructive. Remember that God told Moses that if he were to see Him in all His glory, the brightness of it would kill him? The Lord gave him just a little glimpse, and Moses literally glowed for 40 days afterward. The Israelites asked him to wear a veil because his appearance scared them. And that was the result of only an indirect view of God! So the appearing of Jesus will be glorious beyond comprehension.

Number 5: *His appearing will be climactic.* "For as the lightning comes from the east and flashes to the west, so also will the coming of the Son of Man be" (Matt. 24:27). Those who have had lightning hit near them do not easily forget it. I've had lightning strike close enough for the electrical shock to make my muscles contract. It was behind me. Because I was headed for cover, I didn't look to see what got hit. Another time, I was driving down the road in a storm, and I glanced at a transformer just in time to watch it blow apart. The pole stood there smoking—what was left of it. This kind of event is climactic. You are not going to miss it. "Then the sky receded as a scroll when it is rolled up" (Rev. 6:14). No one will be unaware of the sky disappearing.

"And every mountain and island was moved out of its place. And the kings of the earth, the great men, the rich men, the commanders, the mighty men, every slave and every free man, hid themselves in the caves and in the rocks of the mountains, and said to the mountains and rocks, 'Fall on us and hide us from the face of Him who sits on the throne and from the wrath of the Lamb! For the great day of His wrath has come, and who is able to stand?'" (verses 14-17).

This is the wrap-up of earth's history. You can't miss it. You see it, you hear it, it's glorious, it's climactic, it's awesome!

The coming of Jesus Christ is a rescue mission. It will be the best time of our lives when we look up at Him and He smiles at us and says, "I'm on the way to save you." And remember, if you've been living through the end-times, you've been on earth when the king of the north/beast power has been threatening to kill you. People were out to get you, but now they've got problems of their own to deal with. The rocks and the mountains are starting to collapse, and islands are disappearing. Suppose you had been hiding out in the mountains and suddenly the mountain below you is disappearing. You're going to look up at Jesus and say, "Oh, wow, am I glad to see You!" And then He takes us up into the clouds to meet Him. I will be glad to be out of here.

Death and the Resurrection

On top of all that, not only are we rescued, but also the ones who died trusting in Jesus are resurrected to be taken to heaven with us. Every one of us has lost loved ones. Having already laid one of my children in the grave, I'm looking forward to meeting her again. It's going to be a party on that cloud as we greet each other.

Sadly, most people are not looking forward to that resurrection as they should be, because of one of the deceptions inspired by Satan—what happens when we die. To help you grasp how wonderful the resurrection is, and why all of God's Word is pointing forward to Jesus' coming and the resurrection as the climax of His salvation ministry, you need to understand what He teaches about death.

No Truth From the Dead

A lot of people think they can communicate with the dead. But I have news for you: the Bible says that you cannot. Then who is it that people are contacting? The one who is a liar and a deceiver—Satan. Isaiah 8:19, 20 warns: "When they say to you, 'Seek those who are mediums and wizards, who whisper and mutter,' should not a people seek their God? Should they seek the dead on behalf of the living?" Should you go to God's Word or to a fortuneteller to find out what's coming in the future? You definitely don't go out to cemeteries to find the truth.

"To the law and to the testimony! If they do not speak according to this word, it is because there is no light in them" (verse 20). Anybody who speaks contrary to God's Word has only darkness in them. I've got a lot of prophecy books in my collection that have no light in them, because they are contrary to God's Word. So how do you find out what the truth is? You check with the Word. Jesus is the Word—the Bible is the Word.

Death Is a Sleep

The Bible has a number of things to say about grief and death. Paul writes: "I do not want you to be ignorant, brethren, concerning those who have fallen asleep, lest you sorrow as others who have no hope" (1 Thess. 4:13). He calls death a sleep. The apostle does not say that Christians would not have sorrow, but rather that Christians would not have hopeless sorrow. There is a huge difference. Having been a pastor for many years, I've been involved in many funerals, and I have watched people who had hopeless sorrow. Part of the good news is that we can have sorrow with hope. But we still have to say goodbye for a while.

"For if we believe that Jesus died and rose again, even so God will bring with Him those who sleep in Jesus. For this we say to you by the word of the Lord, that we who are alive and remain until the coming of the Lord will by no means precede those who are asleep. For the Lord Himself will descend from heaven with a shout, with the voice of an archangel, and with the trumpet of God. And the dead in Christ will rise first. Then we who are alive and remain shall be caught up together with them in the clouds to meet the Lord in the air. And thus we shall always be with the Lord. Therefore comfort one another with these words" (verses 14, 15).

Did Paul tell the people in Thessalonica to comfort each other because they would get to meet again as soon as they die? He did not say to them, "I know you lost a loved one, but when you die, you get to meet them in heaven." Nor did he assure us that there would be a reunion in heaven after death. Rather, he spoke of a reunion when Jesus comes in the clouds and resurrects us! How many funerals have you been to in which they state something like "George has been met by his dad up in heaven. They had a wonderful meeting." That is not how Paul said we should have hope. Rather, he told us to have hope in the resurrection.

To make sense of this, look at what Daniel says about the resurrection. "And many of those who sleep in the dust of the earth shall awake, some to everlasting life, some to shame and everlasting contempt" (Dan. 12:2). Again, the Bible calls death a sleep. When your loved one is sleeping in the dust of the earth, they are dead. They receive their everlasting life at the resurrection, when God wakes them up from their sleep.

God in essence told the prophet, "Daniel, you are not going to understand this stuff, so relax. But go your way till the end, for you shall rest [sleep in death], and you will arise to your inheritance at the end of the day" (adapted from verse 12). When was he going to be in heaven? At the end of days, at the end of the time of the end. We haven't finished that period yet. Daniel still has not made it to heaven, according to his own book. He is resting in his dusty grave, waiting for the resurrection.

That is sadly not what the church has taught for most of its history. Early Christian apologists took the pagan idea that when you die, you go right on to heaven or hell, and they brought it into Christianity itself.

What did Jesus Himself say about death being a sleep? One of His closest acquaintances had died, but He said to His disciples, "Our friend Lazarus sleeps, but I go that I may wake him up" (John 11:11). When somebody was dead, all Jesus had to do was ring His alarm clock, and He could wake them up. It was no big deal for Him. "Then His disciples said, 'Lord, if he sleeps he will get well.' However, Jesus spoke of his death, but they thought that He was speaking about taking rest in sleep. Then Jesus said to them plainly, 'Lazarus is dead'" (verses 12-14). Very clearly Jesus calls death a sleep.

The Dead Know Nothing

Elsewhere the Bible tells us the dead aren't aware of anything. "For the living know that they will die; but the dead know nothing, and they have no more reward, for the memory of them is forgotten. Also their love, their hatred, and their envy have now perished; nevermore will they have a share in anything done under the sun" (Eccl. 9:5, 6). Can a dead person come back and haunt you because they did not like you? No. The Bible says that the dead know nothing and that their hatred is forgotten. Can a dead person who loves you give you a warning from the other side? Again, no! Because they do not know that, either. They have no consciousness at all.

Have you ever had a really, really good night's sleep? Exhausted, as soon as your head hit the pillow, you went to sleep, and the next thing you knew it was morning? I like those kinds of nights. Jesus says death is like a good night's sleep. You're not aware of anything. Perhaps you have heard someone say that someone who is sleeping is dead to the world. That's a biblical way of describing the sleep of death.

What is a good way to shorten a long car trip, assuming you're not driving? Go to sleep. The next thing you know, you're there! Think about the beauty of the idea. When you drop off into sleep, you're unaware of everything else, and in death you don't know anything until Jesus wakes you up. So you lie down and sleep in death, and then next thing you realize is that Jesus is there. Not bad—not bad at all.

The Mortal Soul

People sometimes protest, "But, Pastor Tim, what about that immortal soul that I've been taught about for so many years?" Look up the word "immortal" in a concordance. See if you can find where the Bible says that we have an immortal soul. It is not in there. But here's what the Bible does teach: "Behold, all souls are Mine; the soul of the father as well as the soul of the son is Mine; the soul who sins shall die" (Eze. 18:4). If you have an immortal soul right now, can God say that it will die? No! So which will you believe: the traditions that are, unfortunately, taught within the Christian church, or God's own Word? Sadly, most Christians will persist in following traditions and not God's Word.

What about 1 Timothy 6:15, 16? "He who is the blessed and only Potentate, the King of kings and Lord of lords, who alone has immortality, dwelling in unapproachable light." If we have immortality, can the Bible be true if it says that only God possesses it? Would you rather that God be a liar, or that Christian tradition be wrong? Remember, He says that when you worship according to tradition, you worship in vain. It is pretty clear that tradition is not the path to follow.

Paul told the Corinthian believers what would happen at the moment the dead in Christ are resurrected. "Behold, I tell you a mystery: We shall not all sleep, but we shall all be changed—in a moment, in the twinkling of an eye, at the last trumpet. For the trumpet will sound, and the dead will be raised incorruptible, and we shall be changed. For this corruptible must put on incorruption, and this mortal must put on immortality" (1 Cor. 15:51-53). We were mortal at Creation because Adam needed to eat from the tree of life to stay living. Still mortal, we will take on immortality as a gift from God only at the resurrection. If we already had immortality, then why would God have to endow us with it at the resurrection? "So when this corruptible has put on incorruption, and this mortal has put on immortality, then shall be brought to pass the saying that is written: 'Death is swallowed up in victory'" (verse 54).

Now you can see the importance of the resurrection. It is the time of the great reunion. Everything is on the line then. If there is no resurrection, salvation does not work! A lot of Christians have blown by the resurrection because they thought, *Well, I'm going to meet my family when I die, and since they've already died, and we're going to meet in heaven, that's how we get to heaven.* No, we reach heaven by being resurrected by Jesus, and we go there together as a whole human family. And we have a celebration with Jesus on the way to heaven.

The Spirit in a Person

What about the spirit of a person returning to God? "Then the dust will return to the earth as it was, and the spirit will return to God who gave it" (Eccl. 12:7). The spirit does go to God who gave it—I have no question about that. But does that mean we have an immortal soul? Or that we live and know things in heaven after we die? No, because the Bible said the dead know nothing. So, then, what is the spirit? It is the breath of life given in Genesis 2: "The Lord God formed man of the dust of the ground, and breathed into his nostrils the breath of life; and man became a living being" (verse 7). The gift of life—the breath of life—is the spirit. And so when we die, the gift that came from God goes back to Him. It does not mean we live as a spirit in heaven. The gift of life that He has presented us, He holds in Himself after we die, until He comes and wakes us at the resurrection and gives it back.

Genesis 2:7 says that "man became a living soul" (KJV). When an airplane goes down, we may hear in news reports that it had 55 souls on board, meaning 55 people who died. They started out as living beings, and they ended as dead bodies. If the soul were something separate, what do you do with verse 19? "Whatever Adam called each living creature, that was its name." The term "living creature" here is the same term as the Bible uses in verse 7—a living being, a soul. The animals were living beings. Do they have an immortal soul? No. We are all the same in that way—we are living creatures.

According to the Genesis formula, then, body plus breath or spirit equals a soul, which is now a living being. Soul minus the breath, or the living being minus the breath, equals death—a corpse, a pile of dirt. God had taken the body (the dirt) and given it breath, and it became a living person. At death the breath goes out from the living person, and he or she becomes a mound of soil again. It is a pretty simple equation.

Here's another way of looking at it: suppose that a lightbulb represents our body. How much light does the lightbulb give off by itself? It reflects a little bit of light from the outside, but has no light in itself. But if you connect the lightbulb to the electrical power grid—to God's power, His gift of life—what do you have? A light in the bulb. Now what happens when you disconnect that gift of life? All you have is a lightbulb and no light. The light ceases to exist—vanishes. Where does the living being go when the spirit leaves? It too ceases to exist, and what was once a living person is no longer. You have the gift of life waiting in heaven and a dead body on earth. The living person no longer exists because "the dead know nothing."

Remember, in Genesis 3:4, the devil's first lie: "You will not surely die"? "Go ahead, Eve, eat this fruit and you'll become like God (and be immortal)." But only God is inherently immortal. Satan was saying that Eve would become like God, so from the very beginning he was promulgating a lie: follow me, and you'll be immortal. The truth is, if you sin you will die, not be immortal. Eve died, didn't she? So did Adam. So has everybody else since. Who was right—God or Satan? God is the only immortal one. So why does the majority of the world accept Satan and his lie and believe that when you die you become immortal and thus like God? It is contrary to the Scriptures.

No Ghosts

You cannot be haunted by a dead person, nor can you be visited by any kind of dead individual. If that appears to happen, you are dealing with one of Satan's angels, a counterfeit of some dead person. Tell the apparition, "Get behind me, Satan." Have nothing to do with it.

I believe that we're going to encounter more and more of this kind of experience as Satan tries to deceive us and get us to follow something other than God's Word. Satan will tempt us to listen to all kinds of messages from the dead. All you have to do is turn on late-night radio. When I'm driving home late at night, and I've got to stay awake, I turn on one of those stations. I can't take it for very long, as I hear of people seeking to contact the dead and unveil their secrets. Of course, Satan knows those secrets already. He is the one who tempted a person to do a sin, and he was there when they did it. So, yes, he can reveal the secrets of people's lives. He knows way more than we do.

The truth is that you cannot communicate with the dead. The Bible actually tells us in the Old Testament that anyone who tries to do so should be cut off from the nation of Israel, or killed. It was a serious offense. God did not like to have anyone trying to contact the dead, because they are really communicating with Satan. God does not want His people to listen to messages from Satan. Do you blame Him?

The False Christian Tradition

Revelation 17:1, 2 describes "the great harlot who sits on many waters, with whom the kings of the earth committed fornication, and the inhabitants of the earth were made drunk with the wine of her fornication." The world becomes drunk from the stuff in her cup—the corrupted biblical messages that changed into Christian traditions. The world has become intoxicated with it, and it likes spiritual alcohol better than truth. People like having their minds numbed by error, so they don't have to think of the truth. "The woman was arrayed in purple and scarlet, and adorned with gold and precious stones and pearls, having in her hand a golden cup full of abominations and the filthiness of her fornication" (verse 4). The fornications—the spiritual adultery—happened when the early church took human traditions and mixed them with God's Word and created a mix of human ideas (which really means from the devil) and God's Word for the traditions and teachings of the church. It causes people to follow after supposed messages from the dead, to be looking the wrong direction for hope. That's not good, because there is hope only in God's truth.

The State of the Dead

Right before my daughter's death, she asked, "Dad, what's it like to die?"

She said, "I'm not afraid of death, because I know it is just a sleep until Jesus comes. But I'm not so sure about dying."

My daughter was experiencing the uncertainty that we all feel as we approach death. What we do not have to be uncertain about is what happens after death.

The Christian tradition that claims that a person goes to heaven at death has serious consequences. To see the results of this belief, let's take a fictional scenario of a young woman who died and left behind a couple young children. We will let our story play out both in the form that Satan has taught us and the way that God has taught us—the false traditions versus God's truth. Let's present God's version first.

The young mother lies there in the coffin. She's left two little girls, and her husband is in great grief. Buried, she rests there until Christ comes again. The woman is not conscious of anything that happens while she is in that grave for however long, be it days or centuries. Because the dead know nothing, she is not aware of the passing of time.

Her husband does something really foolish. He gets remarried on the rebound to a woman who is a problem. She beats the children and abuses them in all kinds of ways. The husband becomes an alcoholic. How much of that tragedy is the first wife having to deal with? None of it, because she's asleep and knows nothing. Whatever troubles her kids go through, she does not have to deal with it until it's long over and God has taken care of it. You see why His way is really good news?

In my daughter's case, when she died she was ready for it. She didn't want to go through the process of dying, but the thought of going to sleep sounded good, because she had been through way too much already in her fight with cancer. That sleep of death can be a welcome escape when you've suffered a lot. And so, in a way, God gave us a sleep of escape to get us to the resurrection and the coming of Jesus.

Now we will play out the story of the fictional woman again, but this time with the false Christian teaching—the human tradition—that after death she goes straight up to heaven. This time, after she dies, she's not in the casket unaware of anything, but rather she is up in heaven knowing everything. The tradition says that she is immortal like God. That is what the lie teaches. And so she watches events on earth. Haven't you heard at a funeral that the loved one is looking down on us? I have—many times. She observes her little girls and her husband crying, and she sees him lose it. He remarries right away, on the rebound, to a woman who is after his money and trying to destroy him while beating up on the kids and abusing them. The woman who died is stuck in heaven and can't do anything about her kids down on earth. What is heaven now like for her? It just became like hell. Have you thought about where that teaching leads? It is really terrible.

The truth is that the dead rest quietly in the grave. They're not up in heaven being tortured by what they see, but waiting for the resurrection, when they can be reunited with loved ones. God will have already taken care of all the problems of the past. Somebody may try to bring them up, and you say, "Oh, well, it's all history now. Praise the Lord that we are with Jesus. Thank You, Jesus."

Looking at the false teaching from the other direction, how much good news is there for somebody who thinks their loved one had not accepted Christ before they died, which means they're roasting in hell right now? It is better to know that they're resting in the grave waiting for the final judgment to be done. I like Jesus' way of doing things.

I'm looking forward to the resurrection, because that is when I know that Satan has really been defeated. I have been in cemetery after cemetery, and I've helped put lots of people in the ground, including one living funeral director who accidentally slipped and fell in. That was kind of funny. He climbed back up. But the rest have not come out yet. When Jesus returns, I really, really, really want to be near a cemetery, because I want to see the redeemed emerge from the ground. That will be wonderful. I don't know if they're going to shoot out like a rocket, or if the ground is going to ripple and open up. But while I don't know what it is going to be like, I do want to witness it!

Three States of Being

Some might protest at this point, "Pastor Tim, 2 Corinthians 5 declares that to be absent from the body is to be present with the Lord." Does it say that? Kind of. But we should always take things in context. If we read the context in this case, we find that the Paul who wrote this statement is the same one who announced that we will be reunited at the resurrection and not before. Christians who are following the devil's lie believe that there are two states of being—an earthly state and a heavenly one—and that as soon as we leave this one, we go straight to heaven or hell. But are there just two? I'm suggesting there are actually three states of being.

In 2 Corinthians 5 we find that there is not just an earthly life and a heavenly life, but there is also one that Paul calls "naked." "Earthly" means the present life, "heavenly" indicates the future life, and "naked" means without either life. The naked stage is the sleep of death.

"For we know that if our earthly house, this tent, is destroyed, we have a building from God, a house not made with hands, eternal in the heavens" (2 Cor. 5:1). That is God's promise to resurrect your body—to give you an immortal, incorruptible existence. "For in this we groan, earnestly desiring to be clothed with our habitation which is from heaven" (verse 2). I assume you would rather have your heavenly existence than your earthly one. Me too. "If indeed, having been clothed, we shall not be found naked" (verse 3). Oops! Paul would like to be in heaven, and he does not want that in-between state ("naked"), the one without the earthly life that does not yet possess the heavenly one.

"For we who are in this tent [body] groan, being burdened, not because we want to be unclothed, but further clothed, that mortality may be swallowed up by life" (verse 4). Paul is saying, "I want to go to heaven, but I don't really want to die." Can you understand that logic? "But further clothed" means he wants the better life and doesn't want to be without life! He is saying, "I'd like to go straight from this life to the next one, please." But he suspects that he will have to die first and have the next life later. Remember, we're not immortal until Jesus comes back. Paul is saying here that in the future, mortality will be swallowed up by eternal life.

> **Absent/Body = Present/Lord**
>
> **2 Corinthians 5:1-8**
>
> **Earthly = Present Life**
>
> **Naked = Without Life**
>
> **Heavenly = Future Life**

"Now He who has prepared us for this very thing is God, who also has given us the Spirit as a guarantee. Therefore we are always confident, knowing that while we are at home in the body we are absent from the Lord" (verses 5, 6). As long as I walk the streets of earth, I know that I'm not in heaven. "For we walk by faith, not by sight. We are confident, yes, well pleased rather to be absent from the body and to be present with the Lord" (verses 7, 8). Where would you rather be—heaven or earth? That is all Paul says here: "I'd rather be in heaven!" As long as I'm here, I know that I'm not there, and I'd rather be there.

The Thief on the Cross

A comma in Luke 23:43 has led people to believe that Jesus said something He did not. The thief hanging on the cross next to Jesus received a promise. But first look at this paragraph:

thenhesaidtojesuslordremembermewhenyoucomeintoyourkingdom andjesussaidtohimassuredlyisaytoyoutodayyouwillbewithmeinparadise

That is an English version of how ancient Greek was often written, with no spaces or punctuation at all.

I had a Greek teacher who was mean, ornery, and horrible sometimes (not really—it just seemed that way). One of the things he did to us was that if he missed a class, he would say that he believed that we paid good money for that class, so we should have something educational to do if he wasn't there. We did not like it when he was away, for then he would leave us a photocopy of a fragment of some kind of Greek manuscript, possibly from the Bible, possibly not. We would have to figure out what it said by the time he came back.

Why am I sharing this? Because in Luke 23:43 Jesus says to the thief on the cross, "Assuredly, I say to you," and then the word "today," and then "you will be with Me in Paradise." So where does the comma go—before or after "today"? It makes all the difference in the world where we put that comma. One way agrees with what we found to be taught in God's Word, and the other way appears to support the common Christian tradition that crept into the church later.

The verses and punctuation were placed in the English Bible centuries after it was written. So which place do you think the comma went? Translators placed it to reflect Christian tradition. So in your Bible you will probably see it as "Assuredly, I say to you, today you will be with Me in Paradise." This might make it appear that when they died, Jesus and the thief made it to heaven on Friday. But if true, it opens a whole can of worms. We will get to that problem shortly.

Placing the comma the other way, "Assuredly, I say to you today, you will be with Me in Paradise" simply means that Jesus had the authority to tell the thief, "You are forgiven, and you will live with Me forever in Paradise." When Jesus comes back to earth, the thief will be resurrected and go with Him to heaven.

Someone gave me a photocopy from a Lutheran Bible, the Concordant Literal New Testament, that puts the comma where I think it should go. "Verily I say unto you today, you will be with me in paradise." Remember that the translators could not go back to the original Greek to decide where the comma goes. It is not there. And so they could either position it according to the context of the whole Bible, or they could place it using tradition. Most people go by tradition, unfortunately.

Here is a literal translation of the verse: "And he said to Jesus, 'Remember me, Lord, when You come in the kingdom of You.' And said to him Jesus, 'Truly I say unto you, today with Me you will be in paradise.'"

Or is it this way? "And said to him Jesus, 'Truly I say unto you today, with Me you will be in paradise.' " If I'm wrong on that, and the comma did go before "today," and Jesus promised the thief they would be in Paradise together that very day, I have a question about John 20:17.

In John 20 Jesus meets Mary on the Sunday after His death. She grabs hold of His feet, and He says to her: "'Do not cling to Me, for I have not yet ascended to My Father'" (verse 17). Of course, God the Father is in heaven. If Jesus told the thief on Friday that they would both be in Paradise on Friday, then Jesus lied to the thief, because on Sunday He still had not gone to heaven yet. Do you realize that if the comma in most Bibles is correct, Jesus is a liar? But if you understand the comma to have been placed by human tradition, not by the context of God's Word, you know that there's nothing wrong with placing the comma after "today." Suddenly Jesus' words make sense. He was saying to the thief, "Verily I say unto you today, when I come back, you will be with Me in Paradise." Jesus could give that assurance while hanging on the cross, and the thief could relax and die in peace as far as possible. Certainly it still hurt to be on the cross, but the man's soul—his spirit, his being—could be at peace, because he was no longer worried about eternity.

What about the people who have been taken to heaven? It is true that some are already there. For every one of them, the Bible tells us how they got there.

Genesis 5:24 says that Enoch walked with God and was no more. Why? Enoch kept walking with God until he became so in tune with Him that God said, "Let's go back to My house." They had become so close that God just took him with Him to heaven.

In 2 Kings 2 God told Elijah that he would be translated to heaven without seeing death. One day a fiery chariot came down and scooped him up, and he took off in it. Elijah threw his mantle to Elisha, who became the next major prophet in Israel, and Elijah went to heaven. Wouldn't that have been an awesome ride? We will get to do the same thing. Remember that Revelation says that Jesus' coming looks like lightning, so the clouds might have some fire around them too, just as with Elijah's chariot.

And then there is Moses. He was not translated without seeing death, but died on top of a mountain. According to Jude 9 and Matthew 17:3, 4, Moses was resurrected. Jude says that it was Michael, the archangel or commander of the angels, who came to resurrect him, the same one who brings resurrection to us. (Scripture mentions both Jesus and God as being involved in resurrection.) So Moses was resurrected, and Satan argued with

God about it. Michael just replied, "The Lord rebuke you." And He took Moses anyway and raised him to life.

Why would Satan resist? He knows very well that the wages of sin is death. Had Moses sinned? Sure, if murder counts (Ex. 2:12). Doing things contrary to what God asks you to do—yes, Moses had sinned. So Moses was a sinner, and he died. Satan said, "He's mine! You can't have him!"

Jesus said, "Beat it!" and He raised Moses to life anyway. How did Jesus get away with it? In a way, He raised Moses on credit, because He had not yet died to remove the penalty for sin. Because Christ had not yet paid the price for human redemption, Satan naturally protested what the future Savior did.

Isn't it interesting that when Jesus was transfigured on the mountain into His heavenly glory (see Matt. 17:1-12), Elijah and Moses appeared and talked with Jesus. Can you picture the conversation they might have had with Him?

"Jesus, I'm Moses. If You don't go through with dying on the cross, Satan gets me back."

And Elijah might have added, "You know, I have never died, but if You don't go through with the cross, Satan gets me, and You know what he's going to do to me." Both of them realized what was on the line. God sent two human beings from heaven to make sure that Jesus understood the stakes involved with the cross. One of them, Elijah, represents those who are translated alive at the end of time, and Moses, all the rest, who have died and are waiting for the resurrection.

Matthew 27 talks about another interesting group. At the moment Jesus died, "the graves were opened; and many bodies of the saints who had fallen asleep were raised; and coming out of the graves after His resurrection, they went into the holy city and appeared to many" (verse 52). I would love to have seen that. The rabble had gotten away with killing Jesus, and suddenly a bunch of people who had been dead come to talk to them. I can picture the priests and the rulers getting a little shaken up by that. As for how many people were resurrected to life when Jesus died, we just don't know.

According to Ephesians 4, when Jesus went back to heaven, he took "captivity" captive with Him. Paul is using an ancient imagery of a conqueror displaying a few trophies. Here's my belief: Jesus took to heaven with Him that small group of people who were resurrected at His death. And I have a sneaking suspicion it might have totaled 24 people. Revelation 4:10 talks about 24 elders in heaven. While I don't know for sure, they might be those raised to life Resurrection weekend.

Some have asked about Revelation 6:9, 10: "I saw under the altar the souls of those who had been slain for the word of God and for the testimony which they held. And they cried with a loud voice, saying, 'How long, O Lord, holy and true, until You judge and avenge our blood on those who dwell on the earth?'" The suggestion is that the souls under the altar are in heaven. But here is what God said about Abel after his brother Cain killed him: "What have you done? The voice of your brother's blood cries out to Me from the ground" (Gen. 4:10). Here the voice coming from the ground is symbolic of Cain's guilt. Similarly, the blood of those killed by the beast power calls out symbolically from the ground—from under the altar. The death of the saints needs to be avenged. But the saints are not literally stuck under an altar in heaven. Soon Jesus will return and will bring the saints back to life.

You may be wondering, "Is this just what Seventh-day Adventists teach?" Thankfully, the answer is no. I went to a Baptist funeral one day, and at most Baptist funerals I'm used to hearing that the person has gone straight to heaven and is now up there waiting. But in this one the preacher had the person waiting in the grave for the resurrection. I thought, *Wow! This guy is reflecting Scripture. I'm not used to this.* So I waited until everybody had cleared out, and I walked up to the pastor and said, "Sir, I was listening to your presentation very closely. So did you just leave him sleeping in the grave, waiting for the resurrection?" You should have seen his expression. He bristled as he was getting ready to fight with me.

"Well, isn't that what the Bible says?" he replied. As a Baptist pastor, he got hit pretty hard every time he said that, I'm sure.

I said, "Brother," and I felt brotherly right then, because we were agreeing, "I'm just not used to hearing it. I agree with you, sir."

As he relaxed, I said, "I'm just glad to hear it."

You see, it is good news. It is good news for somebody like me, who has lost a loved one. As I walked out of that hospital in Houston, Texas, after my daughter died, I looked up at the moon—it was daytime, but the moon was still out. Turning to my wife, I said, "Karen, from Jennifer's perspective, she's probably about passing the moon by now."

My wife looked at me strangely, so I added, "You know, because she goes to sleep in death, and the next thing she knows is the resurrection. So give her a few minutes after the resurrection, and we're all together on that cloud, going past the moon. Right now I want to think of it from her perspective, not mine." When you die, you are asleep until Jesus rings the alarm, when He comes and blasts His trumpet. He shouts, we wake up and meet our loved ones, then we go home with Him.

CHAPTER 14

The Millennium and the New Earth

A t that time Michael shall stand up, the great prince who stands watch over the sons of your people; and there shall be a time of trouble, such as never was since there was a nation, even to that time. And at that time your people shall be delivered, every one who is found written in the book. And many of those who sleep in the dust of the earth shall awake, some to everlasting life, some to shame and everlasting contempt. Those who are wise shall shine like the brightness of the firmament, and those who turn many to righteousness like the stars forever and ever" (Dan. 12:1-3).

These verses in the Old Testament are the basic outline for Revelation 20, 21, and 22. We have seen how God's people go through the plagues untouched and how, at the end of that time, Jesus returns to rescue them and resurrect those of His followers who have already died. In Revelation 20 we find two resurrections—one for the saved, and one for those who are not saved.

The first resurrection happens at the beginning of the 1,000-year period we call the millennium. You will not find the word "millennium" in a concordance, because it is not in the Bible. But Revelation does present the 1,000 years. The millennium begins with the second advent of Jesus.

The saved ones are happy when Jesus comes. "And it will be said in that day: 'Behold, this is our God; we have waited for Him, and He will save us. This is the Lord; we have waited for Him; we will be glad and rejoice in His salvation'" (Isa. 25:9). When we are God's people and Jesus arrives on His divine rescue mission, we will exclaim, "Yes! Finally! Jesus, I've been waiting for this day. Praise the Lord, You've come back to get us out of here."

On the flip side, the lost are not so happy about it.

"Then the sky receded as a scroll when it is rolled up, and every mountain and island was moved out of its place. And the kings of the earth, the great men, the rich men, the commanders, the mighty men, every slave and every free man, hid themselves in the caves and in the rocks of the mountains, and said to the mountains and rocks, 'Fall on us and hide us from the face of Him who sits on the throne and from the wrath of the Lamb! For the great day of His wrath has come, and who is able to stand?'" (Rev. 6:14-17).

The choices we make in life are important. At the Second Coming we will be either praising the Lord or hiding and pleading for the rocks and mountains to fall on us. Everyone will have already made their decision. "He who is unjust, let him be unjust still; he who is filthy, let him be filthy still; he who is righteous, let him be righteous still; he who is holy, let him be holy still" (Rev. 22:11). From the moment Michael stands up, the judgment is over. It has determined the case of everyone. From that time on there is no chance to change sides. By the beginning of the plagues every person has made their decision as to whether they are going to greet Jesus with joy or flee from Him when He comes.

The millennium commences with the Second Coming and the gathering of the saints at the first resurrection. "I saw thrones, and they sat on them, and judgment was committed to them. Then I saw the souls of those who had been beheaded for their witness to Jesus and for the word of God, who had not worshiped the beast or his image, and had not received his mark on their foreheads or on their hands. And they lived and reigned with Christ for a thousand years. But the rest of the dead did not live again until the thousand years were finished. This is the first resurrection. Blessed and holy is he who has part in the first resurrection. Over such the second death has no power, but they shall be priests of God and of Christ, and shall reign with Him a thousand years" (Rev. 20:4-6).

When does that resurrection happen? First Thessalonians 4 tells us:

"I do not want you to be ignorant, brethren, concerning those who have fallen asleep, lest you sorrow as others who have no hope. For if we believe that Jesus died and rose again, even so God will bring with Him those who sleep in Jesus.

"For this we say to you by the word of the Lord, that we who are alive and remain until the coming of the Lord will by no means precede those who are asleep. For the Lord Himself will descend from heaven with a shout, with the voice of an archangel, and with the trumpet of God. And the dead in Christ will rise first. Then we who are alive and remain shall be caught up together with them in the clouds to meet the Lord in the air.

And thus we shall always be with the Lord" (verses 13-17).

The Second Coming will be the time of the first resurrection and the start of the 1,000 years. The book of John confirms it: "Do not marvel at this; for the hour is coming in which all who are in the graves will hear His voice and come forth—those who have done good, to the resurrection of life, and those who have done evil, to the resurrection of condemnation" (John 5:28, 29).

Notice that Daniel, John, and Revelation speak of two resurrections. But Revelation tells us of a 1,000-year period between them.

The glory of Jesus returning to earth is accompanied by a scene of dying and death. Revelation 19:11 and then verses 17 and following describe what we might call a fowls' feast.

"Now I saw heaven opened, and behold, a white horse. And He who sat on him was called Faithful and True, and in righteousness He judges and makes war. . . . Then I saw an angel standing in the sun; and he cried with a loud voice, saying to all the birds that fly in the midst of heaven, 'Come and gather together for the supper of the great God, that you may eat the flesh of kings, the flesh of captains, the flesh of mighty men, the flesh of horses and of those who sit on them, and the flesh of all people, free and slave, both small and great.'

"And I saw the beast, the kings of the earth, and their armies, gathered together to make war against Him who sat on the horse and against His army."

Jesus will return at the end of the plagues. At that time, Satan and a vast army gather to fight against God, and here He is, heading toward earth. "Then the beast was captured, and with him the false prophet who worked signs in his presence, by which he deceived those who received the mark of the beast and those who worshiped his image. These two were cast alive into the lake of fire" (Rev. 19:20). "The lawless one will be revealed, whom the Lord will consume with the breath of His mouth and destroy with the brightness of His coming" (2 Thess. 2:8). The lawless one is the beast power, and he perishes in the lake of fire at the second advent of Jesus. We have a lake of fire for the beast and the false prophet.

What happens to all the people who followed the two false powers? Rev. 19:21: "And the rest were killed with the sword which proceeded from the mouth of Him who sat on the horse. And all the birds were filled with their flesh." They are not destroyed in the lake of fire but by the sword that comes from the mouth of Jesus Christ. Only the beast and the false prophet get thrown into the lake of fire when Jesus returns. The glory of His coming kills the rest.

Second Thessalonians 1:7, 8 says that at the return of Jesus the brightness of His coming kills those who refused to follow Him. "And to give you who are troubled rest with us when the Lord Jesus is revealed from heaven with His mighty angels, in flaming fire taking vengeance on those who do not know God, and on those who do not obey the gospel of our Lord Jesus Christ."

The Second Coming will divide everyone into four classes:

1. *The righteous who are still alive.* They are changed to their perfect form in a moment, and they go up in the clouds to meet Jesus.

2. *The righteous who have previously died.* Resurrected, they ascend into the clouds to meet Jesus Christ, and He will take them to heaven with Him.

3. *The wicked who are alive at the Second Advent.* In terror they beg for the rocks and the mountains to bury them, only to perish from the brightness of His coming. The symbolic language of Revelation depicts them as being killed by the sword coming from Jesus' mouth—again the brightness of His coming. The living wicked all die.

4. *The wicked who have previously died.* Not resurrected yet, they are still asleep in death, waiting for the end of the 1,000 years.

The saints will live and rule in heaven during the millennium. "They lived and reigned with Christ for a thousand years. . . . Blessed and holy is he who has part in the first resurrection. Over such the second death has no power, but they

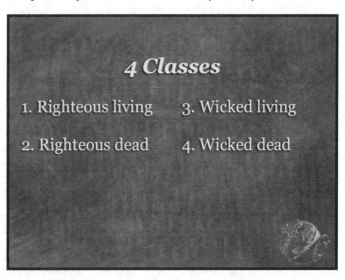

4 Classes

1. Righteous living   3. Wicked living

2. Righteous dead   4. Wicked dead

shall be priests of God and of Christ, and shall reign with Him a thousand years" (Rev. 20:4-6). "You shall rest," God said to Daniel, "and will arise to your inheritance at the end of the days" (Dan. 12:13). The ancient prophet will receive his reward at the beginning of the 1,000 years.

Where will we be during that 1,000-year period? John 14:1, 2: "Let not your heart be troubled; you believe in God, believe also in Me. In My Father's house are many mansions; if it were not so, I would have told you. I go to prepare a place for you." God has promised us some time with Him in heaven. At His coming He takes us to be with Him.

The saints live and reign with Christ, but Revelation 20 tells us that they will also be judging, a role alluded to in 1 Corinthians 6:1, 2: "Dare any of you, having a matter against another, go to law before the unrighteous, and not before the saints? Do you not know that the saints will judge the world? And if the world will be judged by you, are you unworthy to judge the smallest matters?" God's people do not judge anyone now. While God is conducting a judgment in heaven at the moment, His followers do not participate with Him. But during the 1,000 years they will review the case of every person who has ever lived.

Jesus brings His family into the New Jerusalem in heaven. It will be wonderful. I'm really not impressed so much by the streets of gold as what the Bible says about no more pain, suffering, or death. I could happily live on dirt streets in a world with no pain and death, no suffering at all. But God throws in the golden streets and all the rest of it as well.

What happens to Satan at the coming of Jesus and during the 1,000 years? One thing you can be sure of: he will not be in heaven to bother you.

"Then I saw an angel coming down from heaven, having the key to the bottomless pit and a great chain in his hand. He laid hold of the dragon, that serpent of old, who is the Devil and Satan, and bound him for a thousand years; and he cast him into the bottomless pit, and shut him up, and set a seal on him, so that he should deceive the nations no more till the thousand years were finished. But after these things he must be released for a little while" (Rev. 20:1-3).

Some have taught that the millennium has already begun, but that would mean Satan is already bound. I like Billy Graham's answer to that one: if Satan is already confined, it's by a rubber band that stretches from pole to pole. In other words, he is still bouncing all over the place in our world and still tempting people.

The text makes clear that Satan is bound here on earth, and it will be desolate during the 1,000 years. The Greek word for bottomless pit, *abussos,* is the same word that the Septuagint, the Greek Old Testament, used to translate the Hebrew phrase "without form and void" in Genesis 1:2. Before Creation, when the earth was without life, it was "without form, and void." When Jesus returns, the saved are either resurrected or transformed and then taken to heaven, while the wicked who rejected salvation will all die. No living people will remain on earth. The world goes back to its lifeless state, as it was in the beginning.

Jeremiah 25:33: "And at that day the slain of the Lord shall be from one end of the earth even to the other end of the earth. They shall not be lamented, or gathered, or buried; they shall become refuse on the ground." If nobody is left alive on earth, no one will be around to bury what is left of them. Revelation uses the imagery of birds having a feast. So at this time the earth will be full of desolate, empty cities and piles of corpses. Satan is stuck on a lifeless planet with no one to tempt.

Satan had said earlier: "I will ascend into heaven, I will exalt my throne above the stars of God. . . . I will be like the Most High" (Isa. 14:13, 14). He thought he could run the world better than God. And so God says, "You cannot leave the world for 1,000 years, and nobody is left alive on it." I don't know what the devil will look like at this stage. Will he appear as an angel or a demon? I have no idea. But he will be stuck in solitary confinement on a totally ruined planet with no people on it, with plenty of time to think about what's he's done. Satan has read the prophecy. He knows what comes next, and it is not good for him.

The End of the Thousand Years

Satan is bound "that he should deceive the nations no more till the thousand years were finished. But after these things he must be released for a little while" (Rev. 20:3).

"When the thousand years have expired, Satan will be released from his prison and will go out to deceive the nations which are in the four corners of the earth, Gog and Magog, to gather them together to battle, whose number is as the sand of the sea" (verses 7, 8). The devil immediately gathers a huge army. But where does it come from? All those who perished when Jesus returned at the beginning of the 1,000 years, and all those who had died in sin before He came back—all of the wicked from all time—are now resurrected. Once more Satan has people to deceive again.

Daniel 12:1, 2: "At that time your people shall be delivered, every one who is found written in the book. And many of those who sleep in the dust of the earth shall awake, some to everlasting life, some to shame and everlasting contempt." Revelation 20 told us that we want to be in the first resurrection, because those who come back to life at the second resurrection face the lake of fire and the second death—everlasting contempt.

The Holy City Transfers to Earth

At this time the New Jerusalem descends to the earth. "Then I, John, saw the holy city, New Jerusalem, coming down out of heaven from God, prepared as a bride adorned for her husband." "And he carried me away in the Spirit to a great and high mountain, and showed me the great city, the holy Jerusalem, descending out of heaven from God" (Rev. 21:2, 10). The New Jerusalem is a huge city that may be half the size of the United States, and it is as tall as it is wide. In the description in Revelation 21 the wording in the original Greek may be depicting a city approximately 1,400 miles in total circumference, or it may be saying the city is 1,400 miles along each side. Either way, it is a large and beautiful city. You could probably put everyone who ever lived on earth in a city that size.

You may consider a rocket taking off into space as awesome. Just wait until God flies the New Jerusalem down to our world. And it will be a perfect landing. I'm expecting to have fun riding in that city.

Revelation 20 describes what Satan will do next. "Now when the thousand years have expired, Satan will be released from his prison and will go out to deceive the nations which are in the four corners of the earth, Gog and Magog, to gather them together to battle, whose number is as the sand of the sea. They went up on the breadth of the earth and surrounded the camp of the saints and the beloved city" (verses 7-9).

As soon as the city is in place on earth, a vast army of both ancient and modern soldiers from every era in history will immediately surround it. Perhaps they will try to assemble nuclear weapons, doing whatever they can to try to seize God's city that He brought down to our world. Satan with all his hosts is getting ready to attack.

Jesus said that there are more lost than saved. The leaders of the satanic armies know that they outnumber those inside the city. But because God the Father and Jesus are in the city, just those two outweigh Satan's forces. But the hordes of the lost will advance to attack the city. Then fire rains down from God out of heaven and devours them all.

Some people ask me about Gog and Magog attacking the nation of Israel and the rebuilding of the Temple as the fulfillment of Ezekiel 38-48. Remember that for God's people who have accepted Christ and are His true Israel today, the promises for Israel keep getting bigger and better. In Ezekiel 38-48 the enemies that would have attacked God's people if they had been faithful to God were Gog and Magog. That long-ago nation of Israel would have had a wonderful Temple if the people had been faithful after the Babylonian captivity, but they were not. Because the old Israel did not meet the conditions of the prophecy, the promise of Gog and Magog attacking ancient Jerusalem and of deliverance did not happen. Instead, the attack of Gog and Magog has moved down to the end of time—to the New Jerusalem—in Revelation 20. There we find the promise of God raining fire down on the massive armies. He keeps the promise of Ezekiel 38-48 for His true Israel, for those who live by faith. His people in the old nation of Israel did not cash in on the promises. But God's people of faith from all time experience the fulfillment at the end of the 1,000 years.

In times past people kept claiming that God's ways were all based on the Temple, that it was His sole focus. But God said: "'Amend your ways and your doings, and I will cause you to dwell in this place. Do not trust in these lying words, saying, "The temple of the Lord, the temple of the Lord, the temple of the Lord are these"'" (Jer. 7:3, 4). Today many look for a temple to be rebuilt in Jerusalem before Jesus returns. I believe this is the "lying words" again. A widespread contemporary prophetic viewpoint teaches things that do not match the Bible. As we have seen, it predicts a seven-year tribulation after the return of Jesus, offers a second chance for people to choose Jesus during the seven years, teaches that the beast is yet to come sometime in the future, and that a third temple will be built in Jerusalem. As we saw in chapter 12, if someone should erect a third temple and people begin to offer sacrifices again, they will be blaspheming, because Jesus was the sacrifice for all time. They would be denying that Jesus is already our Savior and the Lamb of God. I'm not saying there never will be a temple in Jerusalem again, but if there is, it will not be God's temple.

Revelation said that fire covers the face of the earth at this time. (I think God has a good air-conditioning system in that New Jerusalem.) I have heard some people say the lake of fire is down in the center of the earth somewhere. But the Bible depicts it as on the face of the earth, and it calls it the second death. "Death and Hades were cast into the lake of fire. This is the second death. And anyone not found written in the Book of Life was cast into the lake of fire" (Rev. 20:14, 15). With this fire God erases every trace of sin. He is cleaning up the mess forever.

You do not see the beast and the false prophet at the end of the 1,000 years. Consigned to the lake of fire at the beginning of the millennium, they completely perished. Anything thrown into the lake of fire is never seen again. And now, at the end of the 1,000 years, Satan and all his followers also get cast into the lake of fire, and they will never appear again.

When He is finished burning up all traces of evil and sin, Jesus creates a new world for humanity. "I saw a new heaven and a new earth, for the first heaven and the first earth had passed away. Also there was no more sea" (Rev. 21:1). I wasn't around the first time God created the world, but this time I plan on observing His acts of creation. Can you just picture Him announcing, "Let there be grass and trees" and there they are? "Let there be birds in the sky," and they appear! "Lord, I want to be right where You're going to make that elephant. I want to see an elephant appear out of thin air. Thank You, Lord, that is great!" It's going to be awesome to watch God create a new heaven and a new earth. The lion will lie down with the lamb, and there will be no suffering and no pain, for the former things have passed away. That's the promise God gave us.

Most awesome of all is that we will get to walk and talk with Jesus. The One who died to save us, the One who cleansed our record so that we could live forever with Him, the One who gave us the ability to do good works so that He could reward us according to what He Himself helped us to do—that is the One we get to walk and talk with forever and ever.

But you may wonder about the fate of the lost. "Pastor Tim, don't the wicked people burn forever and ever and ever? for millions and millions of years?" Let's look at the biblical evidence. As we've seen, fire comes down from God, something Scripture calls the second death. But where did the fire go? If flames spread across the face of the earth and now the earth is wonderfully remade, what happened to the fire?

I suggest that we go by the Bible's definition of eternal and unquenchable fire, not by the traditional explanation. It's better to follow Scripture. Second Peter 2:9 declares: "The Lord knows how to deliver the godly out of temptations and to reserve the unjust under punishment for the day of judgment." That means the wicked who died and are now sleeping in the grave are being held for the hellfire. They are not in hellfire yet. That happens at the end of the 1,000 years.

If people went straight to hell for dying in sin to burn and burn and burn, would that be fair? Imagine that I commit a murder now, and Cain murdered somebody 6,000 years ago, and neither of us asks God to forgive us. It would not be fair that Cain suffered 6,000 extra years for the same crime. But if we both die the sleep of death and are resurrected at the end of the 1,000 years, and we receive the same punishment at the same time, then God is fair and just. The Lord is reserving for punishment those who were unjust in times past. They are sleeping in death until He brings them forth at the second resurrection—the resurrection of damnation, as the Bible calls it.

Matthew 13:49, 50 explains that at the end of the world, God will do something just like fishermen sorting the good catch from the bad. The angels will separate the wicked from the just and cast them into the furnace of the fire, and there will be wailing and gnashing of teeth. Is that happening now, or does it come at the end of the world? The Bible says that we do not have an immortal soul, so the wicked cannot be punished now, because the dead know nothing. The wicked never receive immortality. Only God's people do, and then only at the first resurrection. The people of the second resurrection face the second death. They do not have immortality, and they are not punished forever, which is actually kindness on God's part.

Now take a look at what happens to Satan when he gets cast into the fire. Ezekiel 28:12 talks about the king of Tyre. "You were the seal of perfection, full of wisdom and perfect in beauty. You were in Eden, the garden of God." Who was in Eden? Adam, Eve, God—and Satan. But not the king of Tyre. Rather, the king of Tyre serves as a metaphor for Satan as well as a representative of a neighboring people who afflicted Israel.

Satan had been an angel in heaven. "You were the anointed cherub who covers; I established you; you were on the holy mountain of God; you walked back and forth in the midst of fiery stones" (verse 14). He was the guardian cherub. "You were perfect in your ways from the day you were created, till iniquity was found in you. By the abundance of your trading you became filled with violence within, and you sinned; therefore I cast you as a profane thing out of the mountain of God" (verses 15, 16). Repeatedly in Scripture we have a description of Satan being cast or driven out of heaven. (Here Ezekiel shifts back more to the imagery of the king of Tyre, whose people were noted traders in the ancient world.)

"And I destroyed you, O covering cherub, from the midst of the fiery stones. Your heart was lifted up because of your beauty; you corrupted your wisdom for the sake of your splendor; I cast you to the ground, I laid you before kings, that they might gaze at you. You defiled your sanctuaries by the multitude of your iniquities, by the iniquity of your trading; therefore I brought fire from your midst; it devoured you, and I turned you to ashes upon the earth in the sight of all who saw you. All who knew you among the peoples are astonished at you; you have become a horror, and shall be no more forever" (verses 16-19).

What happens to Satan? He is reduced to ashes on the earth. He will be "no more forever."

Did you notice that this passage is written in the past tense? How would you like to be Satan, and God is already talking about you in past tense? If you had been kidnapped and became somebody's captive, for example, and they started talking about you in the past tense, is that a good sign? Remember that when Satan reminds you of your past, you should remind him of his future. That is what God was doing in Ezekiel 28.

The last verse in that passage says Satan will "become a horror, and shall be no more forever." Does this leave him in charge of hell? No! Rather, he is no more. He is gone forever. That should give you a clue about what happened to the fire.

The soul of the sinner shall die, the Bible emphatically declares. We do not have immortal souls. There is only one way out of this dilemma, and that is to have our sins forgiven. After God pardons them, we do not have any sins on our record, so we are no longer sinners and will not die. But if our sins are not forgiven, we will die for ever and be no more.

Remember this famous verse? "God so loved the world that He gave His only begotten Son, that whoever believes in Him should not perish but have everlasting life" (John 3:16). What are the options here? We either have everlasting life or perish. Did Jesus say you have a choice between everlasting life or punishment without end? No, He has never presented the alternative to everlasting life as never-ending torture in a fire. Rather, He said that we would live or perish. Right there in John 3:16 you have a choice between living with Jesus forever or being a scattering of ashes, as Satan will be.

"'Behold, the day is coming, burning like an oven, and all the proud, yes, all who do wickedly will be stubble. And the day which is coming shall burn them up,' says the Lord of hosts. 'That will leave them neither root nor branch. But to you who fear My name the Sun of Righteousness shall arise with healing in His wings; and you shall go out and grow fat like stall-fed calves. You shall trample the wicked, for they shall be ashes under the soles of your feet on the day that I do this,' says the Lord of hosts" (Mal. 4:1-3). Here we have ashes again, this time under the soles of our feet. When the fire is over and the ashes have cooled, you can walk on them. God cleans up the world with fire, burning up all traces of sin. After the fire, God re-creates our planet.

"God will wipe away every tear from their eyes; there shall be no more death, nor sorrow, nor crying; and there shall be no more pain, for the former things have passed away" (Rev. 21:4). Notice that this does not happen at the beginning of the 1,000 years but at the end. I believe there is no pain or suffering in heaven, but I note with interest that God wipes away tears right after that final fire. I think it is because some of us on the inside of the New Jerusalem—perhaps all of us—will have a loved one out there on the wrong side of the wall. Perhaps that power of re-creation, watching God re-create, will help wipe away the tears.

Is there any good news in the fire? The wicked who refuse to trust in Jesus Christ are put out of their misery and will be no more. They will not be tortured eternally. God is love, and He is fair. He is like a good vet who puts a suffering animal out of its misery.

You might wonder where the teaching of eternal torture in hell came from. It emerged in the early church by at least the second century A.D. Several early Christian writers such as Justin Martyr and Irenæus wrote about the eternal punishment of the wicked but asserted that the wicked would finally be destroyed. Unfortunately, many converts to Christianity were educated in pagan concepts. Gradually the idea from Greek mythology (put forward soon after the death of the apostle John) that the disembodied souls of the wicked would stay in Hades found a place in Christian thinking. Sometime after A.D. 200 the Church Father Tertullian wrote plainly that the wicked would be tortured in hell forever. The view caught on and spread in later Christianity.* But the doctrine of eternal torture of the wicked does not appear in the Bible. The God of heaven does not torture people. He cleans up the earth and allows those who refuse to live in a perfect, sinless world to be no more.

What about the phrase that says the smoke ascends "forever and ever" (Rev. 14:11)? We need to find the truth about that kind of "forever" term. More than 50 times the Bible employs the word "forever" for something that had an end. Here is one of the examples. "Then his master shall bring him to the judges. He shall also bring him to the door, or to the doorpost, and his master shall pierce his ear with an awl; and he shall serve him forever" (Ex. 21:6). In ancient Israel you were supposed to set a servant free after seven years. But if a servant really liked his master and said, "I don't want to go free, and I want to be a servant for life," then the master would take an awl, and the servant would put his ear against the door frame of the master's house. The master would drive the awl through the servant's earlobe and into the doorframe, symbolizing that the servant was attached to the master's house for life. However, the ritual did not mean that the servant would stay with the master forever but rather until he died. Again and again in the Bible the word "forever" indicates that something lasted until death.

People often said, "O king, live forever." It was not because they thought the king was never going to die. They meant, "O king, may you have a long and prosperous reign until you die." However, when Jesus says to His people, "You will live forever and ever," and then He adds, "and you will never die," He means that God's people will not finally be overcome by death. The wicked are burned in the lake of fire, but there is an end to their life—the second death. It is not a fire burning them without stop.

What about the unquenchable fire in Jeremiah 17:27? "If you will not heed Me to hallow the Sabbath day, such as not carrying a burden when entering the gates of Jerusalem on the Sabbath day, then I will kindle a fire in its gates, and it shall devour the palaces of Jerusalem, and it shall not be quenched." God would send unquenchable fire against Jerusalem if the people did not obey His commandment. They did not obey, and invaders destroyed their city. But I've been to Jerusalem, and it is not still in flames. If my house caught fire and the fire department could not extinguish the flames, does that mean that 100 years later my house would still be burning? No, the fire consumed all the fuel and left a pile of ashes. Once Satan and all of his people begin to burn, no one can put out that fire until they turn to ashes. Thus once the fire starts, nothing can stop it until it has finished its work.

Jude 7 compares the fate of the wicked with Sodom and Gomorrah: "As Sodom and Gomorrah, and the cities around them in a similar manner to these, having given themselves over to sexual immorality and gone after strange flesh, are set forth as an example, suffering the vengeance of eternal fire." Almost the same thought comes from 2 Peter 2:6: "Turning the cities of Sodom and Gomorrah into ashes, condemned them to destruction, making them an example to those who afterward would live ungodly." Archaeologists know that Sodom and Gomorrah existed, because the records of other cities refer to them and even call them the sin cities. They were somewhere around the Dead Sea. But I have stood on Masada, looking down into the Dead Sea basin, and no cities were on fire down there. These are examples of "eternal" fire, but where do we find them now? The cities are burned up and gone.

Satan will be a pile of ashes and no one will find him, just as happened with Sodom and Gomorrah. Sinners will be gone. If you refuse forgiveness, you end up like those ancient cities and become ashes, and you will be no more. This is eternal punishment, not eternal punishing.

Once I was at a prayer breakfast, and a businessman came in and sat down at the table. "What do you do?" he inquired.

"I'm a pastor."

"Oh, which church?"

"Seventh-day Adventist Church."

"That's the church that doesn't believe in hell, isn't it?"

I smiled and said, "Oh, we believe in a hell, just a hotter one than you do."

Looking at me strangely, he asked, "What? What do you mean, 'a hotter one'?"

"We believe in one hot enough to do the job. It can reduce Satan and sinners into a pile of ashes and put an end to sin and suffering. You believe in a hell that's only partway hot enough and that God isn't really powerful enough to get rid of sin and suffering."

The Bible declares that God is strong enough, and that He reduces wickedness to ashes until it is no more.

Most assume the existence of an eternal hell, because of the belief that sinners have an eternal soul. But the Bible says that they do not. Only those who are forgiven receive immortality, and it begins at the return of Jesus. The sinners thrown into the lake of fire perish because they are mortal. The fire is hot enough to do the job.

What would we say about God's character if He had a fire just hot enough to torture but not hot enough to destroy? Suppose you had a neighbor who liked to torture people, and he had a dungeon in the basement, and you could hear screaming in it. *But,* you think to yourself, *my neighbor is actually kind and nice, because he only keeps people on the edge of death. He never lets anybody die. He tortures them year after year after year, and I can hear their constant anguish.* Would you want to visit that neighbor?

But this is what people have taught about God. The teaching goes all the way back to Satan in the garden. "You won't really die," he lied. "You'll become like God—immortal." This teaching has made God look like a horrible being. The truth is that He allows sinners to have an end to their misery. Then He re-creates the sinless earth, having gotten rid of the sin problem forever. He is big enough and loving enough to have a fire that's hot enough.

The question comes up, Why does God go through all the trouble of bringing the wicked back to life a second time, just to destroy them? Have you ever wondered that?

I visited a church while traveling, and they had a Bible study discussion going. A guy raised his hand and asked, "Why didn't God just get rid of Satan when he had his first sinful thoughts? Why not just take him for a long walk and make sure he never came back?" After all, ultimately that's what God is going to do, isn't He? God will reduce Satan to ashes, and the devil will be no more.

Raising my hand, I said, "Anybody want to go on a long walk with God after that? I mean, if people go on a long walk with Him and they never, ever come back, I wouldn't want to walk with Him at all."

The question to ask is this: What if God wiped out sin and suffering a little too early? If Satan got the message out that God is not fair, and then the Lord eliminated Satan, who would you think was right in the dispute? You would regard Satan as correct. And so God has to let the whole thing play out all the way, in order to make sure that sin does not resurface and so that there will be no questions about it afterward.

Your Questions Answered

Let's say that I am a man who died believing in Jesus. Resurrected, I rise to meet Jesus and my loved ones in the clouds, and then I am taken up to heaven. We go into the New Jerusalem, and God says, "You probably have some questions."

"I have a question. Why isn't my aunt here?"

"OK," God replies, "I'm going to open up the record books, and you can see for yourself. You can view all the records, and you can see all that I tried to do." Remember that the Bible tells us that we will judge everyone during the 1,000 years. So I open up the books, and there I discover how God tried to reach my loved one and how she repeatedly spurned Him. I see when God used me to try to reach her, and she rejected what I sought to share about Jesus Christ. By now I realize that God left no stone unturned to get her into salvation and to bring her into the New Jerusalem. But she would not accept. For 1,000 years God opens the records and answers all of our questions.

You know who is really on trial? God. Was He fair with that earlier judgment, the one that happened before Jesus returned to save His people? Was He fair when He decided whom to resurrect to everlasting life and whom He did not? We now get to examine the records and put our stamp of approval on His decisions.

You might be thinking that if the rebellious ones could only see the New Jerusalem and what they were missing, they would change their tune and accept. Just to make sure you know that He did not mess it up, what does God do at the end of the 1,000 years? "OK, let's go back down to earth," He announces, and He flies the whole city down there. He resurrects all the wicked, and they can watch the New Jerusalem approach. But what do they do? They follow Satan! Then Satan rallies them together, because He is their chosen leader, and they join him in a last attack on God. As they advance on the city, I look over the city wall and see my loved one, the very one about whom I had asked, "Why isn't she here?" My aunt looks up at me, and I realize that she is willing to kill me to seize the city.

That's what sin does. Sin makes us into hard, evil people when we reject the Holy Spirit and no longer allow it to work in our hearts. Sinners become completely devoted to Satan. They are possessed, and they will kill all of us if they get the chance.

Finally, God says, "That is enough," and He pours fire down, something He calls His "strange act" (Isa. 28:21). He does not want to do it—He loves the sinners, too. But He destroys them, reducing them to ashes. Now I turn to God and see tears in His eyes. The Lord has to wipe the tears from His own eyes, too. "Jesus, I understand," I tell Him. "Thank You for stopping them. Thank You." Never again will I question God about whether He was right. If He had pulled the plug too quickly, some people would still be wondering about His justice. Did He really give everyone every chance? But I have seen that the wicked are not interested in changing.

Don't wait for a second chance. It never comes. Now is the time to trust Jesus Christ, to let Him cleanse you from sin.

"Not everyone who says to Me, 'Lord, Lord,' shall enter the kingdom of heaven, but he who does the will of My Father in heaven" (Matt. 7:21). You actually have to do more than just say that you are a Christian—you have to actually live it. To be truly Christian, you have to let Him be Lord and Savior, not just to forgive the past but to take over lordship of the present. As a result you do whatever He asks you to do, and you won't let your boss, your family, or anyone else decide for you.

"Many will say to Me in that day, 'Lord, Lord, have we not prophesied in Your name, cast out demons in Your name, and done many wonders in Your name?'" (verse 22). Remember the false prophet that we said would appear at the end, performing miracles and wonders? It cast out demons in God's name and did many amazing things in His name. Jesus warned that there would be false signs and wonders and counterfeit miracles. But then God declares to those who did them: "I never knew you; depart from Me, you who practice lawlessness!" (verse 23).

If you break one of the commandments, you've dishonored them all, Jesus said. The Sabbath, adultery, lying—don't shrug off any of them. It doesn't matter how many good things you do. Your destiny depends on whether or not you are trusting Him.

"Therefore whoever hears these sayings of Mine, and does them, I will liken him to a wise man who built his house on the rock: and the rain descended, the floods came, and the winds blew and beat on that house; and it did not fall, for it was founded on the rock.

"Now everyone who hears these sayings of Mine, and does not do them, will be like a foolish man who built his house on the sand: and the rain descended, the floods came, and the winds blew and beat on that house; and it fell. And great was its fall" (verses 24-27).

God's Word is the authority. Have you surrendered your life to it? Trust Him completely. You don't have a second chance to change.

---

* The outline of this historical change comes from Thomas B. Thayer, *The Origin and History of the Doctrine of Endless Punishment* (Boston: Universalist Publishing House, 1855), chap. 6. Available online at www.tentmaker.org/books/OriginandHistory.html.

Appendix A

Comparison of Daniel 11:2-12:4 With Historical Events

Prophecy Daniel 11:2–22	Historical/projected Fulfillment
2 And now I will tell you the truth: Behold, three more kings will arise in Persia, and the fourth shall be far richer than them all; by his strength, through his riches, he shall stir up all against the realm of Greece.	1. Cambyses II (530-521 B.C.) 2. Smerdis (521 B.C.) 3. Darius I (521-485 B.C.) 4. Xerxes (486-465 B.C.), excelling in wealth and power, launched an elaborate campaign against Greece and lost.
3 Then a mighty king shall arise, who shall rule with great dominion, and do according to his will. **4** And when he has arisen, his kingdom shall be broken up and divided toward the four winds of heaven, but not among his posterity nor according to his dominion with which he ruled; for his kingdom shall be uprooted, even for others besides these.	Alexander the Great (336-323 B.C.). Four lesser kingdoms emerged from the rubble of Alexander's empire: Greece, Asia Minor, Syria, and Egypt, a four-part breakup indicated in Daniel 7:6 and 8:8. Daniel 11 describes world powers that would attack Palestine from the northern or southern land invasion routes. If not specified, it is from the north.

5 "Also the king of the South shall become strong, as well as one of his princes; and he shall gain power over him and have dominion. His dominion shall be a great dominion. 6 And at the end of some years they shall join forces, for the daughter of the king of the South shall go to the king of the North to make an agreement; but she shall not retain the power of her authority, and neither he nor his authority shall stand; but she shall be given up, with those who brought her, and with him who begot her, and with him who strengthened her in those times.

7 But from a branch of her roots one shall arise in his place, who shall come with an army, enter the fortress of the king of the North, and deal with them and prevail. 8 And he shall also carry their gods captive to Egypt, with their princes and their precious articles of silver and gold; and he shall continue more years than the king of the North. 9 Also the king of the North shall come to the kingdom of the king of the South, but shall return to his own land. 10 However his sons shall stir up strife, and assemble a multitude of great forces; and one shall certainly come and overwhelm and pass through; then he shall return to his fortress and stir up strife. 11 And the king of the South shall be moved with rage, and go out and fight with him, with the king of

Greek kingdoms north (N) versus south (S). 5 (S) Egypt—Ptolemy I (305-283 B.C.); (N) Syria—Seleucus I (305-281 B.C.), who once served under Ptolemy as "one of his princes." 6 (S) Ptolemy II (283-246 B.C.) gave his daughter Berenice in a marriage alliance to his rival (N) Antiochus II (261-246 B.C.). Upon Ptolemy's death, Antiochus returned to his ex-wife Laodice (whom he had divorced in order to marry Berenice). Laodice then poisoned Antiochus and had Berenice and her child murdered so that her son Seleucus II could ascend the throne.

7-9 (S) Ptolemy III (246-222 B.C.), Berenice's brother ("branch of her root"), after Berenice's murder, launched a successful campaign against (N) Seleucus II (246-225 B.C.), who fled. Ptolemy took 40,000 talents' worth of silver, 4,000 talents of gold and 2,500 idols from the Syrians back to Egypt. Seleucus II then recovered Syria.

10-11 (N) Seleucus III (225-223 B.C.) succeeded Seleucus II, raised up an army, and launched a campaign against Attalus I of the Attalid dynasty. Seleucus III was assassinated after a brief two-year reign. His younger brother, (N) Antiochus III, "Antiochus the Great" (223-187 B.C.), succeeded him, amassed an army, and the

North, who shall muster a great multitude; but the multitude shall be given into the hand of his enemy.	marched against (S) Ptolemy IV (221-205 B.C.) of Egypt. He was successful up until his defeat at Raphia in 217 B.C., a loss that nullified his previous gains.
12 When he has taken away the multitude, his heart will be lifted up; and he will cast down tens of thousands, but he will not prevail. **13** For the king of the North will return and muster a multitude greater than the former, and shall certainly come at the end of some years with a great army and much equipment. **14** Now in those times many shall rise up against the king of the South. Also, violent men of your people shall exalt themselves in fulfillment of the vision, but they shall fall. **15** So the king of the North shall come and build a siege mound, and take a fortified city; and the forces of the South shall not withstand him. Even his choice troops shall have no strength to resist. **16** But he who comes against him shall do according to his own will, and no one shall stand against him. He shall stand in the Glorious Land with destruction in his power. **17** He shall also set his face to enter with the strength of his whole kingdom, and upright ones with him; thus shall he do. And he shall give him the daughter of women to destroy it; but she shall not stand with him, or be for him. **18** After this he shall turn his face	**12** (S) Ptolemy IV, his heart being lifted up after his victory in Palestine, sought to enter the Jewish Temple. The Jews resisted him, so he had "tens of thousands" put to death. **13-16** (N) Antiochus III returned to wage war against the (S) Ptolemies, and by 198 B.C., nearly 20 years after his defeat at Raphia, Antiochus had succeeded in taking possession of Palestine. The battle of Panium (198 B.C.) marked the end of Ptolemaic rule in Palestine. **17-19** (N) Antiochus III gave his daughter Cleopatra in marriage to (S) Ptolemy V, hoping to use her to conquer Egypt through intrigue. To his dismay, (S) Cleopatra opposed against her father. Antiochus then turned against Asia Minor ("the coastlands") but was turned back or defeated by the Roman commander Lucius Cornelius Scipo in 190 B.C. Antiochus III was killed while trying to plunder a pagan temple near Susa (187 B.C.) just a year following the peace accords with Rome (188 B.C.); thus he

to the coastlands, and shall take many. But a ruler [or commander] shall bring the reproach against them to an end; and with the reproach removed, he shall turn back on him. **19** Then he shall turn his face toward the fortress of his own land; but he shall stumble and fall, and not be found.	stumbled and fell and was found no more. The role of the king of the north switches to Rome at this point.
20 There shall arise in his place one who imposes taxes on the glorious kingdom; but within a few days he shall be destroyed, but not in anger or in battle.	(N) Augustus Caesar (63 B.C.-A.D. 14), the first Roman emperor, whose taxing or census is recorded in Luke 2:1.
21 And in his place shall arise a vile person, to whom they will not give the honor of royalty; but he shall come in peaceably, and seize the kingdom by intrigue.	Through divorce, remarriage, and killings, Tiberius became the emperor (A.D. 14-37) but was never popular. During his rule Jesus, the prince of the covenant, is broken/killed. The force of a flood is a reference to the coming destruction of Jerusalem, which Daniel linked to the death of Jesus in Daniel 9:26 as well.
22 With the force of a flood they shall be swept away from before him and be broken, and also the prince of the covenant.	Here we have a clear anchor point. Verse 22 is a reference to the death of Jesus, so verse 22 is referencing A.D. 31 and following.
23 And after the league is made with him he shall act deceitfully, for he shall come up and become strong with a small number of people. **24** He shall enter peaceably, even into the richest places of the province; and he shall do what his fathers have not done,	**23** Rise of the Papacy without their own army

24 The pope, a "man of peace," will rule for a limited time. The 1260 days/years of Daniel 7:25; |

nor his forefathers: he shall disperse among them the plunder, spoil, and riches; and he shall devise his plans against the strongholds, but only for a time.	Revelation 12:6,14. The king of the north now enters its papal phase.
25 He shall stir up his power and his courage against the king of the South with a great army. And the king of the South shall be stirred up to battle with a very great and mighty army; but he shall not stand, for they shall devise plans against him. **26** Yes, those who eat of the portion of his delicacies shall destroy him; his army shall be swept away, and many shall fall down slain. **27** Both these kings' hearts shall be bent on evil, and they shall speak lies at the same table; but it shall not prosper, for the end will still be at the appointed time. **28** While returning to his land with great riches, his heart shall be moved against the holy covenant; so he shall do damage and return to his own land.	**25-30** Pagan Rome made no such invasion of Egypt/south after the death of Jesus. So this must be the papal-led Crusades against Islam initiated by Pope Urban II in 1095. Islam now controlled the area to the south of Palestine. The king of the south is now in its Islamic phase. Nine major crusades and many minor ones Armies large and casualties high High intrigue within the armies Both sides lied and broke agreements. **28** The booty from the crusades led to many relics and artifacts being taken to Western Europe.
29 At the appointed time he shall return and go toward the south; but it shall not be like the former or the latter.	"Former": The first conflict between Islam and Christianity including Islamic conquest and Crusades (Dan. 11:25-28; cf. Rev. 9, first woe) Current or "appointed time": The second conflict between Islam and Christianity. This time against the Islamic Ottoman Empire during the time of the Reformation (Dan. 11:29-39). Dan. 11:40-45 (cf. second woe of Rev. 9)

	"Latter": The future third and final conflict between Islam and Christianity (Dan. 11:40-45; possibly the third woe of Rev. 11:15-19 and 12:12)
30 For ships from Cyprus [Kittim] shall come against him; therefore he shall be grieved, and return in rage against the holy covenant, and do damage. So he shall return and show regard for those who forsake the holy covenant. **31** And forces shall be mustered by him, and they shall defile the sanctuary fortress; then they shall take away the daily sacrifices, and place there the abomination of desolation.	Islamic naval victories in the battles of Preveza in 1538 and Dierba in 1560 led to decades of Islamic naval control until Pope Pius V organized the Holy League, which temporarily stopped Islam in one of the largest Middle Ages naval battles. Pope Pius V also reasserted the liturgical Mass, Inquisition, and decrees of the Council of Trent. **31** Same themes as Daniel 8:11-13, the religious phase of the little horn
32 Those who do wickedly against the covenant he shall corrupt with flattery; but the people who know their God shall be strong, and carry out great exploits. **33** And those of the people who understand shall instruct many; yet for many days they shall fall by sword and flame, by captivity and plundering. **34** Now when they fall, they shall be aided with a little help; but many shall **join with them by intrigue.** **35** And some of those of understanding shall fall, to refine them, purify them, and make them white, until **the time of the end; because it is still for the appointed time.**	**32-34** This represents the pre-Reformation and Reformation, with many of the Reformers put to death and burned at the stake. **34** After it became safer to be a Protestant, many joined from false motives. **35** This suggests that verses 36-39 will be a summary of the evils of the 1260-year rule of the Papacy and a description of the Counter-Reformation.

36 Then the king shall do according to his own will: he shall exalt and magnify himself above every god, shall speak blasphemies against the God of gods, and shall prosper till the wrath has been accomplished; for what has been determined shall be done. **37** He shall regard neither the God of his fathers nor the desire of women, nor regard any god; for he shall exalt himself above them all. **38** But in their place he shall honor a god of fortresses; and a god which his fathers did not know he shall honor with gold and silver, with precious stones and pleasant things. **39** Thus he shall act against the strongest fortresses with a foreign god, which he shall acknowledge, and advance its glory; and he shall cause them to rule over many, and divide the land for gain.	**36** The Counter-Reformation and the stronger blasphemous statements of the authority of the Papacy **37** Speaking of celibacy? Pope as final authority **39** The papal practice of deciding who had the right to rule a country within the Holy Roman Empire
40 At the **time of the end** the king of the South shall attack him; and the king of the North shall come against him like a whirlwind, with chariots, horsemen, and with many ships; and he shall enter the countries, overwhelm them, and pass through.	The king of the north continues as the Papacy and allies, and the king of the south continues as Islam, as in Daniel 11:25-39. The **time of the end** begins in the mid-1840s (end of the 2300 days/years of Dan. 8:13-17, 26), and the battle is after the healing of the deadly wound of Revelation 13:3, because the Papacy is able to mount a massive counterattack. It could be said that the developments from 1798 (the end of the 1260 day/year prophecy) to the mid-1840s set up

	the time of the end. The military force comes from an alliance of the Papacy with Europe (Rev. 17:12) and the United States (Rev. 13:11-17). After attacking the Papacy and/or its allies (NATO?), Islam is overwhelmed by the counterattack.
41 He shall also enter the Glorious Land, and many countries shall be overthrown;	The locations listed have both a geographical localized and "spiritual" worldwide application, i.e., the Papacy land invasion route is still from the north of Israel and Islam is still from the south, but both have also joined in a worldwide spiritual struggle. **41** The papal alliance enters Palestine. Many other countries will also be overthrown.
but these shall **escape** from his hand: Edom, Moab, and the prominent people of Ammon. **42** He shall stretch out his hand against the countries, and the land of Egypt shall **not escape.** **43** He shall have power over the treasures of gold and silver, and over all the precious things of Egypt; also the Libyans and Ethiopians **shall follow at his heels.**	These verses suggest a three-way breakup of Islam. **1** Those who "escape" from the papal allianceare represented by modern Jordan, a moderate Islamic state. Spiritually this may represent the Islamic "children of Abraham" spiritually from the line of Lot, Ishmael, and Esau who will accept Jesus (Gal. 3:26-29; Matt. 8:11; Heb. 2:2, 3) and escape the mark of the beast (Rev. 13:8). **2** Those who do **not escape**— Egypt and many others. They are the radical center of Islam that will be defeated. **3** Those that **shall follow at his heels.**

	Libyans and Ethiopians may represent moderate or secular Islamic areas/people that will follow the Papacy (Rev. 13:3, "all the world followed the beast," and verses 13-16, "mark of the beast").
44 But news from the **east** and the north shall trouble him; therefore he shall go out with great fury to destroy and annihilate many.	Just before Jesus comes from the **east** (Matt. 24:27) He speaks a final warning message known as the "loud cry" in Revelation 18:4-20. This will anger the Papacy, and their alliance will enforce its mark (Rev. 13:13-17; see also Eze. 43:1-9 and 44:4-9).
45 And he shall plant the tents of his palace between the seas and the glorious holy mountain; yet he shall come to his end, and no one will help him.	The papal alliance will plant itself in or take control of Palestine and/or spiritual worldwide Israel, the church. The Papacy/king of the north will come to its end at the coming of Christ (Dan. 7:22, 27; 8:25; 2 Thess. 2:8; Rev. 19:20).
12:1 At that time Michael **shall stand up,** The great prince who stands watch over the sons of your people;	Michael (meaning "one who is like God"). Jesus the prince who saves His people (Dan. 9:25-27; 10:13, 21; 11:22). This is in harmony with Martin Luther and many others. The Archangel is not an angel, but over the angels or commander of the angels (Joshua 5:13-15). The pre-Advent judgment concludes when Jesus shall stand up. The judgment started when He sat down in Daniel 7:9, 10. The term "at that time" indicates it is simultaneous with the preceding verse.

And there shall be a time of trouble, Such as never was since there was a nation, Even to that time.	The seven last plagues of Revelation 16. Of interest is Revelation 15:8, in which the temple is filled with smoke and no man can enter. Once the plagues begin, no one changes sides during the plagues or after. God's people go through what Jeremiah 5:1-9 calls Jacob's trouble.
And at that time your people shall be delivered, Every one who is found written in the book. **2** And many of those who sleep in the dust of the earth shall awake, Some to everlasting life, Some to shame and everlasting contempt.	Jesus delivers and/or resurrects His followers at His return (1 Thess. 4:13-18) There are two resurrections: one for the saved, at the beginning of the 1,000 years of Revelation 20, and the resurrection of the lost, at the end of the 1,000 years.
3 Those who are wise shall shine Like the brightness of the firmament, And those who turn many to righteousness Like the stars forever and ever.	The saved will live with God for eternity (Rev. 21:1-7, 27, and 22:1-5).
4 But you, Daniel, shut up the words, and seal the book until the time of the end; many shall run to and fro, and knowledge shall increase.	This verse is currently being fulfilled by the growing interest and understanding of Daniel 11:1-12:4.

Why I Do Not Believe That Atheistic Communism Is the King of the South

Many believe that the king of the south in Daniel 11:40-45 is atheistic Communism. They remember that the atheistic perpetrators of the French Revolution attacked the Roman Catholic Church (the king of the north) and, like Pharaoh, said, "I don't know God." According to such a view, the king of the south in Daniel 11:40-45 denies knowing God. Those who hold such a perspective go on to say that Communism, rooted in the French Revolution, then took the place of the French Revolution as the king of the south. They also assume that the Roman Catholic Church overcame the king of the south in the late 1980s with the fall of Communism at the hands of the United States and the Vatican. This leads them to conclude that Revelation 11 describes the French Revolution. I tend to agree with them in their understanding of Revelation 11 but do not believe, for the following reasons, that the king of the south in Daniel 11 is the same power:

- Daniel 11 is literal/geopolitical from the beginning, so I would expect it to stay that way to the end. On the other hand, Revelation is symbolic, or "signified," from the beginning (Rev. 1:1). We should not apply the same rules to both Daniel 11 and Revelation 11. They are not alike.
- We have no reason to interpret the powers of Daniel 11 as only religious or spiritual, because Daniel 11 already describes them as both geopolitical and religious.
- The historical fit of Islam as the king of the south from verses 25 to 43 is too great to ignore. It fits each of the details throughout the prophecy.
- We should not change the identity of the powers partway through the period between the Roman Empire and the second coming of

Jesus Christ. Both viewpoints understand the king of the north to be the Roman Catholic Papacy. Daniel 2, 7, and 8; 2 Thessalonians 2; and Revelation 13 all indicate that the entity covers the period from the fall of Rome to the second coming of Christ. If this is so, then the king of the south should also extend from the fall of the Roman Empire and last until just before the second coming of Christ. We would expect, based on Daniel 11:29, three eras of conflict between these two powers in the time period between the collapse of Rome and the Second Advent. When we understand Islam to be the king of the south, we do not need to change the identity of the king of the south partway through the prophecy—Islam fits all the way through.

- Some have said that after Christ's death the prophecies become symbolic or spiritual. If this is true of Daniel 11, why do we find such a good description of the Crusades and the Reformation, which are literal and geopolitical and yet after the time of Christ's death? It is not wise to spiritualize a prophecy when it makes sense literally.
- The context of Daniel 11:40-43 lends itself to interpreting the king of the south as Islam. When the king of north launches its strike against the king of the south, what are the names of the countries attacked? They are Egypt, Libya, Ethiopia, and western Jordan (Ammon, Edom, and Moab). What do these countries have in common? They are all predominantly Islamic, not Communist or atheistic. The question should be asked, How does the context of Daniel 11:40-45 indicate Communism? Answer: It doesn't. Those who believe this must find support for their view from outside Daniel 11:40-45.
- Geopolitical consistency: After the demise of the Roman Empire the Papacy takes the northern part of the empire and Islam the southern part. For 1,400 years this has been true. Even today, you can see that it remains so when you look at a map of Europe, Africa, and Asia coded for Christian- and Islamic-controlled countries. Christian nations predominate to the north of Israel, and Islamic nations occupy lands to the south of Israel. Those who believe that atheistic Communism is the king of the south find themselves forced to explain how the king of the south got so far north into Russia. In short, the atheistic Communism view is not geopolitically consistent with the prophecy.

Because the literal explanation fits so well, I am exceedingly reluctant

214

to look for any other supposed meaning. So I firmly believe Islam to be the king of the south in Daniel 11:25-43.

This said, I will agree that some similarities do exist between Islam and atheistic Communism. As I mentioned in the chapter on Islam in prophecy, I believe Islam to be the king of the south, but I also believe that from about 1798 to 1990 Satan used atheistic Communism to keep Christianity in check. In 1798 the French overthrew the Papacy and the Islamic Ottomans became a de facto protectorate of the British in 1840. That meant that the Protestant mission movement had its two major restrictions removed, and the mission and Bible societies flourished. With Islam down, Satan used the rising Communist movement to hold back the spread of Christianity. At the same time that Communism was collapsing in the 1980s, Islam and Islamic terrorism was on the rise. It is interesting to note that the Papacy and the United States apparently worked together to bring down Communism, and as I mention in the chapter on the United States in prophecy, I expect that they will crush Islam at the end. Now that Communism is not holding back Christianity as it was, Islam is once again strong and resisting Christianity in much of the world. Note also that some socialists have sided with Islamic revolutions to fight the West (biblically, the north)—the idea of "the enemy of my enemy is my friend." So I see Islam as the real king of the south, but atheistic Communism, as in Revelation 11, being a temporary substitute for the king of the south and taking the leading role while Islam and the Papacy were recovering from their wounds.

Since Daniel 11 describes the king of the north as both a geopolitical and religious power, as is Israel in the New Testament, I believe we should expect that the final conflict will have both localized geopolitical and worldwide spiritual application.

Appendix C

A Gospel Appeal

As the primary part of this prophecy study, I need to make sure that you understand what Jesus has done for you. It is of the highest importance to me as I share prophecy that people know Jesus Christ as their Lord and Savior. If I just tell you about prophecy, and it is just facts, I have made you a worse sinner than you were before. But if you love Jesus Christ and recognize that He's the great prince who is watching over you, and you realize that no matter what happens, He is the one who died for you and took away your sins and is the star of Bible prophecy, then you have something to live for today! (And if you are already a Christian, please pray for those who might not be.)

Should somebody ask you how to become a Christian, could you answer it? As a teenager, I had a guy inquire, "Do you know how to lead someone to Christ?" And I thought, *H'mmm, I'm a Christian, but I don't know. How would I lead someone to Christ?* So he made a presentation, and I took notes on it. Then I went home and studied my Bible that week, so that I could be ready to tell somebody how to become a Christian. Before the week was over, I was able to lead my first person to Jesus Christ—me. I thought I was a Christian, but I had somehow misunderstood what it really involved and was trying to do it all on my own. When I finally grasped that it was all about Jesus, I just gave myself to Him, and from then on I could have assurance that I would live forever.

Where to Start

To share the gospel with another, you could ask the individual some questions:

How does someone become a Christian? You can expect to get all kinds of answers: by going to church, giving offerings, being a good person. But those aren't it! Should somebody tell you any of these things, you have got good news for them!

How would you spend eternity if you were to die in your present spiritual condition?

If you are like me, before I understood what true Christianity was, I kind of hoped that my good works somehow outweighed my bad works on the scales of divine justice. While I wished that it might be the case, I really had no idea. If you wonder where you stand with God, I've got good news for you. You can know.

When you are ready to share that with someone, ask them, "Would you like me to show you?" If they don't want to hear and you try to present the gospel to them without getting their permission first, they're not going to listen. But if you request, and they say yes, you have a wide-open door to share the good news. Should they respond negatively, then you can accept their answer and reply, "Tell me when you want to know." They might just get curious and say, "Oh, go ahead, tell me." I have had that happen.

Eternal Life Not Earned

Romans 6:23 tells us that we can't earn eternal life—it is a gift. "The wages of sin is death, but the gift of God is eternal life in Christ Jesus our Lord." You already merit death, and the only escape from that is through the gift of God.

How does He give us that gift? First John 1:10 says: "If we say that we have not sinned, we make Him a liar, and His word is not in us." But right before that verse comes this promise: "If we confess our sins, He is faithful and just to forgive us our sins and to cleanse us from all unrighteousness" (verse 9). How much sin does He cleanse? All of it! You might say, "Well, there is something really horrible in my life!" So what? There is something really horrible in all of our lives. Jesus came to save sinners. That's what He announced and what He did. That horrible thing in your life is a sin that He came to forgive!

The only catch is one little word in the middle—the word "if." "If you confess your sins," you can be forgiven. But if you claim that you are not a sinner, you don't have a chance. You have got to admit to Jesus that you have sinned and need forgiveness.

As a kid, I broke into a house with a friend of mine. We took a few old antique bottles that we figured no one wanted anymore. If I said, "Lord, hey, we didn't steal anything of value; it wasn't any big deal," then

I'm making an excuse for it. Thus if I don't confess that I did something wrong, can I be forgiven? No. Or if I said, "My friend Mark actually broke in through the door, so it's his fault, not mine, and I didn't really do anything wrong," can God forgive me for taking things that were not mine? No, because I'm blaming Mark instead. As soon as I come to God and say, "God, I blew it—I did it," He says, "Fine, you're forgiven." Whew! I'm free!

Now, imagine that a couple days later Satan comes along and says, "Tim, remember when you broke into that house with Mark? You're a horrible person. You can't be a Christian." That's going to happen to you, and when it does, don't go back and ask Jesus to forgive you again. Should you ask Jesus to forgive today what He forgave years ago? No, because if you do, it shows you don't believe that He has already forgiven and cleansed you. It will throw you into a cycle of doubt that will cause you to question God's forgiveness. Is that a good cycle to get into? No.

So when Satan tries to push the guilt button on you, here is what you do. If you have already asked Jesus to forgive you for what Satan is trying to make you feel guilty for, say, "Jesus, thank You for already taking care of that for me." That gets rid of the guilt and messes up Satan's plan to ruin your life. I like spoiling Satan's plans.

We can be sure of salvation as long as we continue to trust Jesus. First John 5:11-13 declares:

"And this is the testimony: that God has given us eternal life, and this life is in His Son. He who has the Son has life; he who does not have the Son of God does not have life. These things I have written to you who believe in the name of the Son of God, that you may know that you have eternal life, and that you may continue to believe in the name of the Son of God."

Can you know for sure that you have eternal life? If you trust in Jesus Christ, you will. But should you choose not to trust Him, you will also know that you don't have eternal life. Are you trusting in Jesus? I hope so. If not, surrender to Jesus Christ, and you can be assured that you have eternal life. It is as simple as that.

In John 8:36 Jesus declared that He liberated us to live a new life, one free from sin. And in John 14:15 He says: "If you love Me, keep My commandments." Here is an awesome thought: When He sets you free, you fall in love with Jesus, and now, because you love Him, you want to do the things that please Him. But should you start doing things that don't please Him, and please yourself instead, what does it say about your love for Him? If you were engaged to somebody, and they said, "I don't want to do anything to please you, only what pleases me," should you stay engaged to that person? It suggests a serious problem with their love, doesn't it? If I do what pleases me and what is not pleasing to God, it indicates a problem in the relationship. So Jesus said, "If you love Me, keep My commandments." Do it out of love and for no other reason.

Jesus becomes my Savior. He forgives my sin, and then I let Him reign as my Lord. He leads me, and I follow in everything that He asks me to do. It's interesting that we need both a Lord and Savior. First John 2:1 tells us: "My little children, these things I write to you, that you may not sin. And if anyone sins, we have an Advocate with the Father, Jesus Christ the righteous." Notice, Plan A is Don't sin; follow Jesus. Plan B is When you blow it and you're a Christian, you ask Him to forgive you, and He does. When you have been following Him and you fail, don't give up. You just go back to 1 John 1:9 ("If we confess our sins . . ."), and then you are free.

Jesus continues as your Savior once you are a Christian. Satan will protest, "Oh, you claim to be a Christian, and you messed it up! It shows that you never were a Christian. Just give up!" He will do that to you again and again. But you probably knew that, right? Just don't give up!

After explaining these things to someone, you can ask, "Do you see what Christ wants for you? He wants to set you free and give you assurance of salvation. Have you ever thought of accepting Jesus Christ before? Maybe it is time for you, right now, to commit your life to Him. All you say is, 'Jesus, I blew it. Forgive me. Take control of me and my life.'" It is really not difficult.

And then you can pray with them. Teach them this prayer: "God, I have sinned. Please forgive me and cleanse me. I ask that You take over as Lord of my life. I ask this in the name of Jesus, and I thank You. Amen."

Appendix D

Application of Year-Day Principle, by Centuries, to Respective Trumpet Periods

KEY TO NATIONALITY OF WRITERS:
A—American; B—British; D—Dutch;
F—French; G—German; I—Italian;
S—Scottish.

TIME KEY:
391 days=360+30+1
396 days=365+30+1

No. Expositor	Nationality	Date of Pub.	Fifth Trumpet	Sixth Trumpet	Period Length Years Days
I. Prior to Reformation					
1. Joachim of Floris	(I)	1190	5 months=150 yrs.		
(First to apply year-day principle and first to apply to Mohammedanism.)					
2. Brute of Britain	(B)	1391	5 months=150 yrs.		
3. Luther, Martin	(G)	1545		Sixth Trumpet is Mohammedanism	
II. Sixteenth Century					
1. Foxe, John	(B)	1586	606-756	1051-1573	
2. Napier, John	(S)	1593	1051-1201	1300-1696	396
III. Seventeenth Century					
1. Downham	(B)	1603	630-780	1300-1696	396
2. Brightman, Thomas	(B)	1609	830-930 (630-780)	1300-1696	396
3. Pareus, David	(G)	1618	606-756	1300-1696	396
4. Mede, Joseph	(B)	1627	830-980 (955-1055)	1057-1453	396
5. Goodwin, Thomas	(B)	1639	830-980	1453-1849	396
6. Huet, Ephraim	(A)	1644	606-756	1302-1695	395
7. Parker, Joseph	(A)	1646		1259-1649 (1370-1859)	390
8. de Launay, Pierre	(F)	1651	Saracens	Turkish Invasion	
9. Poole, Matthew	(B)	1666	839-980	1057-1453 (1300-1669)	396
10. Jurieu, Pierre	(F)	1687	622-772	1300-1696	396
11. Cressener, Drue	(B)	1689	637-787	1063-1453	391
12. Knollys, Hanserd	(B)	1689	(150 Yrs.)	(391 "odd days")	391
13. Lloyd, William	(B)	1690	(150 Yrs.)	1302-1698	396
14. Newton, Isaac	(B)	1691	637-936 (300)	1063-1453	391
15. Horchen, Heinrich	(G)	1697	622-1057	1057-1453	396
16. Beverley, Thomas	(B)	1698		1055-1453	391 (+15 days)
IV. Eighteenth Century					
1. Fleming, Robert	(B)	1701	622-772	1067-1458	391
2. Baxter, Richard	(B)	1701	(150 Yrs.)	1300-1696	396
3. Brüssken, Conrad	(G)	1703	606-756	1057-1453	396
4. Vitringa, C.	(D)	1705	Saracens (150)	(Turks)	
5. Whiston, William	(B)	1706	673-823	1301-1697 (1062-1453)	396
6. Mather, Increase	(A)	1709		1300-1699	396
7. Daubuz, Charles	(B)	1712	612-762	1386- (1356-)	
8. Henry, Matthew	(B)	1712	627-779	1075-1453	396
9. Anonymous	(B)	1719	(150 Yrs.)	1057-1453	396
10. Newton, Thomas	(B)	1758	612-762	1281-1672	391
11. Durham, James	(B)	1764		(Period of Time)	391
12. Gill, John	(B)				
13. Kershaw	(B)	1780	629-779	1301-1697	396
14. Wood, Hans	(B)	1787	630-780	1030-	
15. Scott, Thomas	(B)	1791	612-762	1281-1672	391 (+15)
16. Osgood, Samuel	(A)	1794	622-772	997-1388 (1297-)	391
17. Winthrop, James	(A)	1794	"150 yrs."	"391 years"	391+
18. Woodhouse, J. G.	(B)	1794		1055-1453	391
19. Bicheno, James	(B)	1799	606-756	1302-1697	391 (+16)
20. Kett, Henry	(B)	1799	612-762		
V. Nineteenth Century					
1. Mitchel	(B)	1800	622-772	1300-1696	396
2. Evanson, Ed.	(B)	1802	632-782	1057-1453	396
3. Priestly, Joseph	(B)	1804	612-762	1281-1672	391
4. Barnes, Albert	(B)	1805	622-772 (629-779)	1057-1453	391
5. Chamberlin, Richard	(A)	1805	(150 years)	1292-1683	391 (+14)
6. Faber, G. S.	(B)	1806	612-762	1281-1672	391
7. Johnstone, Bryce	(B)	1807	606-756	699-1090	391 (+15)
8. French, Lawrence	(B)	1810	612-762	1065/68-1453 (1299-1685)	391 (+15)
9. Buck, Charles	(B)	1811		1453-1844	391
10. Cunninghame, William	(B)	1813	612-662	1281-1672 (1057-1448)	391 (or 396)
11. Kinne, Aaron	(A)	1814	612-762	1281-1672	391 (+15)
12. M'Lleod, Alexander	(A)	1814	612-762	1281-1672	391 (+15)
13. Armstrong, Amzi	(A)	1815	612-762	1281-1672	391 (+15)
14. Brown, John	(B)	1815	610-760	1281-1672 (1302-1698)	391
15. Frere, James H.	(B)	1815	612-762 (632-782)	1281-1692 (1063-1453)	391
16. Holmes, James I.	(B)	1815	612-762	1281-1672	391 (+15)
17. Cornwallis, Mrs.	(B)	1820	612-762	1281-1672	391 (+15)

220

No.	Expositor	Nationality	Date of Pub.	Fifth Trumpet	Sixth Trumpet	Period Length Years	Days
18.	Gauntlett, Henry	(B)	1821	612-762	1281-1672	391	(+15)
19.	Fry, John	(B)	1822	629-779 (612-762)	1453-1844	391	
20.	Brown, J. A.	(B)	1823	(150 years)	1453-1844	391	
21.	Cooper, Edward	(B)	1825	533 683	1301-1697 (1327-1798)	396	(or 391)
22.	Park, J. R.	(B)	1825	612-762	1453-1844	391	
23.	"Laicus"	(B)	1827	630-930 (300)	1299-1690 (1326-1717)	391	
24.	Cox, John	(B)			1453-1844	391	
25.	Keyworth, Thomas	(B)	1828	612-762	1281-1672	391	(+15)
26.	Addis, Alfred	(B)	1829	786-936			
27.	Homan, Ph.	(B)	1829		1453-1844	391	
28.	Tudor, John	(B)	1829	622-762	391 yrs. & fraction	391	
29.	Anonymous	(B)	1829	632-782	1062-1453	391	
30.	Hales, William	(B)	1830	620-770 (632-782)	1281-1672 (1062-1453)	391	(+15)
31.	MILLER, WILLIAM,	(A)	1831		1452-1843	391	(+15)
			1832	1298-1448	1448-1839	391	(+15)
			1839	1299-1449	1449-1840	391	(+15)
32.	Keith, Alexander	(A)	1832	622-772	1057-1453	396	(+103)
33.	Smith, Ethan	(A)	1833		1453-1818	360	
34.	Habershon, Matthew	(B)	1834	612-762	1453-1844	391	(+15)
35.	Bickersteth, Edward	(B)	1836	637-786	1453-1843/44 (1063-1453)	391	
36.	Bogie, B. D.	(B)	1836	612-762	1300-1696	396	
37.	Jenks, William	(A)	1838	612-762	1281-1672	391	(+15)
38.	**Litch, Josiah**	**(A)**	**1838**	**1299-1449**	**1449-1840 (Aug.)**	**391**	**(+15)**
39.	Wall	(A)	1840		1453-1849	396	
40.	Whitaker & Thurston	(A)	1840		**1453-1844**	391	
41.	Campbell, David	(A)	1840	612-762	1281-1692	391	(+15)
42.	Crandall, A. I.	(A)	1841	606-756	1281-1672	391	
43.	Fitch, Charles	(A)	1842	1299-1449	1449-1840	391	
44.	Birks, T. R.	(B)	1843	632-682		391	
45.	Stone, B. W.	(B)	1843	1299-1449	1449-1840	391	(+15)
46.	Southard, Nath.	(A)	1843	1299-1449	1449-1840	391	(+15)
47.	Anon. (Hyponia)	(B)	1844		1281-1672(Aug.)	391	
48.	Galusha, Elon	(A)	1844	1299-1449	1449-1840	391	(+15)
49.	Elliott, E. B.	(B)	1844	612-762	1057-1453	396	(+130)
50.	Gaussen, Louis	(F)	1844		1453-1844	391	
51.	Guinness, H. G.	(B)	1844	622-762	1300-1699	396	
52.	Junkin, George	(A)	1844	612-762	1281-1672	391	(+15)
53.	Scott, James	(S)	1844		1453-1844	391	
54.	Fysh, Frederick	(A)	1845	612-762 (607-757)	1301-1697 (1453-1849)	396	(+3 mos.)
55.	Scott, Samuel	(A)	1848	622-922(3	1059-1453	396	
56.	Thom, Adam	(B)	1848	606-756	1062-1453	391	
57.	Wickes, Thomas	(A)	1851	612-762	1281-1672	391	(+15)
58.	Jenour, Alfred	(F)	1852	632-786	1062-1453	391	(+15)
59.	Bliss, Sylvester	(A)	1853	622-762	1453-1844	391	(+15)
60.	Jones, Joseph	(B)	1853	Saracens	Turkish Invasion	391	(+15)
61.	Williams, Thomas	(B)	1853	612-762	1281-1672	391	(+15)
62.	L'Hote, J. B.	(A)	1854	622-772	1057-1453 (1302-1698)	396	(+15)
63.	Cumming, John	(A)	1855	612-762	1057-1453	396	
64.	Slight, Benjamin	(Can.)	1855	629-779	1057-1453	396	
65.	Lyon, J. C.	(A)	1859	612-762	1057-1453	365	(+106)
66.	Butler, J. G.	(B)	1860	841-904	1057-1453	396	
67.	Thomas. John	(A)	1861	632-782	1063-1453	391	(+30)
68.	Royse, P. E.	(A)	1864		1250-1641	391	(+30)
69.	Smith, Uriah	(A)	1865	1299-1449	1449-1840	391	(+15)
70.	Gardner, J. P.	(A)	1867	Saracens	Turkish Invasion	391	(+15)
71.	Hunt, E. M.	(A)	1870	612-762	1057-1453	396	
72.	Steele, David	(A)	1870	612-762	1281-1672	391	
73.	Pond, Enoch	(A)	1871	629-779	1062-1453	391	
74.	De Pui, James	(A)	1873	728/30-879	1291-1682	391	
75.	Simons, E. D.	(A)	1875	612-762	1057-1453 (1062-1453)	391	(+15)
76.	Orr, John	(A)	1876	606-	Mohammedanism	396	
77.	Johnson, B. W.	(A)	1881	632-782	1057-1453	396	(+3 mos.)
78.	Kimball, I. E.	(A)	1897		1449-1840	391	(+15)
79.	Moore, T. W.	(A)	1897	Mohammedanism	1070/71-1453 (1095-1478/79)	391	
80.	Tanner, Joseph	(B)	1898	612-762	1062-1453	396	(15 or 30)

VI. Twentieth Century

No.	Expositor	Nationality	Date of Pub.	Fifth Trumpet	Sixth Trumpet	Period Length Years	Days
1.	Hood, J. W.	(A)	1900	612-762	1281-1672	391	(+15)
2.	Smith, F. G.	(A)	1908	Saracens	1281-1672	391	(+15)
3.	Williams, H. C.	(A)	1917	612-672 (632-782)	1057-1453	396	
4.	Briggs, H. C.	(A)	1923	612-762	1057-1453	391	
5.	Rand, H. B.	(A)	1932		1453-1844	391	(+15)
6.	Stewart, Basil	(B)	1934	612-762	1281-1672	391	

Total number of expositors, 124